"A profound and elegant memoir garnished with some of the most delicious and extraordinary recipes you will be blessed to cook and eat."

—RONNI LUNDY, JAMES BEARD AWARD–WINNING AUTHOR OF *VICTUALS*

"*Our South* is destined to be a new American classic—a deliciously compelling cookbook that not only provides an expansive perspective on Southern cooking, but a road map for exploring the vast nuances of Black culinary experience. Ashleigh's recipes and stories are deeply personal, while her mastery of and reverence for the ingredients and foodways of her heritage are on full and vibrant display. With her debut cookbook, she both honors the generations of cooks before her and confidently leads us all into the kitchen, invigorated and inspired to get cooking."

—GAIL SIMMONS, FOOD EXPERT, TV HOST, AND AUTHOR
  OF *BRINGING IT HOME*

"I call the South our richest culinary region in the US, for all the reasons Ashleigh Shanti documents here. Her vibrant recipes and stories shine overdue recognition on Black foodways from Appalachia to the Sea Islands and the countless love-filled kitchens in between."

—OSAYI ENDOLYN, JAMES BEARD AWARD–WINNING FOOD
  AND CULTURE WRITER

OUR SOUTH

OUR SOUTH

Black Food Through My Lens

Backcountry · Lowlands · Midlands · Lowcountry · Homeland

ASHLEIGH SHANTI

UNION
SQUARE
& CO.

NEW YORK

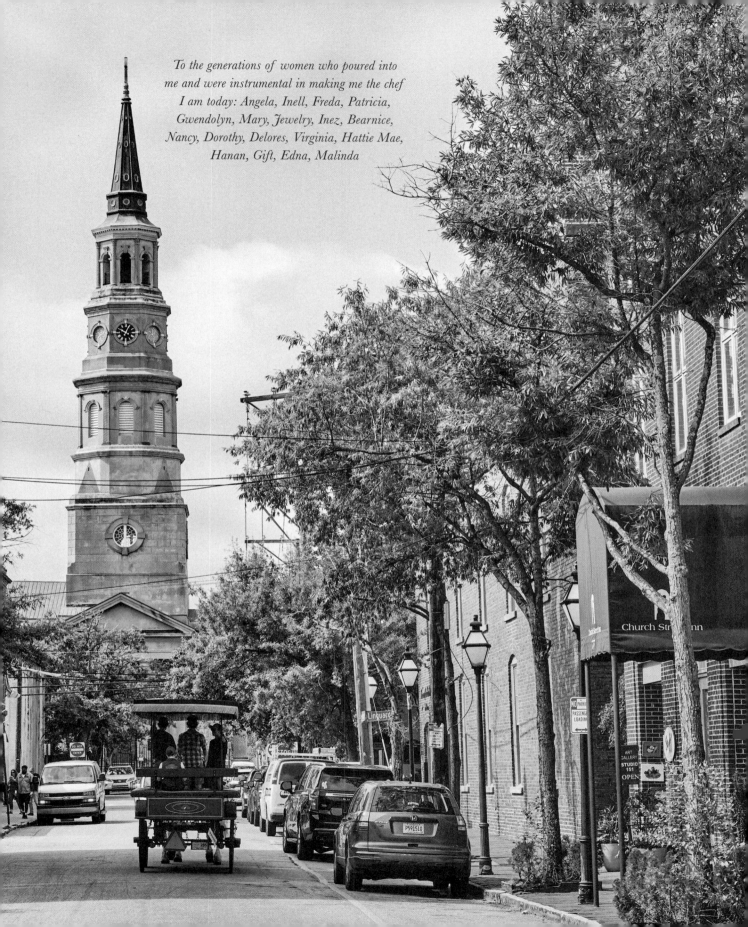

To the generations of women who poured into me and were instrumental in making me the chef I am today: Angela, Inell, Freda, Patricia, Gwendolyn, Mary, Jewelry, Inez, Bearnice, Nancy, Dorothy, Delores, Virginia, Hattie Mae, Hanan, Gift, Edna, Malinda

CONTENTS

AUTHOR'S NOTE

This is not an Appalachian cookbook, nor is it a book full of my family's soul food recipes. This is not a Southern cookbook or a "chef" book. It actually encompasses all of these things—and more. Above all, this book exists to amplify your understanding of the complexities of Black food.

While I'm fully committed to filling your head with thoughts of buttered cornbread still hot from the cast-iron pan; crunchy, juicy lard-fried chicken ready to be torn into; and luscious, sweet shortcake that's as much of a feast for your eyes as for your palate— that's not the beginning and end of this story. In between, I'm out to prove something: I want to dispel the myths of what America thinks Black cooking is and is not.

I hope you'll walk away seeing *Our South* the way I do. You can find thousands of cookbooks that have the word "South" in the title: virtual encyclopedias of cakes by the ladies of Southern Junior Leagues; endless easy, lump-free gravy recipes; and manuals covering every in and out of preserving and canning. With that, the South and the food of the South tell more stories than there is time for, and you'd spend a lifetime eating your way through these unique microregions. For me, and I think for others, too, these vast stories beg the question: Where does this food come from?

What separates *Our South* from most of the other Southern cookbooks is that it specifically seeks to shed light on the Black influence that has uniquely impacted each of these regions and how that influence has defined the individual foodways and cultures of these places.

I am a Black, queer, woman chef who found her identity in cooking. Through my stories, recipes, and experiences, I challenge the belief that Black cuisine is monochromatic, and I show that our diaspora reaches far beyond even the bounds of these thoughtfully crafted pages. By the book's end, I believe we'll land outside the confines and misconceptions of what Black food is. This is Black food through my lens.

INTRODUCTION

From Where and Whom I Come

I was born in the tiny seaside town of St. Mary's, Georgia, making my surprise, early arrival the morning of my aunt Patricia's wedding. When I arrived, my dad and my uncles, still in a post-bachelor-party haze, wildly cheered and drunkenly demanded I be named "Bernard" because it seemed like a good idea at the time. As the first girl born into a family that already had eight boy cousins, my relatives' pent-up desire for someone to carry the torch of our strong matriarchal lineage fell on me. In our culture, the women wear many hats—caretaker, problem solver, house manager, and gardener—and the ideal matriarch nails every task without getting her dress dirty.

Though I do think my becoming a chef fits into that caretaker role, I have to admit that I don't really adhere to the stereotype of a ladylike and proper Southern woman. But that's not to say I resent that history; actually, it's the opposite. The women in my family, whether they defied that stereotype or not, all comprise my culinary lineage. Throughout these pages, I'll tell you even more about them and the places each of them represents to me.

My maternal grandmother, Jewelry Virginia, lived until her forties, when she suddenly became ill and died, leaving behind seven children—but not before teaching the girls what she'd deemed essential skills: sewing, pickling, tending gardens, and caring after orchards. My grandfather, her husband, was a humble peanut and tobacco farmer on someone else's land—getting his boys involved after school—processing tobacco and eventually selling it by the truckload. They had chicken coops and a garden large enough to feed the whole family and preserve a little for seasons to come. They subsisted on a straightforward diet made up of whatever that garden brought in; the pickles and preserves they had saved; and grains, corn, and legumes with a bit of seafood from the Virginia coast dotted in.

My grandmother's mother, my great-grandma Inez, was a force to be reckoned with but was as sweet as the fruit of Midlands. Every time she saw me, she would tear a warm piece of freshly baked white bread, dip it in rich, sticky molasses, and pass it to me behind her back with a wink. Her deep, piercing eyes and distinctive countenance earned her a reverence that could be hard to come by for a woman in the

South. Her smooth, glowing chocolate skin was seemingly unaffected by her years of hard work. She flawlessly managed her household and lived up to her maiden name, Cook, feeding her community. But she defiantly also did "men's work," tending to the smokehouse and overseeing hog killings. It has been said by those who knew her well that I carry her spirit. I cherish that thought and honor her often, especially through my foodways.

A trip a bit farther west leads to my great-aunt Hattie Mae, Jewelry Virginia's sister, who lived right on a brook trout–filled crick off the Dan River in Patrick County, Virginia. Every time my family rolled up in our "fancy car" (as Hattie Mae called it), we'd spot her head, covered with giant pink foam rollers, popping out from underneath a veil of britches. That seemingly infinite supply of goose beans, strung on jute twine and hung up to dry like a greenish shade curtain on the front porch, would sway as the cool breeze of Appalachian spring blew in. Here, pickles are their own food group, vinegar is used as seasoning, a pepper mill and chow chow are constants on the table, and britches are food, not clothing. The end of a visit was always marked with a trip out back to the old larder. Shelves upon shelves were stocked with Ball jars filled with more things than you could possibly imagine. Sent in to pick up jars to take home, I'd return from what felt like a field trip to another world with my lanky arms full.

Humble Lowcountry South Carolina was the home of my God-fearing Southern paternal grandma, Bearnie, and it's where purloo and seafood boils were synonymous with a hug and kiss, and an annual crab-crackin' brought us all together. Rice reigns supreme here, and I credit this place for my confidence to cook it exactly right every time. Time spent here was precious and, unfortunately, too infrequent. While my parents' generation blamed muggy weather and vicious mosquitoes for the rarity of get-togethers, those excuses were a front for the family differences at play. There often seemed to be discomforts looming: old grudges and unspoken grievances that new generations were ready to swat away and forget about, regardless of their roots.

My Culinary Coming of Age

As my parents and I traveled inland from our home base of Virginia Beach to visit the various family homesteads sprinkled throughout the deep, rural South, I would eavesdrop on adult conversations while munching on ripe peaches, warm fried pie, or hot boiled peanuts, depending on where we were going. Salt marshes made way for cotton and tobacco fields as the hours marched along on those drives to Sumter.

Stretched across the back seat, I'd practice my summer reading while also saving my soul as I read aloud the biblical billboards along I-95 to the Lowcountry, where I looked forward to slurping oysters whole and cracking crabs dunked in buttery red sauce on majestic Edisto Island with my cousins. We'd spend the cool summers with my great-aunts up the mountain, snapping and hanging beans on the front porch while "watching pots" of soup beans and salt turnips inside.

I've always loved to eat, but I didn't always have the attention span to remain on the hip or at the feet of the women in my family long enough to learn to construct a carefully stacked cake or the fluffiest biscuits for elaborate Sunday suppers. Instead, I was busy exploring the woods barefoot, delighting in the mushrooms and wild things that were so different from the ones in my backyard. I yearned for each new adventure that would produce that next thrilling, adrenaline-producing bite. Those moments, alone with my thoughts, exposed to different people and places, helped me gather who I'd soon become and how I'd choose to express myself. As a precocious only child in coastal Virginia, my earliest food experiences were birthed here.

My adolescence was spent poring over encyclopedias, *National Geographic*, and travel ads, dreaming of journeying to the world's most fascinating food utopias. To me, that's what travel was, or at least what I wanted it to be. Mostly, though, my travels were relegated to our little Southern bubble: dirt roads spelled jam-filled jars; the mountains led to smells of seasonal flora carried by the cool, brisk air; and gray beaches were an ostreaphile's dream. My hardworking mother, a career woman who stepped into the kitchen when she could, effortlessly merged the practices of various foodways so they sang together in harmony. But we really only ate that way on weekends: a revolving door of guests, elaborate all-day cooking, small bites at the ready. I didn't realize it then, but these formative years taught me a lot about hospitality.

The weekdays, on the other hand, had me slurping gravy-coated spaghetti out of a Chinese takeout container of yock from Mama Chan's or Mak's on the way to gymnastics practice; or tucking into a slow cooker of stew that was awaiting our evening return. Instant grits were magically ready before I even finished brushing my teeth in the morning; juicy chicken and tangy lemon cake from Pollard's Family Restaurant up the street often landed on the table; and frozen Pictsweet sides provided my daily serving of vegetables. Jiffy cornbread was in regular rotation. We enjoyed occasional drop-offs of steamy siopao, or fresh-caught mullet and steamed crabs blanketed in Old

Bay seasoning, gifted as thank-yous to my parents in exchange for their random side hustles: preparing tax returns, replacing a car engine, repairing the church's HVAC. Despite the constant busyness, we never had a bad meal.

At the age of seventeen, I was fortunate enough to finally be able to travel abroad. During a gap year, I traveled to Nairobi, Kenya, with the hope of "finding myself" in ways that certainly didn't involve attending a traditional four-year college. I made fast friends with my host family's cook and shared with her America's latest fleeting food trends—cake balls and chocolate-chip cookies laced with potato chips—but I got the much better end of the deal. In return, she schooled me on the ways of warm chapati, decadent filled samosas, sukuma wiki (which filled my homesick heart with memories of stewed collard greens), and sweet mandazi during noon tea. There, unexpectedly, the food of my ancestors found me.

Back home in Virginia, I spent the summer working my first restaurant job at a fancy seafood spot on the beach. Each day, I'd get up early, spend time on the water, then slip into the kitchen in the afternoon. I was already dreaming of a life filled with wild foods in the woods, busy kitchens on the boardwalk, oyster spats, and chicken necking, but my parents made it clear that I was going to college—that I was going to have a *career*. I was accepted to Hampton University, a nearby HBCU nestled on the Hampton River. "Makes for a good view," I told myself in an attempt to stay optimistic, as I was not thrilled to be just a stone's throw away from home.

I majored in business marketing, but really, I studied Food Network from my tiny, single-occupancy dorm room in W. E. B. DuBois Hall. The residence hall had a community kitchen in which I spent more time than my actual room, at least until I set off the fire alarm one too many times by underestimating the power of an old coil burner. I powered through, and along the way I made some lifelong friends who, for once, could relate to my life experiences. Professors made me feel seen and heard and seemed to want me to succeed. It was nothing I'd ever come across as the only Black girl in class back home.

With a degree obtained by the skin of my teeth, I felt ready for the unavoidable conversation with my parents about grad school. I was armed with research about a few culinary programs up north that I wanted to apply to with the idea of becoming a real chef one day. "Is this not considered a postgraduate education?" I'd ask during our debates about my future. I dreamed of learning to cook ultra-refined restaurant

food; I yearned for an opportunity to utilize my fancy ring molds, which had begun collecting dust; I fantasized about having access to the restaurants I'd been drooling over in the pages of food magazines like *Saveur* and *Food & Wine*. I became convinced that earning the respect of my peers in the kitchen meant cooking THAT food—not my own, not the homey, comforting food I'd grown up on. My parents eventually caved and helped me pack up and move to the farthest school they would let me attend: Baltimore International College.

The Cold Station

To my delight, BIC and Baltimore offered action on every corner and always something to entertain my easily bored mind. Black arabbers sold fresh fruit from their carts; the famous water man outside of Orioles baseball games hawked $1 water bottles with a side of pectoral choreography. I wove my way around film sets in the middle of the street to get from one destination to the next. Here, using words like "finta" and "y'all" made me stick out like a banana on a tuna boat, but I wasn't deterred. Baltimore provided a newness I found inspiring and adrenaline-inducing. I quickly got a job at the Northern Italian fine-dining restaurant Cinghiale, one of the nicest I'd ever stepped foot in, and a convenient bike ride away from my neighborhood and school.

But all was not well in my life as a city girl. My new bike was stolen outside of Lexington Market while I enjoyed my first coddie. I went through an unexpected but necessary breakup. And, perhaps worst of all, I learned BIC was on the verge of losing its accreditation. Instead of saying "I told you so," my parents listened to my nonsensical, tear-filled phone rants, reminding me, "You know you can always come back home." I couldn't bear that thought and wouldn't consider doing that until I'd actually "proved something." But at this point, I wondered if I was just stalling for time with such a vague goal. What was that "something"? A fancy job? A trophy? Deep down, I knew the decision to pursue a culinary career was emotional, not rational. I'd found my calling in the act of cooking; I'd found the way I wanted to express my love for people.

Cooking was about tossing my head back and hearing all of the kitchen folks' laughter bounce off tiled walls. It was about feeling the differences between people—whatever bad blood, gossip, or ill wind they brought with them—melt away as I set a plate of food on a table. I knew that act of bringing people together through food would fill my soul.

Culinary school aside, I thought I would be able to focus on my purpose if I kept working in professional restaurant kitchens. At Cinghiale, however, I quickly noticed I didn't share many of the defining traits I saw in the professional cooks around me. They were meticulous and refined, whereas I felt goofy and clumsy. They understood a task the first time it was explained, whereas I typically had many follow-up questions. Worse, I certainly had been naive to the discrimination I would face. There were so many machines in the kitchen that only I wasn't allowed to touch. And I was relegated to the garde-manger, known affectionately as the cold station, making the same salads, crudos, and desserts night after night.

In their lockers, the kitchen staff hung photos of white men in toques or of tattooed, T-shirt-clad "bad boys" posing in alleys with half-smoked cigarettes hanging from their lips. There'd be these macho quotes on the photos, stuff like "Never allow anyone to pick you up; pick yourself up." Ugh. When I'd ask, "Who the hell is that?" they'd look at me, stunned, and laugh their asses off. I'd be the butt of every joke for the remainder of dinner service. "Sure," I'd think, "*I'm* the strange one for not plastering my locker with notes reminding me I am indeed a part of #cheflife." One day after a refreshing night off, I entered the locker room to find a poster of Rachael Ray sexily bent over as she slid a turkey into an oven, but the poster had been altered to feature my face instead of hers. I laughed just as hard as the others did, not really bothered to be compared to a woman who, like me, had dedicated herself to her craft.

Working garde-manger, however, simply did not light my fire. Extracting pristine wedges of pulp from endless oranges did not, I realized, fill my soul. I wanted to experiment, learn in large strides, and feel like I was feeding people, body and soul.

After Cinghiale, I finally got a sous chef position where I imagined myself thriving. But a mountain of unpaid invoices, too much staff partying, and an absent owner saw that place shutter only months after my arrival. Then there was the pizza spot where I learned to spin dough above my head, a classic family-owned steakhouse, a New American restaurant, and oh, so many seafood shacks. I learned to prove myself through flawless Saturday-night services with hundreds of covers and kept a level head when no one else could. And when things inevitably went awry, to my chagrin, I bit my tongue instead of speaking up and learned to save the tears for the bathroom or a dingy, dark corner of dry storage.

I couldn't find any inkling of myself in the food I was cooking, and these restaurants weren't anything close to the warm, welcoming spaces that I'd always known my family's kitchens to be. I almost left the industry entirely.

Thankfully, I kept looking. At the public library, I entered random strings of words into the digital catalog, hoping they'd conjure up something good. "Wild, Foods, Southern." "African American, Culinary." Whatever thick, dusty cookbook showed up, I'd take home. On visits home, I grilled my parents—especially my dad—for details on what they ate growing up. I gulped in the super-saturated and glamorous culinary spreads in their collection of *Ebony* and *Essence* magazines. After dinner service, I spent my nights writing, then testing, dream menus that I hoped to execute someday. I spent any extra time and money I had to do unpaid stages at restaurants just for the sake of learning, and tasting, more.

In my time of need, one internet search—"Black, Appalachian Recipes"— brought me to Malinda Russell, a Tennessean who in 1866 became the first Black American to publish a cookbook. Just like my peers, I needed a success story to see myself in. I was an oyster spat in a roaring ocean, and Russell was the pier I clung on to. At first, all I found was a blog post summing up her journey, her struggles, and her foodways, but my heart still fluttered at the moments of recognition I felt in her story and the recipes she documented in her *Domestic Cook Book*, which got a much-needed reprint in 2007. She wrote her recipes matter-of-factly, never explaining, because she

A

DOMESTIC

COOK BOOK:

CONTAINING

A CAREFUL SELECTION OF USEFUL RECEIPTS

FOR THE KITCHEN.

BY

MRS. MALINDA RUSSELL,
AN EXPERIENCED COOK.

assumed you knew what she was talking about. (I had to google a lot of the words she used and often came up short.) Like the women in my family, she measured ingredients in pecks and palmfuls, if at all. I saw a shadow of my great-aunt Hattie Mae in the way Russell dressed okra with hot fat and in her one-sentence recipe for chow chow. And though her struggles are so far away from mine, her perseverance and independence felt so reminiscent of the women I grew up with. Black people are so rarely part of the big "important" conversations about food, but the existence of this book proved what I've always known: that we've always been there. Malinda Russell's search for freedom through her artistry gave me hope that I could find my way, too.

Russell was a well-traveled woman—though not by choice. While by law she was born a free Black woman in the rolling hills of eastern Tennessee, she never really felt freedom. In the autobiographical prologue of the cookbook, she writes that at nineteen, she had set out to emigrate from Tennessee to Liberia as part of the Back-to-Africa Movement. But after she was robbed of every penny she had by another traveler, she was forced to stop in Lynchburg, Virginia. What had felt like a small glimmer of hope amounted to a bleak future. So she pivoted.

In Lynchburg, she cooked, maintained a washhouse, and worked as a traveling nurse, making her presence known via the local paper. She soon married and had a son who was born with a disability. Her husband died only four years later. Now a widow and single mother, Russell returned to Tennessee with her son to be closer to family, pivoting once again as she ran a boardinghouse and then a pastry shop on Chuckey Mountain. After a second, devastating robbery and the outbreak of the Civil War, Russell looked north for peace, hearing Michigan was "the garden of the West." It was there, in 1866, that she wrote the *Domestic Cook Book*, a confident culmination of everything she'd learned throughout her childhood, her travels, and her work. In a refreshing act of solidarity, she credited another Black woman, Fanny Steward, with teaching her how to cook. In the prologue, she expressed a wish that the profits of the book could help her and her son return to their true home in Tennessee.

We might not know of Russell's book today if, a century later, curious intellectuals had not come across it after it turned up in the bottom of a box belonging to a cookbook dealer in southern California. Russell's recipes, which reflect her diverse travels and experiences, "are not distinctly Southern," culinary historian

Janice Bluestein Longone noted in the preface of the book's reprint. That is to say, they're not Southern in the way many might define the canon of recipes today. While Russell was a Southern Appalachian Black woman at her roots, her "receipts" defy simple classification and stereotypes—and I wouldn't be where I am without them. As a lost young cook, I felt small while everything around me was big, bright, and loud. But a quiet, still voice inside me insisted that I'd eventually find myself in food. Russell's book was what I didn't know I'd been looking for.

And like Russell, I meandered for a while, working all kinds of food jobs throughout the country. I bartended, catered, taught fermentation classes, worked as a culinary assistant, and staged wherever I felt like I could learn something. Finally, I found my way to Benne on Eagle, a restaurant in a historically African American neighborhood in Asheville, North Carolina. I rekindled my connection to Southern Appalachian foodways in that kitchen, where I served as chef de cuisine for a little over two years. Before, I was cooking other people's food. At Benne on Eagle, I got a chance to figure out what *my* food could potentially look like. I experimented with West African flavors, Appalachian heritage techniques and ingredients, and the global mishmash of recipes that I grew up eating at home. There were leather britches (page 72) cooked in buttermilk, Nigerian akara fritters (page 259) made up like hush puppies, and luscious plates of braised oxtail that practically flew out of the kitchen. Our menu got us plenty of awards and press, which was so unexpected and affirming; but for real, seeing a dining room full of Black faces in a town as white as Asheville was the biggest compliment of all.

I could have stopped there, but I still wanted more—in a city where Black and brown business ownership was and still is a rarity, it meant a lot to me to do something that could lead to me owning my own restaurant. So in 2020 (like many other people during the COVID-19 pandemic), I left my job and found inspiration in other places. I collaborated with chef friends and for a while put on pop-up events where I cooked whatever I wanted, from tasting menus to fish fries. It struck me that I wasn't the first in my family to patch a life together with a bunch of side hustles: I was just the latest in a long lineage of women, mostly homemakers, who used their talents in the kitchen to make their families' lives better. Great-grandma Inez, a champion pickler, sold pickles to make some extra money. And my maternal great-aunts worked together to sell brown bags of piping-hot fried fish and hush puppies at waterside fish camps, shouting "Good hot fish!" to draw in customers.

So I decided that Good Hot Fish, a modern-day fish camp and my first foray into full restaurant ownership, would be a direct descendant of my predecessors' ingenuity. Modeled after the pop-ups that I did leading up to the restaurant's opening, the menu leans into the classics that you'd find at my great-aunts' tents: hush puppies, leather britches, baked beans, and, of course, crisp fried fish. The restaurant continues to expand the boundaries of what we call Southern food, spinning local North Carolina ingredients through the culinary techniques and styles of places as distant as Japan and Cameroon.

It might seem, then, like I would defy being reduced to *just* a Southern chef, but I don't mind being labeled. I don't even think labels are bad—I wear all of mine proudly. I'm a Chef, a Southerner, and a Gay Black Woman. These words do define my identity. But labels shouldn't feel binding, nor should they reiterate any sort of stereotypical ideologies. They shouldn't limit and contain us. Like Malinda Russell, I, too, am on a quest for freedom, to be freed from the confines of what is expected of me, cooking while Black, in twenty-first-century America.

This food—my food, my family's food, the food of my heritage and culture—is the food I am here to cook. It carries many labels despite being defined by so many regions, ideas, crops, and cultures. I'll tell you again and again that Southern food isn't a monolith; but even so, I've learned several truths to be evident when it comes to how we eat and cook here:

- Seasonality and food connectivity occur seamlessly in the name of community.

- Shopping centers, chain restaurants, and grocery stores are less sources of food and more places to catch up with your neighbors.

- The influences of the African diaspora are woven into each narrative and recipe and have made a unique imprint on the way we cook and enjoy food.

- We develop dishes around fruits and vegetables and treat meat like a condiment.

- Simple ingredients like rice, cornmeal, and the humble sweet potato are exalted.

Our food tells a story, and it's capable of producing feelings and emotions deep within one's inner being. That is the food of our South.

The dishes documented in *Our South* represent approachable recipes and techniques from numerous kitchens, and I have articulated the food of these microregions in a produce-driven, traditional way. The regions are then organized by the courses and customs of that place, so each chapter flows from small bites or snacks through to the end of a meal. None of these recipes requires intimidating restaurant stuff like vac sealers or tech powders. The recipes, while chef-driven, aren't necessarily written with chefs in mind. Some require a fair amount of time to complete, while others have only a few simple ingredients and take under ten minutes. Then there are what I call the "Supreme" recipes, or the backbone of Southern cooking: standard components and techniques that you'll use throughout the book. You'll have plenty of opportunities to practice those. The recipes chosen for the book translate well for large-format entertaining and speak with a seasonal sensibility.

These are recipes generated from stories of substance and value. The dishes here are quintessentially me and call deeply to my roots. Each adds up to my argument that the South is made up of many parts, each with its own distinct flora and fauna, dialects, and regional dishes. The parts of the South I take you through are the ones closest to my heart. When I cook now, I can't help but express a little piece of each place every time.

NECESSITIES

After sharpened knives and my trusty sauce spoons, if you want a good meal out of me, I'll likely need a few of these gems to really *make* it. The following ingredients are the tools of my trade. You should find some version of these simple items in any good Southern kitchen—and in the true spirit of the simplicity of Southern cooking, you likely already have the majority of these necessities at home, so we're off to a good start. As we explore several microregions that make the South what it is, you'll take note of common ingredients utilized across each chapter, but you will also notice how they have different purposes—and meanings—depending on where they're being cooked. The tone of *Our South* encourages shopping at farmers' markets, for sure, but almost all the ingredient lists can be sourced at your average grocery store. Let's look at the versatility in these simple Southern staples.

Carolina Gold Rice

Carolina Gold is the only rice variety you'll find in this book. Southerners don't play when it comes to rice, and you shouldn't, either. As we make our way through the precious, historic rice fields of the Lowcountry, you'll see this variety utilized throughout. While Carolina Gold is the standard, I also treasure other heirloom varieties like heritage red rice, which has a super-complex and earthy flavor. It's just really cool to think about my ancestors eating what I'm eating.

Seasoning Meat

Ham hocks, salt-cured fatty pork, and smoked turkey tails and necks are cuts that often go unmentioned by chefs outside of the South, but entire warehouses throughout Virginia and the Carolinas are dedicated to these delicacies, which add so much flavor to soups and braises. Finding little chunks of seasoning meat in your bowl feels like finding the little plastic baby inside the Mardi Gras king cake. Not only does this meat add intense smoky, salty flavor, its collagen also lends a luscious and velvety texture to whatever it graces.

Chicken Stock

My recipe for the ideal base for all kinds of Southern soups and stews is in the Supreme Recipes chapter; you'll find it on page 41. You'll want to prepare gallons of this liquid gold, as you'll go through plenty of it. If time isn't on your side, feel free to make yours with a chicken bouillon base.

Cornbread

You'll find several versions of the South's favorite bread throughout these pages. The versatility of Classic Cornbread (page 40) comes in handy; it freezes and reheats well, so make a double batch.

Dried Beans and Field Peas

To save yourself a step when you're cooking dried beans or field peas, soak a big batch of them overnight, then drain the beans and freeze them in airtight bags. When you're ready to make a pot of beans, just thaw your already-soaked legumes.

Vinegar

Vinegar spans a wide range, from mild to sweet to subtle to ultra-mouth-puckering. I own more vinegars than I'll ever be able to use up in my lifetime, but you can get away with just a sweeter apple cider vinegar for cooking and a more acidic, punchy wine vinegar for salad dressings and other cold applications.

Animal Fats and Oils

When I was visiting my grandma in Virginia, I'd get my scalp greased with bear fat or my burns soothed with cold butter. Fat has many uses, and my kitchen contains quite an array of types for cooking and grandma-inspired applications. Schmaltz and bacon fat are at the top of my list for animal fats. They impart lots of good flavor and create a mean sear with the help of a neutral oil. I like that neutral oils like canola and grapeseed oil provide a high smoke point without adding any competing aromas. When I want to finish a dish with oil, like a charred vegetable or crudo, I look to a robust extra-virgin olive oil that could be fruity or peppery depending on what flavor profile I'm after.

Sorghum Molasses

This African grass is most commonly seen in grain form or as a syrup pressed from the sorghum cane. I often utilize sorghum syrup (or sorghum molasses) as a sweetener instead of sugar or honey. It provides a sour and earthy complexity that varies by the region from which it hails.

Hot Sauce

Hot sauce is important for its ability to simultaneously and effortlessly introduce heat and acid to a dish without one flavor profile showing up the other. Tabasco, Texas Pete, and Valentina are three great examples—and the top three hot sauces in our household collection of forty-plus.

Duke's Mayonnaise

If you read "Duke's" and think "any store-bought mayo," then consider this paragraph a persuasion piece. As a chef, I've made my fair share of mayonnaises and aioli. These words are not meant to negate the high quality that can be yielded by a perfect emulsion. Rather, they are to say that Duke's, which is noticeably brightened up with a hit of apple cider vinegar, is simply unmatched. It is synonymous with tomato season. I've folded it into cakes and dipped fries into it. It has saved my ass as a last-minute marinade. For God's sake, I've seared pork chops slathered with Duke's to create the most incredible, foolproof crust. It is my magic. Just use Duke's.

Flaky Salt

Flaky salt does double duty by introducing both an element of crunch and subtle bites of salinity. It makes sense to splurge here, since salt structure and texture are what you're paying for. Stretch your dollar and flex your control by using it strictly for finishing. I usually go for J.Q. Dickinson Salt-Works Heirloom Finishing Salt for maximum pinchability.

SUPREME RECIPES

Nailing these recipes and methods will yield the best results as you cook from *Our South* and, generally, make you a better home cook or chef overall. Load up your larder with what you see here as you cook through the seasons, and you'll find yourself cutting recipe times in half.

You could certainly use a can of stewed or diced tomatoes where a recipe calls for it, but these tomatoes, bursting with ripe, juicy flavor, are far better. **Makes 1 gallon**

STEWED TOMATOES

1 tablespoon unsalted butter

2 teaspoons canola oil

2 yellow onions, diced

2 green bell peppers, diced

2 teaspoons kosher salt

6 large heirloom tomatoes, quartered, juices reserved

3 tablespoons dark brown sugar

1 tablespoon fresh lemon juice

¼ teaspoon red pepper flakes

1 tablespoon dried parsley

In a heavy-bottomed pot or Dutch oven, melt the butter and oil over medium-low heat. Add the onions and bell peppers and cook, stirring occasionally, until the onions are translucent and beginning to brown, 7 to 9 minutes.

Stir in the salt, tomatoes with their juices, brown sugar, lemon juice, red pepper flakes, and parsley. Increase the heat to high, cover with the lid ajar, and bring to a boil.

Reduce the heat to medium and cook, uncovered, until the liquid begins to reduce and the mixture thickens, about 40 minutes.

Remove from the heat and let cool. Store in an airtight container in the refrigerator for up to 5 days. (For long-term storage, use the Hot Water Bath Canning technique opposite.)

Hot Water Bath Canning

This method for hot water bath canning is used specifically for ingredients that are high in acidity like chow chow (page 53) or Grape Jelly (page 160). You'll need:

A wire rack

A deep stockpot

Canning jars with lids and bands

A jar lifter or canning tongs

Pickles, stock, or preserves (see pages 000, 000, and 000), hot

A silicone spatula or wooden chopstick

To sterilize the jars, fit a wire rack into the bottom of a deep stockpot and set the jars, lids, and bands on the rack. Fill the pot with enough water to fully submerge the jars and bring it to a boil over high heat. Boil the jars for 10 minutes. Using a jar lifter or tongs, carefully lift the jars, lids, and bands from the water (use caution, as they will be slippery). Pour any water out of the jars and set aside, though keep in mind that the jars should still be hot when you fill them. (Alternatively, sterilize the jars by running them through a sanitize cycle in the dishwasher.)

Fill the hot jars with the hot pickles, stock, or preserves, leaving 1 to 2 inches of headspace. Run a spatula or chopstick around the inside of the jar to release any air bubbles and wipe the rim clean for a good seal. Cover the jars with the lids and tighten just until you feel some resistance—do not overtighten.

Fill your stockpot halfway with water and bring to a simmer over medium heat, 8 to 9 minutes. Using the jar lifter or tongs, carefully lower the sealed jars into the simmering water one at a time; the water in the pot should cover the jars by 1 to 2 inches. Increase the heat to high, cover, and bring to a rolling boil. Boil for 10 minutes (add another 5 minutes if your jars are 16 ounces or larger). Turn off the heat and leave the jars in the water for 10 minutes before removing them from the pot. Set the jars upright on a dry towel, spacing them 2 inches apart. Let cool overnight.

The next day, test the seal by pressing down on the center of each jar's lid. If it doesn't pop up, it's sealed. If it does pop up, or if the lid is easily removed, it's not sealed. Any jars that did not seal properly can be stored in the refrigerator for up to 4 weeks. Store properly sealed jars out of sunlight for up to 1 year. After opening, store in the fridge for up to 4 weeks.

Around these parts, cornbread is the sixth love language. And much like love, it comes in plenty of different forms. This classic version is the most common and recognizable. It's THE ONE, a trusty vehicle, the most approachable, the basis of all others—and it deserves to wear its haughty title. Use warm cornbread as a vehicle for jams and butters or open-faced-anything. Crush toasted cornbread bits onto salads or soups for crunch and texture. Utilize it finely crumbled as filler for recipes like Oyster Dressing Cakes (page 131) or sub for breadcrumbs for a more complex flavor. Not to dismiss other cornbread types you'll find here, like spoonbread (page 305), Cracklin Cornbread (page 161), johnnycakes (page 114), and Hot Water Cornbread (page 79), but classic is just my type. **Feeds 6 to 8**

CLASSIC CORNBREAD

6 tablespoons (¾ stick) unsalted butter, melted, plus more for greasing

1 cup fine yellow cornmeal

¾ cup all-purpose flour

3 tablespoons sugar

1½ teaspoons baking powder

½ teaspoon baking soda

¼ teaspoon kosher salt

2 large eggs, at room temperature, lightly beaten

1½ cups buttermilk

Preheat the oven to 425°F. Grease an 8-inch cast-iron skillet with butter.

In a large bowl, mix together the cornmeal, flour, sugar, baking powder, baking soda, and salt. In a separate large bowl, mix together the eggs, buttermilk, and melted butter. Pour the buttermilk mixture into the cornmeal mixture and fold together until no dry spots remain (the batter will still be lumpy). Pour the batter into the prepared skillet.

Bake for about 20 minutes, until the top of the cornbread is golden brown and a toothpick inserted into the center comes out clean. Remove the cornbread from the oven and let cool for 10 minutes before serving or using otherwise.

I don't balk at the use of chicken bouillon; it lives in my pantry just the same as it does yours. However, this homemade chicken stock allows you to take the reins, controlling the salt content and flavor intensity. Unlike the concentrated version, the depth of chicken flavor is pronounced without overpowering your palate with salt. The flavor profile is exactly what it should be: chicken. **Makes about 16 cups**

CHICKEN STOCK

4 to 5 pounds chicken bones

2 yellow onions, halved

4 carrots, coarsely chopped

4 celery stalks, coarsely chopped

7 garlic cloves, smashed

4 dried bay leaves

1 bunch parsley

6 thyme sprigs

1 tablespoon whole black peppercorns

2 tablespoons apple cider vinegar

In a large stockpot, combine the chicken bones, onions, carrots, celery, garlic, bay leaves, parsley, thyme, peppercorns, and vinegar. Add enough water to cover by 2 inches. Bring to a boil over high heat, then reduce the heat to low.

Simmer, uncovered, for 6 to 7 hours, until the chicken bones are softened, the vegetables are pretty much obliterated, and the stock is starting to turn golden brown. Every 2 hours as the stock simmers, use a spoon or ladle to scrape off and discard the foamy scum that rises to the surface.

Using tongs, carefully remove the bones from the pot and discard. Carefully strain the stock through a fine-mesh sieve into a large storage container and discard the solids. Let it cool in the refrigerator, uncovered, for at least 5 hours.

Skim off the fat that has solidified on the surface of the chilled stock (see Note). Cover the container of stock and store in the refrigerator for up to 4 days or in the freezer for up to 3 months.

Note: The rendered chicken fat, or schmaltz, can be stored in a separate airtight container for use in other recipes; it will keep in the refrigerator for up to 4 days.

Like the story of the North Carolina woman cleaning out her family's kitchen after her mother's death and finding pink bush beans—a variety we all believed to be extinct—saved in the back of the freezer and preserved in time, similar anecdotes have been shared by my dear farmer friend, Chris Smith, about how he has happened upon long-sought-after heirloom seeds. I'd consider myself a legume nerd, and the discovery of something my ancestors held closely really gets me going. Heirloom varieties are all subtly different in flavor, showing off bright pink speckles, slick textures, and deep shades of purple and black like tiny marbles waiting to be played with. I add these by the spoonful to pirloos such as Spiced Shrimp and Field Pea Pirloo (page 138) or fold them into Black-Eyed Pea Hominy Fritters (page 259), but a warm bowl of Soup Beans and Hot Water Cornbread (page 79) on a chilly night is self-care. **Makes about 4 cups**

FIELD PEAS AND BEANS

1 cup dried field peas or beans, presoaked and frozen (see page 31) or soaked in water overnight and drained

1 (2-inch) chunk smoky bacon

1 yellow onion, chopped

1 bay leaf

1 teaspoon freshly cracked black pepper

1 teaspoon kosher salt

Place the field peas in a large stockpot. Add the bacon, onion, bay leaf, and pepper and fill the pot with enough cool water to cover the peas by 3 inches. Bring to a boil over high heat, then let her rip for a full minute before reducing the heat to low to keep the water at a simmer. Cover the pot and cook for 1½ hours, checking occasionally and adding more water if needed to ensure the peas are fully covered, then do the doneness test: Take a single pea and pop it into your mouth. If you can effortlessly smash it against the roof of your mouth using your tongue, they're done; the peas should be smooth and creamy, not too firm. If they aren't done, cook for 30 minutes more, then test again.

When the peas are completely cooked, stir in the salt. Remove from the heat and let rest for 20 minutes. Serve immediately or store in a covered nonreactive vessel in the refrigerator for up to 4 days. Reheat before serving.

When I think about the Black diaspora's seemingly universal love of rice, a crop disseminated with us throughout the world via the slave trade and migration, I think about sankofa. Part of a famous proverb from Ghana's Akan tribe, it's a word that reminds us that knowing your history is the key to knowing yourself. Fittingly, the traditional symbol of sankofa is a bird stretching its neck to grab a single precious egg from its back—but to me, that egg looks like a perfectly pearly grain of rice. Southern rice, the irreplaceable foundation of the hoppin' John, pirloo, and hash that I ate growing up, connects me to the generations of ancestors who relied on African expertise and tradition to painstakingly cultivate an enormously influential and valuable industry from a few imported grains. And in the South, starchy and nutty Carolina Gold is the queen: a Lowcountry heirloom and staple of the Gullah Geechee, descendants of the same West Africans forcibly brought to the Carolinas to work on those plantations. As a tribute to how folks in Charleston refer to it, I call cooked Carolina Gold rice "Charleston ice cream" throughout this book. Served piping hot (despite the nickname), Charleston ice cream gets loaded into bowls in large scoops with globs of butter running down their sides faster than any hands can get to it. **Makes about 2½ cups**

CHARLESTON ICE CREAM, OR CLASSIC CAROLINA GOLD RICE

2 teaspoons kosher salt
1 cup Carolina Gold rice
Unsalted butter, for serving

Preheat the oven to 300°F. Line a baking sheet with parchment paper.

Fill a medium pot with 6 cups water, then add the salt. Quickly stir in the rice and bring the water to a boil over high heat, then immediately reduce the heat to low. Simmer gently, uncovered, stirring occasionally, until the rice is just past al dente, 11 to 13 minutes. Drain the rice through a fine-mesh sieve and rinse under cool water until the water runs clear. Shake the sieve to drain any excess water.

Distribute the rice in a single layer on the prepared baking sheet. Place in the oven to dry for 8 to 10 minutes, gently turning the grains a few times with a spatula, ensuring they remain in an even layer. You can stop when you're able to suss out the individuals grains of rice, which should now be on the drier side. Remove the rice from the oven and fluff with a fork. The rice should not be clumpy; each grain should be fluffy and distinguishable from the others. Use immediately or serve on its own, with butter.

Middlins are the broken-up, supposedly low-end cousins of pristine and polished grains of Carolina Gold rice. These crushed, broken, hulled, bottom-of-the-barrel kernels were historically written off as "slave food." It was anybody's guess why and how we'd make something good of this starch, so unidentifiable it led to comparisons to grits. But years ago, enterprising cooks discovered that the starchy, boggy rice was the ideal base for pirloo, a creamy, risotto-like side dish, and for meals where a stickier rice was more appropriate. **Makes about 3 cups**

RICE MIDDLINS

1 cup middlins or rice grits (preferably
    Carolina Gold)
¼ cup thinly sliced fresh chives

Place the middlins in a fine-mesh sieve and rinse under cool running water for 8 to 9 minutes, until the water is no longer cloudy. Shake off any excess water.

Transfer the middlins to a 4-quart pot and add 1¾ cups cool water. Cover the pot and cook over high heat until small bubbles begin to form, then reduce the heat to low and cook, without lifting the lid, for 16 to 18 minutes, until the middlins take on the appearance of a stiffer risotto. Remove the pot from the heat and let rest, covered, for another 10 minutes, then uncover and fluff the middlins with a fork.

Garnish with the chives and serve warm.

Potlikker is the bitter, earthy green broth left inside the pot after greens have been stewed for hours. This liquid is important in a lot of Southern cultures; in fact, some people deem it medicinal, a cure-all of sorts. Stewing greens could be any type of cruciferous greens that require long cooking times to tenderize. Collards are the usual suspect for producing potlikker, but since a lovely mess of greens is the by-product of this broody green liquid, I always throw in a bit of my other favorites—mustard and turnip—and enjoy them, too.
Makes about 1 gallon

POTLIKKER

1 pound salt pork

2 yellow onions, halved

1 garlic head, halved crosswise

2 pounds stewing greens

¼ cup vinegar (I typically use a combination of sherry vinegar and apple cider vinegar)

2 teaspoons kosher salt

2 teaspoons whole black peppercorns

1 teaspoon red pepper flakes

1 teaspoon cayenne pepper

In a large stockpot, combine the salt pork, onions, garlic, greens, vinegar, salt, peppercorns, red pepper flakes, and cayenne. Add enough water to cover the greens by 2 inches. Bring to a boil over high heat. Boil for 30 seconds, then reduce the heat to low. Weigh down the greens with a heatproof plate, cover the pot, and simmer for 1½ hours, until the liquid has taken on the color of the greens and the greens have become tender. Remove from the heat.

Strain the rich liquid (you can reserve the greens, without the peppercorns, to stir into soup or eat with rice). Store the potlikker in an airtight 4-quart container in the refrigerator for up to 4 days or in the freezer for up 3 months. (For long-term storage, use the Hot Water Bath Canning technique on page 39.)

BACKC

OUNTRY

I don't have children, but I imagine picking a favorite regional cuisine is as impossible as choosing a favorite child. I will say, though, that something about the Appalachian South sets it apart from the rest of the South. Perched thousands of feet above its neighboring counterparts, its rolling hills bring a sense of peace, at least for me. Some of my warmest and most vivid memories are from here, right alongside those of my great-aunt Hattie Mae. If I close my eyes and think about her, I feel a yearning for her voice and her little Appalachian home, where the afternoon sun was always filtered through curtains of drying britches and the walls were lined with enough jarred remedies to bring discomfort to a licensed medical professional. While there was no hot water (or really any people, for that matter), a younger me understood this step back in time to be utopia. During our short visits to "check up on Hattie," the adults would talk for hours while I explored deep enough into the woods for their voices to disappear. I'd run off for hours; here, that was okay. I'd bring back my foraged finds, and Hattie Mae would name every single mushroom, branch, berry, and leaf I held in my dirty hands. She taught me all the things I didn't know I needed to learn.

Hattie Mae was one of the last relatives in my maternal family who insisted mountain life was just better. Stubborn, the other adults often called her, just like her mama (my late great-grandmother Inez, whom I'd only ever met when I was a child). Even though three generations on this side had lived and owned land in Carroll County in southwestern Virginia, "Appalachian" was not a title they wore proudly. "Why would she insist on this hard mountain life when she could just come to the coast with us?" they'd wonder. "Why would anyone insist on living this way?" Those words and conversations stuck with me. And as I got older, my desire for the Backcountry life waned, and I happily took any opportunity to get out of going up the Dan River. But the mountains were waiting to welcome me home, and all I'd learned from Hattie Mae would eventually come flooding back to my soul.

Chow chow is much like Southern Appalachia itself: colorful and profound. It contains plenty of quirky things that work together to create some form of semblance. No batch is made the exact same way, but key qualities and characteristics usually remain unchanged. Gripped by pungent flavors, it's typically sweet and often funky, too. It was born out of the dilemma of not having enough of one thing to make a whole anything. For instance, those end-of-the-week days in which you're faced with a quarter of a head of leafy cabbage, half a green bell pepper, a withering carrot, and an onion in the back of the fridge—those are the moments chow chow is waiting for. **Makes 1 gallon**

CLASSIC CHOW CHOW

2 pounds vegetables (such as cabbage, bell peppers, onions), finely chopped

¼ cup kosher salt

4 cups distilled white vinegar

2 cups sugar

1 (1-inch) piece fresh ginger, peeled and minced

2 teaspoons celery seeds

2 teaspoons ground turmeric

2 teaspoons fennel seeds

2 teaspoons red pepper flakes

1 teaspoon whole black peppercorns

1 teaspoon mustard seeds

4 whole cloves

Set a colander over a large bowl. Place the chopped vegetables in the colander and toss with the salt. Set aside at room temperature for at least 3 hours or up to 8 hours; this will draw out excess liquid from the vegetables to prevent the brine from becoming diluted.

In a 2-quart saucepan, combine the vinegar, sugar, ginger, celery seeds, turmeric, fennel seeds, red pepper flakes, peppercorns, mustard seeds, and cloves. Bring to a boil over high heat for about 30 seconds. Reduce the heat to low and simmer for another 15 minutes to dissolve the sugar and infuse the vinegar with the spices.

Meanwhile, pack the vegetables into a sterilized 1-gallon glass jar (or other nonreactive heatproof vessel with a tight-fitting lid). Pour the hot brine over the top, leaving 1 inch of headspace, and let cool. Seal the jar and store the chow chow in the refrigerator for up to 30 days. (For long-term storage, use the Hot Water Bath Canning technique on page 39.)

This earthy beet version of chow chow adds both sour and sweet components to the table. Its flavor is more amplified than common beet pickles, and grating the beets helps them retain their crunch and stand up nicely to the punchy horseradish. I like to enjoy this chow chow on sandwiches, boiled eggs, or Loaded Twice-Baked Sweet Potatoes (page 280).

Makes 1 gallon

SPICY BEET CHOW CHOW

3 large beets with their greens, coarsely shredded, greens minced

4 cups coarsely shredded cabbage

2 garlic cloves, grated

¼ cup prepared horseradish

2½ tablespoons kosher salt

2 cups sugar

2 cups white wine vinegar

1 tablespoon yellow mustard seeds

2½ teaspoons red pepper flakes

2 teaspoons coriander seeds

2 whole cloves

2 dried bay leaves

In a large bowl, combine the beets, beet greens, cabbage, garlic, horseradish, and salt.

In a 2-quart saucepan, combine the sugar, vinegar, mustard seeds, red pepper flakes, coriander, cloves, and bay leaves. Bring to a boil over high heat. Cook for 1 minute, then reduce the heat to low and simmer for 10 minutes, until the sugar has dissolved.

Meanwhile, pack the beet mixture into a sterilized 1-gallon glass jar (or other nonreactive heatproof vessel with a tight-fitting lid). Pour the hot brine over the top, leaving 1 inch of headspace, and let cool. Seal the jar and store the chow chow in the refrigerator for up to 14 days. (For long-term storage, use the Hot Water Bath Canning technique on page 39.)

Sour Corn Chow Chow,
page 57

Classic Chow Chow,
page 53

Spicy Beet Chow Chow,
page 54

SEVEN SWEETS AND SOURS

An Appalachian tablespace is full of jars, crocks, and other nameless vessels of varying sizes filled with bright, bracing, sweet, and colorful preserves, pickles, and fermented wild foods. This tradition is known as Seven Sweets and Sours. Some form of cornbread is required to sop up any gravies or sauces. A sticky jar of sorghum molasses is a key condiment. Large-format meals, served family style, are commonplace because this type of eating beckons the masses to come share. What happens next is a sight to behold: reaching, passing, dipping, scooping.

With its seemingly bland and basic foodways, Appalachian cooking often gets dismissed as unworthy. While there is some truth to the perception that the food here is subdued and executed in its simplest form, the Seven Sweets and Sours are essentials that make even the simplest foods sing, allowing the humblest ingredients to come to life on the Appalachian table. My usual trick is pairing sweet flavors with savory braised meats or stews—like Hattie Mae's sweet cucumber salad blanketing a juicy pork chop—and introducing sour ones when I want that extra kick of umami, like sour corn (page 59) and soup beans (page 79).

Chow chow (see pages 53, 54, and 57) and apple butter (page 67) are also excellent sweet and sour complements. Stay awhile and maybe enjoy a bowl of buttered hominy, complete with vittles, that will change your perspective of Appalachia.

The thought of souring for preservation might seem backward, as Westernized palates often associate funky, bubbling flavors with spoilage. But souring is a type of lacto-fermentation witnessed in the making of yogurt, sauerkraut, and sourdough, in case you need convincing. Moreover, Indigenous people have been utilizing this technique for ages, and this form of fast fermentation can also be found in many old techniques in Black cookery, often signifying for enslaved people a form of empowerment that long remained a mystery to their owners. **Makes 1 gallon**

SOUR CORN CHOW CHOW

1 pound firm green tomatoes, diced

1 red bell pepper, diced

1 medium red onion, diced

4 garlic cloves, chopped

2 tablespoons kosher salt

2 cups apple cider vinegar

1 cup packed light brown sugar

1 teaspoon juniper berries

½ teaspoon allspice berries

½ teaspoon ground turmeric

½ teaspoon red pepper flakes

1 cinnamon stick

2 bay leaves

Sour Corn (see page 59)

Set a colander over a large bowl. Place the tomatoes, bell pepper, onion, and garlic in the colander and sprinkle with the salt. Set aside at room temperature for at least 3 hours and up to 8 hours; this will draw out excess liquid from the vegetables to prevent the brine from becoming diluted.

Meanwhile, in a high-sided medium saucepan, combine the vinegar, brown sugar, juniper, allspice, turmeric, red pepper flakes, cinnamon stick, and bay leaves. Bring to a boil over high heat. Cook for 1 minute, then reduce the heat to low and simmer for 15 minutes, until the brown sugar has dissolved.

In a large bowl, combine the salted vegetables with the drained sour corn. Pack the vegetable mixture into a sterilized 1-gallon glass jar (or other nonreactive heatproof vessel with a tight-fitting lid). Pour the hot brine over the mixture, leaving 1 inch of headspace, and let cool. Seal the jar and store in the refrigerator for up to 30 days. (For long-term storage, use the Hot Water Bath Canning technique on page 39.)

I learned this technique at the Baltimore restaurant Cinghiale early in my professional cooking career. We'd use an old wooden tool created specifically for shucking corn to make what we called "fresh polenta." "That's totally creamed corn," I thought aloud when we went over new dishes for service; largely ignored, I just went to my station and got right to it. The end result was a face absolutely covered in corn carnage, but my efforts also produced a creamy, rich, crazily corn-forward side dish. I believe in the power of the sour, so that's what I like to use here. **Feeds 4 to 6**

CREAMED SOUR CORN

8 ears corn, shucked

2 cups Sour Corn (recipe follows), drained

1 teaspoon kosher salt

1 teaspoon freshly ground black pepper

¼ cup heavy cream

1 tablespoon unsalted butter

Using a paring knife, score the corncobs from top to bottom all along the kernels of corn. Using a metal spoon with a large bowl set underneath, vigorously scrape the "corn milk" into the bowl, making sure to scrape the entire cob free of kernels and to capture any liquid that releases. (You can discard the cobs or reserve them for another use, such as the Family Reunion Watermelon Punch on page 193.)

In a blender or food processor, puree the sour corn until smooth. Pass the sour corn mixture through a fine-mesh sieve set over a high-sided medium saucepan, using a ladle to push it through. Pass the collected "corn milk" through a sieve into the same pot. Discard the solids.

Add the salt, pepper, and cream to the strained corn milk mixture. Place the pot over high heat. When the mixture begins to gently boil and sputter, reduce the heat to medium-low. Cover and simmer until thickened, 20 to 25 minutes. Stir in the butter to melt, then serve immediately.

Sour Corn

Makes 8 cups

    6 ears corn, shucked, kernels cut from the cobs
    4 dill sprigs
    2 quarts room-temperature distilled water
    5 tablespoons kosher salt

Pack the corn kernels into a sterilized 1-gallon glass jar (or an equivalent nonreactive vessel with a tight-fitting lid), leaving 2 inches of headspace. Add the dill to the jar.

In a large bowl, stir together the distilled water and salt until the salt looks evenly distributed. Slowly pour 2 quarts of this brine into the jar. Using a glass weight or small plate, weigh down the corn kernels so they are fully submerged. Cover the jar with muslin cloth and secure it with a rubber band or kitchen twine. Set aside to ferment for 5 days, until the corn smells a bit funky and tastes a little sour. (A layer of white yeast may form at the top—this is normal; use a spoon to remove and discard it.) If the taste of the corn is to your liking, seal the jar with its lid and refrigerate; if not, ferment the corn on the counter for 2 to 3 days more.

Store the sour corn in the refrigerator for up to 2 weeks. Every 5 or 6 days, wipe the top and inside of the jar with a clean paper towel and ensure the corn is submerged in the brine.

My friend and fellow chef Yakiim Sano taught me about preserving fish with vinegar. In the inland mountains of his grandparents' region, Shizuoka, Japan, people have done so for centuries—long before the invention of sushi. While we spoke, my mind drifted toward memories of cold Appalachian winters, when seafood and fresh produce were rarities on the dinner table. There, as in Shizuoka, food preservation was key to survival. The two worlds convene in this dish in which punchy vinegar is both functional and flavorful. **Feeds 4**

VINEGAR-CURED TROUT AND SOUR APPLES

For the Sour Apples

Juice of 1 lime

2 teaspoons honey

½ teaspoon kosher salt

2 Granny Smith apples, cored and thinly sliced

½ cup apple cider vinegar

1 thyme sprig

1 dill sprig

1 garlic clove, peeled

½ teaspoon yellow mustard seeds

For the Trout

4 steelhead trout fillets

½ cup kosher salt

¾ cup sugar

Rice vinegar

For Serving

1 Gala or Fuji apple, cored and thinly sliced

Extra-virgin olive oil

Freshly cracked black pepper

Make the sour apples: In a nonreactive medium bowl, whisk together the lime juice, honey, and salt. Add the apples, toss to coat, and let stand for 15 to 25 minutes.

In a small high-sided saucepan, combine the vinegar, thyme, dill, garlic, mustard seeds, and ½ cup water. Bring to a rolling boil over high heat. Boil for 1 minute, then reduce the heat to low and simmer for 5 minutes. Remove from the heat and let cool. Pour the brine over the apples and let sit for at least 10 minutes to lightly pickle them. (They get even better if you leave them at room temperature overnight.)

Make the trout: Place one trout fillet skin-side down on your cutting board. Using a sharp knife and holding the skin tightly, remove it from the trout by situating the blade between the skin and its flesh. Point the blade downward, being sure not to cut through the flesh or tear the skin. Reserve the skin, then slice the flesh lengthwise into 2-inch strips. Repeat with the remaining fillets.

In a small bowl, combine the salt and sugar. Pour half the salt-sugar cure over the bottom of a large nonreactive baking dish. Lay the trout over the cure and cover with the remaining cure. Refrigerate for 30 minutes.

Preheat the oven to 325°F. Set a wire rack over a baking sheet.

Rinse the fish well, pat dry with paper towels, and place in a shallow nonreactive dish. Sprinkle with rice vinegar. Set aside to cure for 10 to 15 minutes.

Using a small spoon, gently scrape the reserved skins clean of any residual flesh and lay them flat, scaled-side up, on the rack. Cover with parchment and top with another baking sheet to keep them flat. Roast for 25 to 30 minutes, until crispy. Remove from the oven, uncover, and let cool.

To serve, layer the cured trout, sour apples, and raw apples on a plate. Drizzle generously with olive oil. Garnish with the crispy trout skin and freshly cracked black pepper.

I grew up beachside, which means the texture and taste of saltwater taffy are forever imprinted on my brain. So, too, are hush puppies: they will never exit my olfactory memory. Well-seasoned, fragrant, and crisp hush puppies are married with a ketchup that contains the nuances of sweet corn but the intense smoked umami of Heinz. Where I'm from, hush puppies make their home on fried-fish plates, so I suggest you try these pups at your next fish fry—or just snack on them all on their own. **Makes 24 hush puppies**

FISH CAMP HUSH PUPPIES
WITH SOUR CORN KETCHUP

For the Sour Corn Ketchup

2 cups Sour Corn (see page 59), drained, 1 cup liquid reserved

1 tablespoon unsalted butter, melted

1 teaspoon kosher salt

1 teaspoon freshly ground black pepper

1 tablespoon honey

A few dashes of hot sauce

For the Hush Puppies

1 cup fine yellow cornmeal

½ cup self-rising flour

1 teaspoon kosher salt, plus more as needed

½ teaspoon sugar

½ teaspoon garlic powder

¼ teaspoon paprika

½ cup (1 stick) unsalted butter, melted

1 large egg, at room temperature, lightly beaten

¾ cup cold buttermilk

1 small onion, grated

Peanut oil, for frying

Make the ketchup: Preheat a smoker to 225°F. Line a rack with aluminum foil.

In a small bowl, toss the sour corn with the melted butter, salt, and pepper. Spread the mixture over the prepared rack and smoke the kernels for 35 to 40 minutes, until the corn smells smoky.

Transfer the smoked sour corn to a blender or food processor and add the sour corn liquid, honey, and hot sauce. Puree until smooth, then pass the mixture through a fine-mesh sieve set over a small high-sided saucepan using a ladle to push it through. Discard the solids. Bring to a simmer over low heat, then cook, stirring occasionally, until thickened, about 15 minutes. Remove from the heat and let cool to room temperature.

Meanwhile, make the hush puppies: In a large bowl, combine the cornmeal, flour, salt, sugar, garlic powder, and paprika. In a small bowl, whisk together the butter, egg, buttermilk, and grated onion. Add the wet ingredients to the dry ingredients and stir until just combined.

Fill a Dutch oven with 2 inches of oil and clip a deep-fry thermometer to the side. Heat over medium heat to 350°F.

Using clean hands, grab about 1 tablespoon of the batter and quickly rub it between your palms to form a cylinder, them drop it into the hot oil. Add more to the pot (I like to do about 8 at a time) and cook until golden brown, flipping halfway through, about 2 minutes total. Use a slotted spoon to transfer the pups to a plate lined with paper towels. Immediately season lightly with salt. Repeat with the remaining batter, letting the oil return to 350°F between batches.

Serve the hush puppies warm, with a sidecar of sour corn ketchup.

Malinda Russell, author of the 1866 *Domestic Cook Book*, might call my version of her recipe a bit wordy. Known for using no more than a few lines even for the most detailed of processes, she might come off as a woman of few words. But I'd guess the opposite, in fact. I think Russell's recipes left room for the conversations she intended to have and the questions she longed to hear. I imagine many readers invited her over to dinner to taste-test their versions of her recipes and identify exactly where they went wrong or how they should add this or that. To tell it, of all my kitchen feats, it's my confidence in baking that leaves me wishing I had some sort of recipe club, too. There was something I found very comforting in being faced with this recipe of Russell's, which is just a few words. Short and sweet, it didn't leave much room for overthinking: no paragraphs to lose myself in or lines to read between. That's how I got drawn in. And I stayed there, with those few words, until I got it right. Since I can't meet you at your dinner table and answer your burning questions, I'll leave my very, very detailed adaptation of Miss Malinda's salt-rising bread recipe here for you. **Makes 12 rolls**

MALINDA RUSSELL'S SALT-RISING BREAD
WITH COUNTRY HAM RAMP BUTTER

For the Butter

½ pound smoked country ham,
    center-cut, diced

1 pound (4 sticks) unsalted butter,
    at room temperature

3 ramps, green parts only, minced

1 teaspoon white wine vinegar

½ teaspoon kosher salt

¼ teaspoon freshly ground
    black pepper

For the Bread

¼ cup whole milk

2 tablespoons fine yellow cornmeal

1½ teaspoons sugar

1 cup hot water (about 120°F)

1 teaspoon kosher salt

½ teaspoon baking soda

4 cups all-purpose flour, plus more for dusting

3 tablespoons lard, plus more for greasing

Flaky salt

Make the butter: Place the diced country ham in a medium cast-iron or other heavy-bottomed skillet. Set the pan over medium-low heat and cook, stirring occasionally, until crisp, 10 to 12 minutes. (This is an important step! It crisps up the bits of ham, which will add a crunchy texture to the smooth butter.) Remove from the heat and let cool, then transfer to a food processor and pulse a few times to form crunchy little ham bits.

In a stand mixer fitted with the paddle attachment, beat together the butter, ramps, vinegar, salt, pepper, and ham bits on medium-high speed until fully incorporated, about 5 minutes. Scoop the butter onto a length of wax

Recipe continues

paper and shape it into a log, twisting the ends to seal. Refrigerate until firm, at least 1 hour. (Store the butter in the refrigerator for up to 5 days or in the freezer for up to a few months. Thaw for 15 minutes before serving, until just soft enough to slice into rounds.)

Make the bread: In a small saucepan, gently heat the milk over medium-high heat, stirring frequently to be sure not to scorch the bottom of the pot, until small bubbles form around the edges of the pan, 2 to 3 minutes. Remove the pot from the heat.

In a small bowl, stir together the cornmeal and 1 teaspoon of the sugar, then vigorously whisk in the scalded milk. Cover the bowl with plastic wrap and place it somewhere warm (between 90° and 100°F) to ferment for at least 9 hours or up to 12 hours (see Note), until the mixture begins to bubble and smell cheesy.

In a large bowl, stir together the hot water, ½ teaspoon of the salt, the baking soda, and the remaining ½ teaspoon sugar. Slowly add 1½ cups of the flour, stirring until everything is thoroughly combined. Stir in the fermented

cornmeal mixture. Cover the bowl with plastic wrap and place it in a warm spot (see Note). Let rest for 3 to 4 hours, until the starter is bubbling and has nearly doubled in size.

Grease and flour an 8-inch round baking pan.

Transfer the starter to a stand mixer fitted with the dough hook. With the mixer running on medium speed, add the lard, the remaining ½ teaspoon salt, and remaining 2½ cups flour and knead until the dough is soft and stretchy; this will just take a couple minutes—do not overknead.

Using a dough cutter, divide the dough into 4 equal pieces. Divide each piece evenly into thirds, each weighing about 2 ounces (60 g). Working with one piece at a time, lay the dough flat on a cutting board and pull the edges into the center to form a roll. Place the roll seam-side down in the prepared baking pan and repeat with the remaining dough.

Add a pinch of flaky salt to the top of each roll, then cover the pan loosely with a tea towel or muslin cloth and place it in a warm spot. Let the dough rise for 2 to 3 hours.

Preheat the oven to 350°F. Bake the rolls for 25 to 30 minutes, until the tops are browned. Remove from the oven and place the pan on a wire rack to cool slightly.

Serve the warm rolls with the ham butter alongside.

Note: If you're not making this during a muggy Southern summer, preheat your oven to its lowest temperature, turn it off, then place the bowl with the cornmeal mixture inside. After about 8 hours, the mixture should begin to bubble and smell cheesy; if it doesn't, move the bowl to a warmer spot to ferment for 8 hours more. During cooler months, place a small pan filled with 2 cups water on the bottom rack in your oven, preheat the oven to its lowest temperature, then turn the oven off and place the bowl with the cornmeal mixture inside. This creates a warm, moist environment for fermentation.

Making apple butter in the Mountain South is a hillbilly rite of passage. The end of the apple season right around November usually spells heavy labor—peeling, coring, and hours-long stewing of these cool-weather gifts. Through this process, I learned that pectin is stored not only in the seeds but also in the flavor-packed ruby-red skins, which produce a jammy, caramelized texture all on their own. To amp up the pectin-production abilities and save yourself a laborious step, we'll skip the peeling. **Makes 3 cups**

APPLE BUTTER

3 pounds apples (I like a sweet variety such as Gala or Fuji), cored and cut into 1-inch chunks

1 cup packed dark brown sugar

1 teaspoon kosher salt

1 teaspoon ground cinnamon

½ teaspoon freshly grated nutmeg

¼ teaspoon ground cardamom

¼ teaspoon ground cloves

In a Dutch oven or other heavy-bottomed pot, combine the apples, brown sugar, salt, cinnamon, nutmeg, cardamom, and cloves. Add ½ cup water, cover, and cook over low heat, stirring occasionally, for 1 hour, until the apples begin to break down and become fork-tender.

Using an immersion blender, puree the apples directly in the pot until smooth; the apple butter should be thick and scoopable. Store in an airtight container in the refrigerator for up to 10 days.

Kilt, as in "killed," is how mountain folk describe once-lively lettuce that has been forgotten and left to wilt on the counter (or in the back of the fridge for the modernists). Either way, ditching it is sacrilege in the "waste not, want not" era. In the days of old, prior to common, convenient refrigeration, this tried-and-true recipe revived wilted garden lettuce with bacon grease and vinegar—two of my own lifelines. **Feeds 4 to 6**

KILT LETTUCE

½ pound slab bacon, or 5 thick-cut slices bacon, diced

1 small yellow onion, thinly sliced into rounds

¼ cup apple cider vinegar

1 tablespoon honey

1 head iceberg lettuce, preferably a few days old, maybe even left on the counter for a day, coarsely chopped

Kosher salt and freshly ground black pepper

In a large, high-sided cast-iron skillet or Dutch oven, cook the bacon over medium heat until golden brown, about 15 minutes. Using a slotted spoon, transfer the bacon to a plate lined with paper towels, leaving the rendered fat in the pan.

Add the onion rounds to the pan and cook, stirring occasionally, until soft and translucent, 4 to 5 minutes. Carefully and slowly pour in the vinegar, then the honey. Bring to a rolling boil and boil for 30 seconds.

Add the bacon to the vinegar mixture. Remove from the heat and add the lettuce. Let stand for 3 to 4 minutes to wilt, then toss to coat. Season with salt and pepper and serve.

In Southern Appalachia, root cellars and larders are spoken of with great pride, much like the esteemed underground wine cellars of some of the world's greatest wine connoisseurs. When I prepare this soup on a cold night, I imagine my great-aunt Hattie Mae making her way down those crumbly old brick stairs to that cool, otherworldly place where the year's produce magically stands still in time. **Feeds 6 to 8**

PEPPERY TURNIP SOUP
WITH DANDELION PESTO

For the Soup

4 tablespoons (½ stick) unsalted butter

2 teaspoons canola oil

2 pounds turnips with greens, diced, greens removed and chopped

4 leeks, white parts only, well washed and chopped

3 garlic cloves, smashed and minced

1 yellow onion, diced

2 teaspoons kosher salt

2 teaspoons freshly ground white pepper

¼ teaspoon freshly grated nutmeg

5 cups chicken stock, homemade (page 41) or store-bought

2 dried bay leaves

2 teaspoons dried sage

1 Parmesan cheese rind

For the Pesto

1 cup dandelion flowers and greens

1 cup extra-virgin olive oil

4 garlic cloves, smashed and peeled

Juice of 2 lemons

½ cup blanched almonds, toasted

2 teaspoons kosher salt

2 tablespoons freshly grated Parmesan cheese

Freshly ground black pepper

Make the soup: In a Dutch oven, combine the butter, canola oil, turnips, turnip greens, leeks, garlic, onion, salt, white pepper, and nutmeg. Cook over medium-low heat until the vegetables begin to soften, 10 to 12 minutes. Stir in the stock, bay leaves, sage, and Parmesan rind. Cover and cook for 1 hour more, stirring occasionally, until the flavors are melded.

Meanwhile, make the pesto: In a food processor, combine the dandelions, olive oil, garlic, and lemon juice. Process for 1 to 2 minutes, keeping the mixture a bit chunky. Add the almonds, salt, and Parmesan and pulse a few times to fully incorporate. Transfer the pesto to a small bowl.

To serve, ladle the hot soup into bowls and garnish with a few dollops of pesto and a couple of turns of black pepper.

Leather britches are something the Appalachian South can undeniably and proudly claim as its own—our very own version of hoshigaki, if you will. Unlike that Japanese technique, which uses persimmons, we use green beans, the kind we are accustomed to snapping, or greasy beans—a western North Carolina specialty—and a needle and thread. A nearly forgotten art, there ain't much fighting over this one. The creation of leather britches is a long, meditative one. You'll want to grab a chair to sit in while you string green beans before hanging them to dry in a sunny spot. They'll develop a shriveled appearance, making them look like little leather pants on a clothesline, hence the goofy name. The results of this old-time practice, combined with smoky seasoning meat, create a dish with a depth of umami-rich flavor. **Feeds 4 to 6**

LEATHER BRITCHES

1 pound ham hock

1 onion, quartered

½ pound britches (2 cups; see sidebar)

1 teaspoon kosher salt

¼ teaspoon freshly ground
　black pepper

In a medium pot, combine the ham hock and onion and add water to cover completely. Bring to a boil over high heat and cook for a full minute. Reduce the heat to medium-low to maintain a simmer, cover, and cook for 45 minutes to 1 hour, until the ham hock becomes tender.

Uncover the pot and add the britches. Using a glass weight or small plate, weigh down the britches so they are fully submerged. Simmer for 1 hour, adding water as necessary to keep the britches submerged, then remove the weight and the ham hock. Set the ham hock aside to cool while the britches simmer for 1 hour more, until tender.

When the ham hock is cool enough to handle, pull the meat from the bone and coarsely chop, discarding the bone. Return the meat to the pot of britches and season with the salt and pepper. Serve the britches in bowls with a ladleful of the hot liquid.

Britches

To make britches, thread a needle with about 2 feet of darning thread or fishing line and tie a knot at one end to secure it. Thread about ½ pound of green beans onto the line, passing the needle through the center of each pod. Continue until the thread is filled with beans, leaving about 4 inches of space at each end. Tie the excess thread at each end into a loop; the threaded green beans will look like garland. Using the loops, hang the britches in a sunny window for at least 7 days or up to 14 days, until the green beans have shriveled and dried. Remove the britches from the string before using.

Every good Southern chef has a grits recipe they believe is the best. This one is mine, and they really are that. These creamy, rich grits are special because I start with dried hominy, which gets soaked to double its size, then cooked slowly in butter, then blended to a smooth, velvety texture. These buttery bad boys are generous in umami and taste like they've got cheddar cheese running through them. **Feeds 4 to 6**

BUTTERY HOMINY GRITS

1 cup dried hominy, soaked
   in water overnight and drained

2½ teaspoons kosher salt

½ cup (1 stick) unsalted butter,
   plus more for serving

Freshly cracked black pepper, for serving

In a medium heavy-bottomed pot, cover the hominy with water by about 1 inch. Bring to a boil over high heat, then reduce the heat to low and simmer for about 90 minutes, until the hominy is fork-tender. Turn off the heat and, using an immersion blender, puree the hominy directly in the pot until smooth.

Return the pot to medium heat. While stirring continuously with a wooden spoon, add 1 cup water and the salt, being sure to scrape the bottom of the pot to prevent the grits from sticking. Add another 1 cup water, continuing to stir. The grits should be the consistency of a loose porridge; if necessary, add another ¼ cup water to achieve the desired consistency.

Fold in the butter to melt. Serve the grits hot, spooned into bowls with additional pats of butter and black pepper over the top.

I can't call this a family recipe, but I can certainly trace it back through my lineage. While I didn't grow up practicing the methods of preservation through pine rosin, I know my people did—it's one of the lesser known foodways of Black culture, and one that deserves recognition. These days, all most people know about this substance is that violin players coat their bows with it. The thought that anyone would use it to cook is far out of mind, though pine rosin potatoes used to be featured in historic cookbooks and even on Southern restaurant menus. But where do you even get pine rosin? To start, you'd tap pine trees to harvest their resin, a sappy, sticky, tacky substance. Then you'd boil the resin to distill and separate out the oil of turpentine. Turpentine camps and tar burners were all over the pine forests of North Carolina in the eighteenth and nineteenth centuries, earning it its "Tar Heel State" moniker. Most of these camps were worked by Black people born into slavery, which would explain why the history of enslaved people is ripe with stories of sap collecting for sustenance and preservation. They were survivalists through and through.

Perhaps you're wondering why one would go through all this trouble for a potato. The obvious reason is that it was likely done out of need—dropping a couple of potatoes into lava-hot sap made for an easy lunch so you could keep working without stopping. The fact that the end result was actually incredibly delicious was a lucky coincidence.

This recipe is a massive undertaking, and I urge you to take in every bit of it. You've got to cook this outside, because rosin is super flammable and when heated, its fumes are toxic, and you'll need everything listed below to make this recipe work. While I won't ask you to tap a pine tree to get rosin, you can get the required 5 pounds online or at a music store for about $50 (don't worry—it's reusable). Pine rosin cookers are available to purchase for this task, but if you don't want to invest in one, I'd suggest using a pot you don't mind designating the "rosin pot" from here on out. You will be able to get it mostly clean—with patience and elbow grease—but usually it just ends up being the rosin pot.

After a few fascinating trials, I can say that cooking in rosin yields the most pure, potato-y potato a human could ever have. What I love most about this recipe is what I love about most recipes in general: the rich history that can be seen in so many avenues of preservation. **Feeds 6 to 8**

ROSIN-COOKED POTATOES
WITH SPRUCE TIP BUTTER

5 pounds pine rosin

1 cup (2 sticks) unsalted butter, at room
   temperature

¼ cup fresh spruce tips, minced

2 teaspoons minced garlic

1 teaspoon kosher salt

¼ teaspoon freshly ground black pepper

4 pounds small russet potatoes

You *must* cook this recipe outside.

Melt the rosin in your rosin pot (a medium stockpot) over medium heat until it is completely liquefied, about 25 minutes.

Meanwhile, using a handheld mixer, whip together the butter, spruce tips, garlic, salt, and pepper for 2 minutes, until fully combined. If you're not planning on using the butter right away, keep it in the refrigerator.

Reduce the heat under the rosin pot to low, then use tongs to carefully lower the potatoes into the hot rosin. Turn the potatoes to coat them in the rosin and cook, uncovered, until the potatoes begin to float, about 1 hour. Remove the potatoes with the tongs, carefully allowing excess rosin to drip back into the pot. Turn off the heat.

Place each potato directly onto a single sheet of newspaper, then wrap it and twist each end to seal. Let cool slightly, about 10 minutes, then peel back the newspaper. The pine rosin will have hardened and remain stuck to the newspaper. Break the potatoes open and serve with the butter. Eat the flesh of the potato only, discarding the rosin-covered potato skin.

To clean the rosin pot, reheat it and clean carefully while the rosin is liquefied. The rosin can be stashed in plastic quart containers and reused indefinitely; let it cool slightly before storage. The tongs can be boiled to remove the excess rosin.

Soup beans are a staple in the mountains. Warming on cold nights, this unfussy side dish, which has seasoning meat in the pot, plus a few fixings on the table, makes a meal complete. Chow chow adds bites of acidity, and the cornbread enables sopping. Pinto beans are commonly used, and in my household, butter beans are another favorite. But the magic here is less about the beans and more about the method. You'll want to ladle generous portions of that rich "beanlikker" into each bowl you serve to make them true soup beans. Get out your sweets and sours (see page 56) to make your Appalachian table complete and dig in. **Feeds 4 to 6**

SOUP BEANS AND HOT WATER CORNBREAD

For the Beans

1 cup dried beans (my preference is a blend of pinto and black-eyed peas), soaked in water overnight and drained

½ pound anything fatty, cured, smoked, and from a hog

1 yellow onion, chopped

2 teaspoons freshly cracked black pepper

2 teaspoons kosher salt

For the Hot Water Cornbread

1 cup fine yellow cornmeal

2 teaspoons kosher salt

2 teaspoons sugar

1 cup boiling water

1 tablespoon bacon grease, plus more for frying

For Serving

1 small white onion, finely diced

Sour Corn Chow Chow (page 57)

Make the beans: In a large stockpot, combine the drained beans, seasoning meat, onion, and pepper. Fill the pot with enough cool water to cover the beans by 3 inches. Bring to a boil over high heat. Cook for 1 minute, then reduce the heat to low to keep the water at a simmer. Cover the pot and cook the beans for 1½ hours, checking to add more water, if necessary, to ensure beans are fully covered. Test the beans for doneness: Take a single bean and pop it into your mouth. If you can effortlessly smash it against the roof of your mouth using your tongue, they're done; the beans should be smooth and creamy, not firm. If they aren't done, cook for 30 minutes more, then test again. Once the beans are completely cooked, stir in the salt. Remove from the heat and let rest for 10 minutes.

Meanwhile, make the cornbread: In a large bowl, combine the cornmeal, salt, and sugar. Add the boiling water and bacon grease and stir to melt together.

Fill a large cast-iron skillet with ½ inch of bacon grease and clip a deep-fry thermometer to the side. Heat over medium-high heat to 350°F. Add batter to the hot grease by the heaping tablespoon and fry until crisp and golden brown, turning halfway through, about 4 minutes total. Transfer to a plate lined with paper towels.

To serve, ladle the soup beans in bowls, being sure to add plenty of the beanlikker. Top each bowl with a heaping spoonful of white onion. Serve with the cornbread and sour corn chow chow alongside.

Schnitzel was introduced to the South by German settlers in the 1800s, weaving its way into country fried steak and what is often referred to as "fried pork chops." With sauerkraut and apple butter on many Appalachian tables, the influence of these settlers is hard to miss. The unlikely melting pot of cultures witnessed in the Backcountry often sees many regional influences on one table, and I'm all about it. Bologna crept into our foodways much in the same way as German influences, and we wisely held on to that, too. Giving it the schnitzel treatment makes this recipe read like it came out of a stoner cookbook, but it's what I think of when someone mentions fried bologna sandwiches to me (I somehow didn't discover the beauty of those until college). So I created what I thought a bologna schnitzel sandwich might be. Whether you're looking for lunch or are indeed experiencing late-night munchies, this sandwich is the answer. **Feeds 4**

BOLOGNA SCHNITZEL SANDWICH
WITH SOUR COLLARDS

For the Sour Collards

1 bunch collards, stems trimmed ½ inch

4 garlic cloves, peeled

5 tablespoons kosher salt

2 teaspoons whole black peppercorns

For the Schnitzel

½ cup all-purpose flour

2 large eggs, lightly beaten

1 cup panko breadcrumbs

1 teaspoon kosher salt

2 teaspoons freshly ground black pepper

4 (1-inch-thick) slices bologna (ask for this at your deli counter)

Canola oil, for frying

8 slices white bread, for serving

Duke's mayonnaise, for serving

Make the sour collards: Pack the collards, garlic, salt, and peppercorns into a sterilized 1-gallon jar (or other nonreactive heatproof vessel with a tight-fitting lid), leaving 2 inches of headspace. Slowly pour 2 quarts water into the jar. Using a glass weight or small plate, weigh down the collards so they are fully submerged. Cover the jar with muslin cloth and secure it with a rubber band or kitchen twine. Set aside to ferment for 5 days, until the collards smell a bit funky and taste a little sour. (A layer of white yeast may form at the top—this is normal; use a spoon to remove and discard it.) If the taste of the collards is to your liking, seal the jar with the lid and refrigerate; if not, ferment the collards on the counter for 2 to 3 days more. (For long-term storage, use the Hot Water Bath Canning technique on page 39.)

Make the schnitzel: Place the flour in a shallow dish. In a separate shallow dish, place the beaten eggs. In a third shallow dish, combine the panko, salt, and pepper. Dredge each slice of bologna in the flour mixture, shaking off any excess, then coat in the egg, allowing any excess to drip off, and finally dredge in the panko mixture, shaking off any excess. Set aside the breaded bologna on a wire rack.

Fill a large high-sided cast-iron skillet with ½ inch of oil and clip a deep-fry thermometer to the side. Heat over medium-high to 350°F. Add a few slices of bologna to the hot oil and fry for 1 to 2 minutes per side, until golden brown. Return the fried bologna to the rack to cool (this keeps them from steaming and getting soft) and repeat with the remaining bologna, letting the oil return to 350°F between batches.

On one side of each slice of bread, spread some mayo. Add a leaf of sour collards to the slathered sides and sandwich a slice of bologna schnitzel between every two.

In the old Southern Appalachia, crocks of sauerkraut with cornbread made from the freshest milled corn were served on tables alongside each other, and spaetzle tossed with sun-warmed yellow squash and herbs picked that morning felt something like a decadent pasta dish. These nuances have kept our region intriguing. In an atmosphere of many cultures finding a sense of place, it's easy to see how food, as an extension of those intersections, became an obsession for our people. **Feeds 4 to 6**

SCHMALTZY SPAETZLE AND BLISTERED YELLOW SQUASH
WITH CELERIAC

For the Spaetzle

2 cups all-purpose flour

7 large eggs

¼ cup whole milk

Kosher salt

1 cup small-diced peeled celeriac

1 cup small-diced yellow squash

3 teaspoons extra-virgin olive oil

1 tablespoon chicken schmaltz
(see Note, page 41)

Leaves of 3 tarragon sprigs, minced

Make the spaetzle: In a large bowl, combine the flour, eggs, and milk. Cover with plastic wrap and refrigerate for at least an hour or up to overnight.

Fill a stockpot with water and bring to a boil over high heat. Season the water with salt until its taste mimics the ocean. Fill a large bowl with ice and water and set it nearby.

Add the celeriac to the boiling water and count to 60, then add the yellow squash and cook for 60 seconds more. Using a slotted spoon, transfer the celeriac and squash to the ice bath to cool, then drain and set aside.

Refill the ice bath with water and ice. Return the same pot of water to a rolling boil, adding more water and salt as necessary. Carefully set a colander over the pot. Add one-quarter of the rested spaetzle batter to the colander and quickly press it through the holes with a rubber spatula. Boil for 2 to 3 minutes, then use a slotted spoon

to remove the spaetzle and drop it into the ice bath. Repeat with the remaining batter. When the spaetzle has cooled completely, drain it, transfer to a baking sheet, and toss with 2 teaspoons of the olive oil to prevent sticking. Spread it into a single layer on the baking sheet.

In a large cast-iron skillet over medium-high heat, combine the remaining 1 teaspoon olive oil and the squash and celeriac. Cook, stirring occasionally, until browned, 4 to 5 minutes. Remove the vegetables from the pan and set aside.

Add the schmaltz and the cooled spaetzle to the same pan (no need to wipe it out). Cook, stirring occasionally, until the spaetzle is golden brown and toasted, 5 to 6 minutes. Add 1 teaspoon salt, the squash-celeriac mixture, and the tarragon and toss to combine. Remove from the heat.

Serve hot or at room temperature. Spoon the spaetzle onto plates, being sure to scoop up some of the vegetables as well.

Pork and apples are paired together as frequently in the South as summer tomatoes and Duke's mayonnaise, but the history of this partnership is a bit murky. One notion is that sugar, largely expensive and not readily available, was substituted with sugar-laden, stewed fruits. The idea I like better speaks to the quintessence of Southern cooking—that is, if it grows together, it goes together. I have no difficulty imagining a farmer taking the hogs out to pasture to feast among the apple orchards. Maybe, then, a lightbulb just went off for someone: simply put, apples taste good with pork. These pork chops gain nuttiness from brown butter, and the tartness of those apples cuts right through the rich, fatty pork—ideal complements. **Feeds 4**

BROWN BUTTER APPLE POR CHOPS

4 tablespoons (½ stick) unsalted butter

2 thyme sprigs

1 cinnamon stick

1 dried bay leaf

1 yellow onion, thinly sliced

2 Gala apples, cored and sliced

2 teaspoons light brown sugar

1 cup apple cider

Juice of 1 lemon

1½ teaspoons canola oil

4 thick-cut bone-in pork chops

2½ teaspoons kosher salt

1 teaspoon freshly ground black pepper

Preheat the oven to 400°F.

In a medium saucepan, melt the butter over medium heat, stirring occasionally, until it begins to foam. Reduce the heat to medium-low, then add the thyme, cinnamon stick, and bay leaf. Simmer for 5 minutes, until fragrant. Add the onion, apples, brown sugar, apple cider, and lemon juice. Cover and continue to simmer, stirring occasionally, for 10 minutes, until the onion starts to become translucent.

Meanwhile, in a large cast-iron skillet, heat the oil over medium-high heat. Pat each pork chop dry with a paper towel. Season all over with salt and pepper. Sear on each side until golden brown, 8 to 10 minutes total, then pour the butter-apple mixture over the pork chops and stir, using a wooden spoon to scrape up any browned bits from the bottom of the pan.

Transfer the skillet to the oven and bake, uncovered, for 11 to 13 minutes, until a meat thermometer inserted into the pork chops registers 145°F. Remove from the oven and discard the bay leaf, cinnamon stick, and thyme sprigs. Serve each pork chop with some of the brown butter sauce spooned over the top, plus a helping of apples and onions.

The consumption of small game is common in the lands of Appalachia: squirrel, raccoon, rabbit, or even whole game birds on the table wouldn't warrant the squeamish reaction they might elsewhere. Even with the rapid industrialization that hit the area, hunting is still an everyday thing there. During my childhood visits to Hattie Mae's, I'd occasionally hear a loud, rusty truck full of camouflage-clad hunters clank its way up to the house. These men, her neighbors, shared their kills with us in exchange for being allowed to stalk wild game in her woods. While they worked, I stayed on the porch, peering through the morning fog to watch the hunting dogs act more obedient and disciplined than I could ever be. Out in the woods, the same men who conscientiously and shyly hid their rifles behind their backs while talking to my family transformed into new beings who could silence the brush under their feet with the intimidating grace of mountain lions. Their ritual taught me early on that the land was sacred—that there was so much humanity, so much life, invested in the food on our plates. **Feeds 4**

BLACK PEPPER QUAIL AND LEATHER BRITCHES

1½ teaspoons kosher salt

¼ teaspoon baking soda

1 teaspoon fish sauce

1 tablespoon sorghum molasses

1½ teaspoons canola oil

2 teaspoons dry sherry

4 semi-boneless quail (1 pound total)

2½ tablespoons cornstarch

1 tablespoon freshly ground black pepper

½ cup chicken stock, homemade (page 41) or store-bought

1 tablespoon soy sauce

Leather Britches (page 72), for serving

In a medium bowl, whisk together the salt, baking soda, fish sauce, sorghum, ½ teaspoon of the canola oil, and the sherry. Place the quail in a nonreactive medium dish and pour the marinade over the top, turning the quail to coat. Cover the dish with plastic wrap and marinate in the refrigerator for at least 5 hours or up to overnight.

Set a wire rack over a rimmed baking sheet. Remove the marinated quail from the refrigerator and transfer it to the rack. Let stand at room temperature for 20 minutes.

In a small bowl, combine the cornstarch and pepper. Coat the marinated quail in the cornstarch mixture.

In a large high-sided skillet, heat the remaining 1 teaspoon canola oil over medium heat. When the pan begins to smoke, add the quail and sear until golden brown on both sides, 1 to 2 minutes per side. Reduce the heat to low and add the stock and the soy sauce. Cover and cook for 6 to 7 minutes.

Serve the quail alongside the leather britches, with the pan sauce spooned over the top.

To make a good meal in Southern Appalachia, you start with a successful hunting day in the woods; later that night, you pull your best preserves out of the larder to complement your finds. Earthy and sweet aromas of lean game meats and stewing vegetables fill the air and mix with wholesome chatter. This is Southern cooking. I hate to admit it, but I once or twice saw something like this dish hit the table and wrote it off as unexciting. In my ignorance at the time, I was unable to appreciate the immense care that went into creating such a dish: early mornings setting traps in the woods and lively canning sessions in summer. **Feeds 4**

STEWED RABBIT
WITH PRESERVED CARROT PUREE

For the Carrots

3 pounds carrots, tops trimmed

3 celery stalks

Rind of 1 orange

3 tablespoons kosher salt

2 teaspoons coriander seeds

2 teaspoons celery seeds

½ cup (1 stick) unsalted butter

For the Rabbit

8 rabbit hind legs

2 teaspoons kosher salt

1 teaspoon freshly ground black pepper

2 tablespoons canola oil

3 shallots, thinly sliced

5 thyme sprigs, tied together with
    kitchen twine

4 garlic cloves, thinly sliced

½ cup apple brandy

2 cups apple cider

1 cup chicken stock, homemade
    (page 41) or store-bought

1 tablespoon unsalted butter

¼ cup whole-grain mustard

½ cup Apple Butter (page 67)

Make the carrots: In a large bowl, combine the carrots, celery, orange rind, salt, coriander, and celery seeds. Transfer to a vacuum-sealed bag or a 1-gallon zip-top bag with the air pressed out completely. Refrigerate for at least 10 days or up to 1 month.

In a small saucepan, cook the butter over medium-low heat until it becomes golden brown and smells nutty, 8 to 10 minutes. Using a spoon, skim off and discard the foamy solids that rise to the top. Remove from the heat.

Remove the carrots from the salt brine and rinse; discard the brine. Transfer the carrots to a blender and puree until smooth, slowly drizzling in the brown butter as you blend.

Make the rabbit: Season the rabbit legs with the salt and pepper. In a Dutch oven or heavy-bottomed skillet, heat the oil over medium heat. When the oil is just starting to smoke, add the rabbit and cook until golden brown on

both sides, 4 to 5 minutes per side. Transfer the rabbit to a plate. Reduce the heat to low and add the shallots and thyme. Cook, stirring occasionally, until the shallots are soft and translucent, 5 to 6 minutes. Add the garlic and cook, stirring, until fragrant and softened, 2 minutes. Add the apple brandy, cider, and stock and use a wooden spoon to scrape up any browned bits from the bottom. If you're brave, tilt the pan just slightly toward the flame to allow the brandy to ignite (or turn off the heat and ignite the sauce with a barbecue lighter). The fire will go out after several seconds. Whisk in the butter, mustard, and apple butter and cook over low heat, whisking frequently, until the mixture emulsifies, 10 minutes more. Return the rabbit legs to the pan, cover, and cook for 45 minutes, until the meat is tender.

Spoon a generous portion of the carrot puree into the centers of each of four plates. Top each with 2 rabbit legs and spoon the pan sauce over the top, then serve.

Chewy, flat, slippery, noodlelike dumplings swimming in fatty, collagen-rich, garlicky broth—that's what we call "chicken and slicks" around here. The dish is what I'd consider to be Appalachia's soup for when you're feeling sick, but I regularly have it just to make me feel good. Either way, it's a quick and easy one-pot meal. **Feeds 8 to 10**

CHICKEN AND SLICKS

For the Chicken

2 chicken bouillon cubes

6 garlic cloves

3 tablespoons apple cider vinegar

1½ tablespoons kosher salt

5 thyme sprigs

5 dried bay leaves

2 teaspoons whole black peppercorns

½ teaspoon red pepper flakes

1 (4-pound) whole chicken

2 teaspoons canola oil

2 yellow onions, diced

1 cup diced celery

1 cup diced carrots

For the Slicks

2 cups all-purpose flour, plus more for dusting

1 teaspoon baking powder

½ teaspoon kosher salt

2 tablespoons cold chicken schmaltz (see Note, page 41)

1 tablespoon bacon fat

For Serving

Thinly sliced fresh chives

Freshly ground black pepper

Make the chicken: In a Dutch oven, combine the bouillon cubes, garlic, vinegar, salt, thyme, bay leaves, peppercorns, and red pepper flakes. Fill the pot halfway with water. Bring the water to a rolling boil over high heat, then add the chicken. (If the water doesn't cover the chicken by 1 inch, add more.) Boil for 5 minutes, until the meat is beginning to lose its pink. Reduce the heat to medium-low and simmer until the chicken is cooked through, about 1 hour 20 minutes, carefully turning the chicken halfway through. Remove from the heat.

When the chicken is cool enough to handle, remove the meat from the bones; shred the meat and discard the bones. Strain the stock and discard the solids. Let the stock cool, then skim the layer of fat from the surface and reserve the stock and fat separately.

Make the slicks: In a medium bowl, combine the flour, baking powder, and salt. Add the reserved chicken fat, the schmaltz, and the bacon fat. Work the mixture together with your hands. Slowly add broth, 1 tablespoon at a time. You want a soft dough that can be easily rolled out thin. Add up to ½ cup of broth, if necessary.

On a floured surface, roll out the dough to ⅛ inch thick. Using a pizza cutter or paring knife, cut the dough into 2 by 5-inch rectangles (you should have about 24 slicks).

In a large skillet, heat the canola oil over medium heat. Just as the pan begins to smoke, add the onions, celery, and carrots. Cook, stirring occasionally, until the onions are fragrant, 4 to 5 minutes, then transfer to a stockpot. Add the remaining stock and bring to a rolling boil over medium-high heat.

Drop the slicks into the pot a few at a time so they don't stick together. Boil for 15 to 20 minutes, until cooked through. Your broth should reduce and thicken into a velvety gravy. Return the shredded chicken to the pot, reduce the heat to low, and simmer just long enough to get the meat hot, about 5 minutes.

To serve, ladle the stew into bowls, scooping up generous portions of the chicken and slicks. Garnish with chives and black pepper.

Summers up the mountain meant trading bacon and sausage on the breakfast table for scrapple and fatback. Birthed out of both necessity and sheer creativity, scrapple showed up on the scene long before whole-hog utilization became a high honor in culinary communities. It's a forcemeat of sorts, utilizing all the pig parts and bound together into loaf form via natural gelatin and cornmeal. Dispelling the idea that Southern cooking requires little technique and precision, this age-old method, which traditionally includes offal, is also used to create the finest of French pâtés and terrines. If scrapple isn't seared and served as a breakfast meat, you'll find it sneak its way into bowls of grits or made portable by tucking into bread and graced with condiments like apple butter, grape jelly, or mustard. **Feeds 9**

SCRAPPLE SANDWICH
WITH APPLE BUTTER MUSTARD

1 tablespoon unsalted butter, plus more for greasing

2 pounds bone-in, skin-on pork butt

2 fresh pig's feet or necks

1 yellow onion, quartered

2 celery stalks, chopped

2 carrots, chopped

2 tablespoons kosher salt

1 teaspoon celery seeds

2 dried bay leaves

1 tablespoon freshly ground black pepper

2 teaspoons cayenne pepper

2 teaspoons dried sage

1 teaspoon garlic powder

1 teaspoon dried parsley

1 cup fine yellow cornmeal

1 cup Apple Butter (page 67)

½ cup yellow mustard seeds, toasted

¼ cup apple cider vinegar

White bread or biscuits, for serving

Grease a 9 × 5-inch loaf pan with butter.

In a large stockpot, combine the pork butt, pig's feet, onion, celery, carrots, salt, celery salt, and bay leaves. Add water to cover by ½ inch. Cook over low heat for about 2 hours, until the pork is tender and the meat is falling off the bone. Using a slotted spoon, transfer the solids to a baking sheet to cool. Strain and reserve 2 cups of the cooking liquid. When the pork is cool enough to handle, remove the bones and bay leaves and discard. Working in batches, transfer the mixture to a food processor and pulse a few times to chop; don't overprocess—the mixture should remain coarse.

Return the pork mixture to the pot. Add the 2 cups cooking liquid, black pepper, cayenne, sage, garlic powder, and parsley. Bring to a simmer over low heat. Vigorously stir in the cornmeal, breaking up any lumps that form.

Cook, stirring occasionally, until smooth and thick, 10 to 12 minutes. Pour the mixture into the prepared pan and refrigerate to set for at least 5 hours or up to overnight.

In a blender, combine the apple butter, mustard seeds, and vinegar. Blend until smooth, about 3 minutes. Transfer to a small bowl.

Once the scrapple has set, turn it out of the pan onto a cutting board. Cut into eighteen ½-inch-thick slices.

In a small skillet, melt the butter over medium heat. Working in batches, cook the scrapple slices until they're browned and the edges are crisped, 3 to 4 minutes per side.

For each serving, spread apple butter mustard on two slices of white bread or both sides of a split biscuit. Sandwich about 2 slices of seared scrapple between bread slices and serve immediately.

You always knew when my Appalachian aunties were making a stack cake. By virtue of living no more than a quarter of a mile from each other, they'd come together to make it for every party or special occasion, each toting a round layer of cake they'd baked at home from flour, molasses, and eggs from the neighbors' chickens. As they built up the patchwork of mismatched layers on a special cake stand they'd dug out of storage, they filled the host kitchen with loud cackling, blues playing, clouds of flour dust, and plenty of arguing about what special touch to add this time. As the crumbly, cookielike layers soaked up the moisture from the applesauce, the cake would transform into a fluffy and soft masterpiece overnight. But owing to the fact that no two layers ever looked the same, it was always a crazy-ass lookin' cake.

More of the quiet, meditative, less precise type in the kitchen, I never quite fell in love with baking cakes the way my aunties did, but it would be a shame not to share this recipe, which is as much about community building as it is about the end product. Apple stack cake is a labor of the love of many hands—by design, it's a real pain in the ass to make by yourself. The more friends and family you had and the more people you knew, the taller your cake was. So for this recipe, enlist your folks to each bake a layer so you can finish the cake together. **Feeds 8**

PAWPAW APPLE STACK CAKE

For the applesauce

1 pound dried apples

¼ cup packed dark brown sugar

For the Cake

½ cup sorghum molasses

½ cup plus ¼ teaspoon granulated sugar

½ cup buttermilk

1 large egg, lightly beaten

1 teaspoon baking soda

1 teaspoon baking powder

½ teaspoon kosher salt

⅓ cup lard or vegetable shortening

4½ cups all-purpose flour, sifted, plus more for dusting

To Finish

¼ cup pawpaw puree

Confectioners' sugar

Make the applesauce: In a large high-sided saucepan, combine the dried apples, brown sugar, and 4 cups water. Cook over high heat for 5 minutes, then reduce the heat to low and cook until the apples begin to rehydrate and break down, 25 to 30 minutes, adding more water as needed (there should be at least 3 inches of water in the pot). Remove from the heat. Using an immersion blender, puree the rehydrated apples directly in the pot, or, alternatively, run them through a food mill. Store in the refrigerator until needed, up to 5 days.

Recipe continues

Make the cake dough: This recipe makes 6 cake layers, so you can mix up one big batch and split the dough between six people (and six ovens) to bake.

In the bowl of a stand mixer fitted with the paddle attachment, beat together the sorghum, ½ cup of the granulated sugar, the buttermilk, and the egg on medium speed to combine, 1 to 2 minutes. Add the baking soda, baking powder, salt, and lard and beat for 1 minute more. Add the flour, 1 cup at a time, and mix until a stiff dough forms, 3 to 4 minutes. Separate the dough into 6 even balls and distribute them to family (or chosen family), along with instructions for baking.

Bake the cake layers: Position an oven rack in the center of the oven and preheat the oven to 350°F. Dust a 13 × 18-inch baking sheet with flour. Cut out a 9-inch circle of parchment paper.

On a floured surface, with a floured rolling pin, roll out your dough ball to about a ¼-inch thickness, then stretch the disc of dough to fit the prepared parchment circle.

Transfer the dough on the parchment to the prepared baking sheet. Use the tines of a fork to prick the round of dough all over, then sprinkle it with the remaining ¼ teaspoon granulated sugar.

Bake until golden brown, 9 to 12 minutes, rotating the baking sheet halfway through the cook time. Remove from the oven and transfer the cake layer from the pan to a wire rack to cool completely, about 45 minutes.

Assemble the cake: Place one layer on a cake stand. Spread ½ cup of the applesauce over the top, leaving a ½-inch border. Stack another layer on top, and continue alternating cake and applesauce (½ cup each time), ending with a cake layer on top. Cover and refrigerate for 1 to 2 days to let the cake layers soften.

Remove the cake from the fridge and top with the pawpaw puree. Slice and dust with confectioners' sugar. Serve at room temperature. On the off chance that there are leftovers, they'll keep in the fridge, covered, for up to 24 hours before turning to mush.

Drawing on connectivity to our land, Appalachian traditions are rich with teas, tinctures, and the good people doing the Lord's work by brewing these ancient concoctions.

Birch is a key ingredient in the wild mountain teas I swear by. I had a great uncle, Sco, who used birch twigs as a natural toothbrush and breath freshener for as long as he had teeth, which was an impressively long while. For birch tea, you'll want to use fresh birch twigs. With just the twist of a twig in hot water, you'll inhale and almost immediately encounter the essence of green tea. In Southern Appalachia you're surrounded by endless varieties—most commonly yellow birch and sweet birch trees. You'll notice it out in the woods first by its papery bark, which can double as campfire tinder, then by its small green mintlike leaves that grow in tight clusters. **Serves 1**

WILD MOUNTAIN TEA

1 tablespoon assorted wild ingredients (my favorite combinations are black walnut leaves and spruce needles; see sidebar, page 98)

1 yellow birch twig,

1 cup steaming-hot (not boiling) water

2 teaspoons honey

Place the wild ingredients in a 10-ounce mug (or use a tea ball, if you have one). Twist the birch twig (if using) to bruise it and then add it to the mug. Pour the water into the mug and steep for 8 minutes. Strain the tea and return it to the hot mug (or remove the tea ball and birch twig). Stir in the honey. Drink warm.

WILD INGREDIENTS

Some would consider the practice of foraging adventurous, but I experience it as a freeing way to stay connected to nature. Our land has always been a food source, especially the flora and fauna of the mountains. But unlike a continually restocked grocery store, the land has to be taken care of so that it can continue to provide for the next generation. Don't take more than what you can eat in a day, and if you have any doubts about something that could be poisonous or inedible, leave it alone. Even after a lifetime of developing comfort with the outdoors, I still consult a trusted expert when I'm unsure of what I've picked. And don't just listen to me: consult vetted field guides for your area, like Chris Bennett's *Southeast Foraging*.

Sumac: This is best as a late-summer harvest. You're looking for staghorn sumac, not to be confused with the poisonous variety. Staghorn has fuzzy hairs on its twigs, while poison sumac has smooth twigs. You'll also notice staghorn sumac has toothed leaves, where, again, poison sumac is smooth. As mountain nights start to cool even further, you'll see that sumac is ready to go when it shows an almost crystal-like citric acid coating all over its berries. That's the good stuff, so try not to touch it too much. Clip it by the bundle and use it fresh for the application found here. I should tell you to rinse the surface dirt off the berries before using, but that would be rinsing off a good bit of the citric acid. My way is to give them a little shake and lay them outside to give the critters a good while to run off. To make sumac powder, you'll want to use a completely different method for harvesting and processing, so I'd recommend sourcing a really good version of the already-ground stuff and using the fresh for infused-type applications.

Black Walnut Leaves: From early spring to late summer, I like to harvest underripe black walnuts for nocino-making. To make a pot of black walnut leaf tea, snip 3 large (3-foot-long) leaves off the branches of a tree (or 4 leaves for a stronger tea). You can dry these in a few ways; I usually bundle them up with twine, then hang them upside-down for 5 to 7 days, until they're dry. Very carefully transfer the dried leaves to a blender or spice grinder and grind, or use a mortar and pestle for a coarse grind. Store in an airtight glass jar.

Spruce and Pine Needles: For spruce, look for short, individually attached needles. You'll find that pine needles attach to their branches in large clusters. Pick both spruce and pine needles during the height of spring while they're tender and young, with bright green tips. The citrusy astringence of pine needles is immediately identifiable, while spruce gives more woodsy, earthy undertones. When foraging, harvest from shorter branches sparingly to maintain the health of the trees you're sourcing from. Place the needles on a baking sheet, cover with cheesecloth, and leave them in the sun for a few hours, until the needles feel dry to the touch and are crushed easily between your fingertips. Store in an airtight glass jar.

Red Clover: These bushy little pinkish-purple flowers are often found growing in lawns and fields and along roadsides. Tie their stems together tightly with kitchen twine and hang them upside down to dry for a couple days. Then remove the flowers and leaves, discarding the stems, and crush with a mortar and pestle or give them a couple quick pulses in a spice grinder. Store in an airtight glass jar.

I believe sumac to be the premier spice of Appalachia. It grows wildly on nearly every mountaintop, coated in icy crystals of naturally occurring citric acid that provide a signature sour acidity. This simple but refreshing two-ingredient drink highlights one of my favorite wild foods superbly. You'll end up with a botanical-tasting, tart summer bev.
Serves 4

SUMAC-ADE

½ cup sugar

1 cup fresh staghorn sumac berries
   (see opposite)

In a small saucepan, combine the sugar and ½ cup water. Cook over medium heat, stirring occasionally, until the sugar is dissolved, 8 to 9 minutes. Remove from the heat and let cool.

Meanwhile, place the sumac berries on a piece of cheesecloth and secure into a bundle with kitchen twine. Place the bundle in a glass pitcher. Pour 2½ cups cool water over the sumac. Using a muddler or a wooden spoon, smash the berries inside the cheesecloth to release their flavor; the water will begin to turn pink. Let sit for 20 minutes, then stir in the simple syrup. Chill in the refrigerator for 3 hours. Remove the cheesecloth bundle, squeezing any excess liquid back into the pitcher.

Fill tall glasses with ice and pour in the sumac-ade, then serve.

When I was growing up, I was never given any cough medicine; instead, the remedy was this honey—and I can understand why. The team-up of the antimicrobial properties in the honey and the allicin in the onion's juices really did work, wildly enough. I won't pretend to swear by this recipe to get me through all ailments, but it does stay on my counter. I've had success creating versions with ramps and honeysuckle or sorghum and garlic. I also found it to be an easy way to preserve ramps while producing a fermented honey worthy of barbecues and glazes everywhere. I've used the honeyed onion additives finely chopped up as a condiment for pizza and sandwiches, as well as in dressings. That's all to say that this simple, two-ingredient recipe is a triple threat. The most common way to prepare this elixir is using readily available yard onions. Also known as wild onions or onion grass, these pungent alliums can be harvested wild in areas untreated with pesticides. With some patience and a firm grip, they can be pulled up right from the root. You'll notice instantly by the aroma if you've found your onion patch. **Makes 1½ cups**

YARD ONION HONEY

1 cup packed well-cleaned yard onions or
    ramp bulbs (roots trimmed to 1 inch)
1½ cups honey

Place the yard onions in a sterilized 1-pint jar (or other nonreactive heatproof vessel with a tight-fitting lid). Slowly pour the honey over the top and give the jar a shake to remove any large pockets of air. Twist the lid onto the jar loosely; it should not be airtight. Let sit out on the counter to ferment; after 4 to 5 days, the honey will begin to form small bubbles and thin out. The honey will be ready to use after 5 days.

Tighten the lid on the jar and store in a cool, dry place; the honey will last eternally as long as you ensure the onions are completely submerged at all times, feeding them more honey as the jar is depleted.

Vinegar pie was known as a "make do" pie during the Depression. Just as that name implies, desserts like these were born from a need to make do with whatever you had—even if that meant few ingredients and no refrigeration. Vinegar wisely took the place of lemon juice wherever acidity was needed in a recipe. I find this "MacGyver-ing" honorable. Black Southern cooking saw incredible recipes and methods, many still widely used and practiced, come from a place of need and desperation. These vinegar bars are a respectful nod to that desperation cooking. **Makes 15 bars**

VINEGAR BARS

For the Crust

Neutral oil, such as canola or grapeseed, for greasing

1 cup (2 sticks) unsalted butter, at room temperature

½ cup sugar

2 cups all-purpose flour, plus more for dusting

⅛ teaspoon kosher salt

For the Filling

4 extra-large eggs, at room temperature

2 cups sugar

⅔ cup apple cider vinegar

⅔ cup all-purpose flour

Sorghum molasses, for drizzling

Make the crust: Grease a 9 × 13 × 2-inch baking dish with oil.

In a stand mixer fitted with the paddle attachment, cream the butter and sugar on medium speed until light and fluffy, 2 to 3 minutes.

In a medium bowl, combine the flour and salt. With the mixer running on low, add the flour mixture to the butter mixture and beat until just combined, about 45 seconds. Turn out the dough onto a well-floured surface and gather it into a ball. Flatten the dough with floured hands and press it into the prepared baking dish, building up a ½-inch edge on all sides. Chill in the refrigerator for 35 to 40 minutes.

Preheat the oven to 350°F.

Bake the crust for 15 to 20 minutes, until very lightly browned. Let cool on a wire rack. Leave the oven on.

Meanwhile, make the filling: In a medium bowl, whisk together the eggs, sugar, vinegar, and flour. Pour the filling over the crust.

Bake for 30 to 35 minutes, or about 5 minutes beyond the point where the filling is set. Remove and let cool slightly. Cut into rectangles and drizzle with sorghum, then serve. Store the bars in an airtight container in the refrigerator for up to 4 days.

LOWCO

OUNTRY

St. Mary's, Georgia, a tiny, unassuming seaside town that is not known to many, is my place of birth. I was born here unexpectedly, the morning of my aunt Patricia's wedding. My mom was visiting from Virginia Beach and out I came, a month early. As the story goes, I didn't want to miss the crab boil happening that weekend (this was true). Food of the Coastal South, I learned early on, is different from that of its inland counterparts: chicken bog takes the place of pirloo, and rice for grits. It's still familiar.

All through my childhood, we would travel down the coast for the holidays to visit my dad's family in St. Mary's and on South Carolina's Edisto Island and the other barrier islands. Here, the smell of seawater hung in the air; my uncles caught and ate fish and other seafood, then set fires just for the sake of roasting oysters and telling stories—so many stories—that taught me a lot about myself and my family. After a while, the family remaining there began to dwindle, and by the time I was around thirteen, they seemed to have disappeared altogether, and I wondered why.

In order to say what I'm going to say next, I have to believe my family won't ever read this (which I know isn't true) for fear of offending them. But for the elders in my family, and for so many Black Americans, the South is equated with pain and oppression—and understandably so. Skilled trades began to feel like slave labor. Long-preserved cultural practices were now worn with a shameful stain. A trip "down south" was an invitation for a tense car ride, tightening its grip the farther south we traveled. I didn't realize the bumpy, unpaved dirt roads that were fun for me were painful for my parents. They led the way to a place where my dad felt we could never thrive and my mom feared was too politically backward to try to raise a modern family.

I remember playing with my cousins on Edisto Island one summer and my aunt Helen overhearing me teasing them about how their speech sounded funny. Before the next joke even had time to land, I felt the most painful pinch to my arm as Aunt Helen led me away from the group with a loud "Come yuh" and spun me around to find her leaning over me with a finger in my face. "Don' you ebbuh talk bad about the way your cuz'ns talk'um. Things might be different weh you lib, but this is the langwidge here!" Even at age six or so, I knew there was more to what she was saying. While I didn't understand Gullah language, I understood that whatever I did not know I had better learn. I suddenly felt like an outsider—because I was. I was the "city girl" who knew nothing about my own culture.

Despite the weight the past held over us, my parents realized they had to create these experiences for me every chance we got so I could learn to value and appreciate them. They wanted me to be proud of who I am and of my culture in a world that would try to mute that. It took me time to gain the perspective I have now. And looking back, it made sense why the elder relatives chose to stay, as the torch bearers, in a land full of erasure. For too long, I operated under a sense of shame that almost felt like a family tradition. While that truth stings because it perpetuates the erasure of our own history, I don't know what I could have done to change things then. But now I note the importance in grappling with parts of the past that can't be looked at with longing eyes. Hurt and erasure don't equal shame anymore. I remember the idea of sankofa and how those ugly moments of the past have the power to drive us forward into the future.

If I'm not slurping freshly shucked oysters from their shells, that means they're probably smoking over a fire because I had some patience that day. Next time you roll out a Lowcountry boil, get some friends and set up a fire next to it—though an outdoor grill will work just as well. You'll want to use the smokiest ham you can find for this; Benton's has some of the best. **Feeds 4 to 6**

SMOKY HAM BBQ OYSTERS ON THE HALF SHELL

1 cup apple cider vinegar

1 cup Stewed Tomatoes (page 38) or canned stewed tomatoes

1 pound smoked country ham (preferably Benton's), diced

1 tablespoon yellow mustard

½ cup packed dark brown sugar

1 teaspoon freshly ground black pepper

1 teaspoon kosher salt

1 teaspoon red pepper flakes

4 tablespoons (½ stick) unsalted butter

2 dashes of hot sauce

24 raw oysters, scrubbed

Prepare an open fire with a grate over the coals or heat a grill to medium-high (400°F).

In a small saucepan, combine the vinegar, tomatoes, country ham, and ¼ cup water. Bring to a simmer over medium-low heat and cook, stirring occasionally, until the sauce begins to thicken, about 20 minutes. Whisk in the mustard, brown sugar, black pepper, salt, red pepper flakes, butter, and hot sauce and cook until the sugar has dissolved and the butter has melted, 7 to 8 minutes more. Remove from the heat and transfer the barbecue sauce to a glass dish while you prepare the oysters.

Place the oysters on the grill grates with their flat side facing up. Cover the grill (if using an open fire, cover the grate loosely with a big sheet of aluminum foil) and cook until the oysters begin to open, 2 to 3 minutes. Transfer the opened oysters to a tray to cool, discarding any that have not opened.

Once they're cool enough to handle, use an oyster knife to pry the shells completely open, taking care to retain the oyster liquor inside. Using the oyster knife, free the oyster meat from the muscle connecting it to its shell, but leave the meat in the shell for serving.

Serve the warm oysters in their shells with a helping of the barbecue sauce spooned over them, being sure to pick up bits of country ham.

This recipe is a respectful nod to all those late-night fried crab rangoons and Westernized shrimp toasts that I believe can only be topped by the simplicity of the crab-filled bites the Geechee in me craves. I've enjoyed my fair share of crab, in many different forms: crab fritters and crab balls, always with more sweet lump crabmeat than crushed saltines and always a family favorite. Benne is another nod to the culture. Imported, en masse, to Charleston by our enslaved ancestors and often referred to as the "goodwill" plant, warding off evil spirits, benne was also grown for its earthy, oil-packed seeds. Here they lend nutty flavor, complexity, and solid crunch. **Feeds 6 to 8**

BENNE SEED CRAB TOAST
WITH SPICY SORGHUM-MISO MUSTARD

For the Crab Toast

1 red bell pepper (see Note)

Neutral oil

Kosher salt

1 (8-ounce) package cream cheese, at room temperature

½ cup Duke's mayonnaise

3 large egg yolks

1 tablespoon fish sauce

Zest and juice of 2 lemons

1 pound jumbo lump crabmeat, picked over

¼ cup fresh parsley, minced

1 bunch scallions, green parts only, thinly sliced

½ teaspoon cayenne pepper

1 teaspoon freshly ground white pepper

8 slices white bread, crusts removed

½ cup benne seeds

For the Spicy Sorghum-Miso Mustard

½ cup yellow mustard

3 tablespoons sorghum molasses

1 tablespoon gochujang

1 tablespoon white miso paste

Make the crab toast: Preheat the oven to 400°F. Line two baking sheets with parchment paper.

Place the bell pepper in a bowl, coat with oil, and season with salt. Transfer to one prepared baking sheet and roast for 40 to 45 minutes, until it deflates and the skin becomes charred and blistered. Transfer the roasted pepper to a glass bowl (keep the oven on), tightly cover with plastic wrap, and let stand for 10 minutes. Remove the pepper from the bowl and, holding the pepper under running water, use your fingers to gently remove the skin. Discard the seeds and membrane, then finely chop the flesh.

In a medium bowl, mix the cream cheese, mayonnaise, 2 egg yolks, the fish sauce, lemon zest, and lemon juice and stir until smooth and fully combined. Stir in the crab, parsley, scallions, roasted pepper, cayenne, and white pepper.

Arrange the bread on the second prepared baking sheet, spacing the slices far enough apart that they don't touch. Spread the crab mixture evenly over each slice. Beat the remaining egg yolk and brush it over the tops, then sprinkle 1 tablespoon of benne seeds over each. Bake for 20 minutes, or until the toasts are puffed and golden. Transfer to a wire rack and let rest for about 5 minutes before serving.

Make the spicy mustard: In a small bowl, whisk together the mustard, sorghum, gochujang, and miso until smooth.

Cut each piece of crab toast diagonally into triangles. Serve on a platter with the spicy mustard alongside.

Note: If you'd rather not roast the bell pepper, a jarred roasted pepper is fine.

The sweetness of tender, white shrimp complements the tartness of green mango in these lettuce wraps. The Lowcountry diet isn't rich in bread—and it's not missed much, either. Here, lettuce wraps serve as vehicles for this bright and herbaceous mix of flavors. Scoop up that shrimp just as you would Korean ssam, and don't miss out on the vinegar—it adds subtle spice and sweetness along with complex acidity that rounds out every bite. **Feeds 4 to 6**

WHITE SHRIMP AND GREEN MANGO LETTUCE WRAPS

1 pound white shrimp, peeled and deveined

2 teaspoons extra-virgin olive oil, plus more for drizzling

1½ teaspoons kosher salt

2 underripe mangoes

2 ripe plantains

1 white onion, diced

2 avocados, diced

Leaves from 4 mint sprigs, torn

Zest and juice of 1 lime

1 head Bibb lettuce

For the Dipping Vinegar

1 cup distilled white vinegar

1 jalapeño, minced

2 tablespoons packed dark brown sugar

1 teaspoon fish sauce

1 tablespoon honey

1 garlic clove, grated

1 (1-inch) knob fresh ginger, peeled and grated

Heat a charcoal or gas grill to medium (425° to 450°F) or heat a grill pan over medium-high heat. If using an outdoor grill, designate hot and warm zones.

In a medium bowl, combine the shrimp with the olive oil and salt and toss to coat.

Working with one mango at a time, hold the thinnest part toward you and slice lengthwise along either side of the pit; repeat with the second mango. Place the mango halves on a baking sheet, flesh-side up. Slice both plantains lengthwise (leaving the skins on) and place them cut-side up on the same baking sheet. Drizzle the mango and plantain halves with olive oil.

Over direct heat, grill the shrimp, mangoes, and plantains (placing the fruit cut-side down) for 2 to 3 minutes.

Remove the plantains and mango halves from the grill. Flip the shrimp and grill until pink and opaque all over, about 1 minute more, then transfer to a cutting board and coarsely chop. Remove and discard the skin from the plantains and mangoes and coarsely chop the flesh.

In a medium bowl, combine the shrimp, mango, plantains, onion, avocados, mint, and lime zest and juice.

Make the dipping vinegar: In a small bowl, whisk together the vinegar, jalapeño, brown sugar, fish sauce, honey, garlic, and ginger.

To serve, take a leaf of lettuce and fill with a spoonful of the shrimp mixture. Pinch the sides together to close, dip into the vinegar mixture, and enjoy.

No one knows for sure who invented johnnycakes, though the theory I like the best is that they were a creation of enslaved Black people stocking up on provisions before fleeing the Antebellum South via the Underground Railroad. Regardless of who really deserves credit, their alleged original name, journey cakes, holds a clue as to why they came about in the first place. They're unique in their hardiness and stand up well to being packed. Compared with hardtack, another historic traveling carb, they have a softer bite and slowly develop a cakier texture as they sit at room temperature. I imagine this was cornbread before it had a name—the pioneer. Whether traveling or comfortable at home, I find johnnycakes pair well with anything spreadable—especially this savory, jammy, pork-and-pepper situation. **Feeds 12**

CLASSIC JOHNNYCAKES
WITH PORK AND PEPPER JAM

For the Jam

2 pounds pork shoulder

1 smoked ham hock

2 cups white wine

4 garlic cloves, peeled

4 thyme sprigs

2 teaspoons kosher salt

2 teaspoons whole black peppercorns

¼ cup light brown sugar

3 tablespoons unsalted butter

1 small yellow onion, diced

2 green bell peppers, diced

1 tablespoon all-purpose flour

¼ cup white wine vinegar

For the Johnnycakes

1 cup all-purpose flour

1 cup coarse yellow cornmeal

2 teaspoons baking powder

2 tablespoons granulated sugar

½ teaspoon kosher salt

2 large eggs, at room temperature, lightly beaten

¾ cup buttermilk

4 tablespoons (½ stick) unsalted butter, melted

Canola oil, for frying

Sliced fresh chives, for garnish

Make the jam: In a large pot, combine the pork shoulder, ham hock, wine, garlic, thyme, salt, and peppercorns. Add water to cover by ½ inch. Bring the mixture to a boil over high heat, then reduce the heat to low to maintain a simmer. Cover and cook until the meat is tender, about 3 hours. Using tongs, transfer the pork to a bowl and let cool, reserving the cooking liquid. When cool enough to handle, remove the meat from the bone and shred it. Place the meat on a baking sheet and transfer to the refrigerator to cool completely, at least 7 hours or up to overnight.

Strain the cooking liquid, discarding the solids. Return the liquid to the pot and whisk in the brown sugar. Bring to a boil over high heat, then reduce the heat to medium and simmer, uncovered, until reduced by half, about 30 minutes.

In a large skillet, combine the butter, onion, and bell peppers. Cook over medium-low heat until the onion is soft and translucent, 6 to 7 minutes. Stir in the flour and cook, stirring frequently to prevent burning, until thickened, 3 to 4 minutes. Add the vinegar and cook, stirring and scraping up the browned bits from the bottom of the pan, then add the mixture to the pot with the strained liquid. Place the mixture into a nonreactive dish and refrigerate for at least 3 hours to cool. Once cooled, remove the pork from the refrigerator and stir together with the cooled mixture.

Make the johnnycakes: In a medium bowl, whisk together the flour, cornmeal, baking powder, sugar, and salt. In a separate medium bowl, whisk together the eggs and buttermilk. Add ½ cup water and the melted butter to the egg mixture and whisk until just combined. Add the dry ingredients to the wet ingredients and stir until just combined.

Heat ¼ inch of canola oil in a large cast-iron skillet over medium heat. When the oil shimmers, working in batches, drop the batter into the pan by the tablespoon, spacing the johnnycakes about 1 inch apart. Cook until bubbles form on the surface, 3 to 4 minutes, then flip and cook on the second side until the edges are crispy and golden brown, 2 minutes more. Transfer the johnnycakes to a plate lined with paper towels. Repeat with the remaining batter, adding another teaspoon of oil to the skillet between each batch.

To serve, spread a generous portion of the pork and pepper jam on the hot johnnycakes and garnish with chives. Store leftover johnnycakes in an airtight container with layers of paper towels between them; they will keep at room temperature for a couple days. Store any leftover jam in an airtight container in the refrigerator for up to 1 week.

I'm not ashamed to admit I'm okay with the ever-controversial cheese-and-seafood pairing, and I'm hoping to convert you, too. As a certified seafood lover, it's a thing I'd only honor and never bastardize. Cheese-seafood pairings are not all created equally. It's important to understand that delicate seafood does not really belong here. In order for a dish to be successful, we need to lean into heartier, fattier seafood varieties that can stand up to oily, fat-driven cheeses. Think shaving Manchego over charred shrimp, pouring a nice Parmesan cream sauce over flounder, or the time I blew my own mind by griddling cheddar over otoro. These combinations' appeal lies in the way the salty-sweet brininess of seafood cuts through the fattiness and complements the saltiness and sharpness of the proper cheese. If I were you, I'd make this dish for someone I wanted to impress; it gives the illusion of a hard day's work in the kitchen, but how quickly it cooks will just buy you more time to preach the cheese-seafood gospel. **Feeds 6 to 8**

CHEESY CRAWFISH CROUSTADE

4 tablespoons (½ stick) unsalted butter, melted, plus more at room temperature for greasing

1 pound cooked crawfish tail meat

1½ teaspoons kosher salt

2 tablespoons Dijon mustard

2 sheets frozen puff pastry, thawed

½ cup shredded sharp white cheddar cheese

½ cup shredded Muenster cheese

Place a rack in the lower third of the oven and preheat the oven to 375°F. Grease a 10-inch tart pan with butter.

In a medium bowl, combine the crawfish, salt, mustard, and 2 tablespoons of the melted butter. Toss to coat well.

Place one sheet of puff pastry on a clean work surface. Using a rolling pin, slightly roll it out to a size 1 inch larger than the tart pan. Transfer the puff pastry to the pan and trim off the excess dough, leaving just ½ inch of overhang all around.

Add the crawfish mixture to the dough, top with both cheeses, and fold the edges of the dough toward the center.

Place the second sheet of pastry on your work surface and roll it out so it's about 1 inch larger than the tart pan all around. Using a 2-inch ring mold or the rim of a standard shot glass, punch a hole directly in the center of the pastry. Place the pastry over the top of the tart pan and crimp the edges to seal, pinching the dough around the edge of the pan. Trim any excess overhang. Brush the top of the pastry with the remaining 2 tablespoons melted butter.

Bake for 35 to 40 minutes, until the top of the croustade is golden. Remove from the oven and set the pan on a wire rack. Let cool for about 5 minutes, then serve, in or out of the pan.

In April 2022, the much-anticipated *Gullah Geechee Home Cooking: Recipes from the Matriarch of Edisto Island* by the late Ms. Emily Meggett was published. It is a cookbook we all needed, canonizing her place in history as the Lowcountry culinary icon. Her talent and stature and impact unquestionably put her in line with the famous Jacques Pépin, who is heralded as America's premier chef of French cuisine. If I could meet Ms. Emily, I'd invite her into my kitchen and feed her these stuffed deviled eggs, the exchange being the opposite of what she'd come to know in her selfless life. A take on Jacques Pépin's Oeufs Jeannette, which were created as a nod to his mother, these are filled with lump crabmeat and seared until crispy in the same fashion—my ode to Ms. Emily. **Makes 12**

EGGS EMILY
WITH SPICY ROUILLE VINAIGRETTE

For the Eggs

2 teaspoons kosher salt

6 large eggs

4 ounces jumbo lump crabmeat, picked over

1 tablespoon Duke's mayonnaise

2 teaspoons yellow mustard

1 teaspoon freshly ground white pepper

1 tablespoon unsalted butter

1 teaspoon canola oil

For the Rouille Vinaigrette

1 roasted red bell pepper (see page 110), chopped

1 garlic clove, peeled

1 teaspoon cayenne pepper

½ teaspoon red pepper flakes

2 tablespoons rice vinegar

3 tablespoons chile oil

Juice of 1 lime

1 tablespoon sorghum molasses

¼ cup fresh cilantro leaves

1 teaspoon kosher salt

¼ cup roasted peanuts, crushed

½ cup thinly sliced fresh chives

Extra-virgin olive oil (optional)

Make the eggs: Fill a small pot with water, add 1 teaspoon of the salt, and bring to a boil over high heat. Fill a large bowl with ice and water and set it nearby. Carefully drop the eggs into the boiling water. Boil for 6 minutes, then use a slotted spoon to remove and transfer to the ice bath to cool. When the eggs are cool enough to handle, peel them and slice them in half lengthwise.

Carefully remove the egg yolks using a spoon, placing 4 in a medium bowl and the remaining 2 in a separate small bowl; set the small bowl aside. Smash the 4 egg yolks using the back of a fork, then fold in the crab, mayo, mustard, remaining 1 teaspoon salt, and the pepper. Arrange the egg whites cut-side up on a plate and spoon the yolk mixture into the whites, leveling out the yolk so it remains flat.

Combine the butter and oil in a large cast-iron skillet over medium heat. When the butter is foamy, add the filled egg whites, face down, and cook without moving until a golden brown crust forms, 2 to 3 minutes. Remove from the pan.

Make the rouille vinaigrette: In a blender or food processor, combine the reserved 2 egg yolks, the bell pepper, garlic, cayenne, red pepper flakes, vinegar, chile oil, lime juice, sorghum, cilantro, and salt and blend until emulsified and smooth, about 2 minutes. Transfer to a small bowl, then fold in the peanuts and chives. Add olive oil to loosen, if needed.

To serve, arrange the eggs on a proper deviled egg platter and drizzle some vinaigrette onto each.

I thought the phrase "everything but the kitchen sink" was specific to the way my mom prepared stews. If I listened closely some nights from my upstairs sanctuary, I could hear her long red acrylic fingernails clacking against the stockpot as she pondered what would land in the pot next. Leaning into her knowledge from recent restaurant experiences, taking inspiration from the pages of lifestyle magazines, and letting her background in Appalachian cuisine guide her, she'd throw in whatever she thought made sense, building layer upon layer of flavor, all with her hand on her hip to show her confidence. These all-in soups often included seasoning meat as the common denominator of flavor and were always chock-full of fresh vegetables and seafood from the Virginia coast. Other than that, there weren't many constants besides the outcome tasting delicious, homey, and well seasoned. Every weekend, she would transform from successful career woman to Southern belle, presiding over the kitchen to conquer the cravings of our family, from my traditional South Carolinian dad to my own finicky self. And yet my mom swears she is not a good cook, just because she doesn't pull from an arsenal of tried-and-true recipes or fancy techniques. "I'm just making it good as I go," she always says, cooking by taste and feel, which I love. I think that is the mark of a good cook. **Feeds 6 to 8**

BLACKENED FLOUNDER CHOWDER
WITH TURKEY TAILS

1 pound smoked turkey tails

2 teaspoons smoked paprika

2 teaspoons cayenne pepper

2 teaspoons onion powder

1 teaspoon garlic powder

1 teaspoon freshly ground black pepper

3 teaspoons kosher salt

1 pound flounder fillets

2 teaspoons canola oil

4 ears corn, shucked

2 cups heavy cream

4 thyme sprigs

3 bay leaves

2 cups chicken stock, homemade (page 41) or store-bought

1 pound new potatoes, quartered

½ cup chopped fresh parsley

Classic Cornbread (page 40) or Malinda Russell's Salt-Rising Bread (page 65), for serving

Place the turkey tails in a small pot and add 3 cups water. Bring to a boil over medium-high heat and cook until the turkey begins to soften, at least 15 minutes. Reduce the heat to low and cook until the turkey is fork-tender, about 45 minutes more. Remove from the heat.

Using a strainer, transfer the turkey tails to a large bowl to cool slightly. When the turkey tails are cool enough to handle, remove the meat from the bones, discarding the bones, and return the meat to the liquid.

Recipe continues

In a small bowl, combine the smoked paprika, cayenne, onion powder, garlic powder, black pepper, and 2 teaspoons of the salt. Coat the fish on both sides with seasoning blend.

In a medium skillet, heat the oil over medium-high heat. When it just begins to smoke, add the fish and cook until the spices begin to blacken, 3 to 4 minutes, then flip the fish over and immediately remove the pan from the heat, letting the fish rest in the pan for 4 to 6 minutes (you can get the charred corn started in the meantime), until it flakes easily and is no longer opaque.

Meanwhile, in a large skillet, cook the corn over medium-high heat, rotating occasionally, until charred on all sides, about 8 minutes total. Remove and let cool slightly, then slice the kernels off the cobs; set the kernels aside. Place the spent cobs in a medium stockpot and add 2 cups water. Bring to a boil over high heat, then reduce the heat to medium, cover, and cook for 30 minutes. Remove the cobs from the corn stock and discard them.

Meanwhile, in a 4-quart stockpot, combine the cream, thyme, bay leaves, and remaining 1 teaspoon salt. Cook over low heat, stirring occasionally, until reduced by half, about 40 minutes. Add the corn stock and chicken stock. Increase the heat to high to bring the mixture to a boil, then reduce the heat to medium to maintain a simmer. Add the potatoes and cook until they are beginning to soften, 18 to 20 minutes. Add the turkey tail mixture and the charred corn. Reduce the heat to low and cook until completely warmed through, 7 to 8 minutes. Flake the blackened fish directly into the chowder. Add the parsley and stir to combine.

Ladle into bowls and serve with cornbread or salt-rising bread alongside.

Coming up in Coastal Virginia, I ate my fair share of seafood. While mussels were never part of our at-home diet, they were always the thing we ordered when dining at "fancy" places. Every menu on the boardwalk featured mussels, but it wasn't until I started cooking on the beach as a teen that I saw them prepared pound after pound, nonstop, each night. I was intrigued. I always found simplicity in eating these bivalves. Hot out of a pot, swimming in their own broth, they sauced themselves. There was no violent cracking or layers of newspaper beneath your elbows, but there was bread sopping to make up for it. To me, mussels seemed elevated—classy, even. Through my own trials and experimentation, I'll say that, as with everything, quality and freshness are important here. Enjoy these little porch pounders—and for the full experience, serve them with johnnycakes (page 114) to sop up all that precious broth. **Feeds 4 to 6**

BROTHY MUSSELS AND TURNIP GREENS

3 tablespoons unsalted butter

4 ounces slab bacon, diced

1 yellow onion, chopped

1 bunch turnip greens, chopped

4 garlic cloves, chopped

1 tablespoon light brown sugar

1 teaspoon red pepper flakes

1½ teaspoons yellow mustard seeds

1½ teaspoons fennel seeds

2 tablespoons white wine vinegar

2 pounds mussels, cleaned and debearded

Flaky salt

Lemon zest and juice, for serving

In a large stockpot, combine the butter, bacon, and onion. Cook over medium-low heat, stirring occasionally, until the onions are soft and translucent (but not brown), 4 to 5 minutes. Add the greens, garlic, brown sugar, red pepper flakes, mustard seeds, fennel seeds, and vinegar. Add 5 cups water, cover, and cook, stirring occasionally to ensure the greens remain submerged, until the greens are tender but still have some bite, about 30 minutes.

Add the mussels, cover, and cook until they open, 7 to 8 minutes, giving everything one good stir halfway through. Using a slotted spoon, transfer the mussels and greens to serving bowls; discard any mussels that have not opened.

Return the broth to a boil over high heat and cook, uncovered, until reduced by two-thirds, 4 to 5 minutes. Ladle hot broth over each serving of mussels. Finish with flaky salt, some lemon zest, and a squeeze of lemon juice.

I admit this isn't a true panzanella, as it swaps cornbread for sourdough, and it will surely earn a side-eye from Italian-cuisine purists—but try to ignore that. What you should *not* ignore about this panzanella-ish salad is the quality of the tomatoes you choose to make it with. I need you to completely avoid the grocery store here. It is imperative that you use in-season tomatoes, ripened by the summer sun. Bonus points if you shake the farmer's hand that grew them. When you do it right, toasted cornbread soaks up the tomatoes' juices, and a simple white wine vinaigrette and fresh summer herbs top it all off. You'll think Tuscan sun but find yourself in magical Lowcountry instead. **Feeds 4**

TOMATO AND CORNBREAD PANZANELLA

2 cups diced Classic Cornbread (page 40)

1 small heirloom tomato, left whole, plus 2 medium heirloom tomatoes, cut into wedges

2 teaspoons kosher salt

2 teaspoons freshly ground black pepper

1 tablespoon whole-grain mustard

1 tablespoon white wine vinegar

¼ cup extra-virgin olive oil

Handful of cherry tomatoes, halved 1 cup diced summer squash

Flaky salt

Torn fresh basil leaves, for serving

Torn fresh mint leaves, for serving

Preheat the oven to 400°F. Line a baking sheet with parchment paper.

Arrange the cornbread in a single layer on the prepared baking sheet. Toast until golden brown, 8 to 10 minutes. Remove from the oven and set aside to cool.

Over a large bowl, use your hands to crush the small tomato. Use your fingers to work the pulp and seeds free from the skin, discarding the skin. Add the salt, pepper, mustard, vinegar, and oil and whisk to combine with the pulp. Add the tomato wedges, cherry tomatoes, and summer squash and gently toss to combine.

Spread the toasted cornbread cubes in a serving bowl, then pour the dressed tomato-squash mixture over the top, letting the liquid soak into the bread. Finish with flaky salt, basil, and mint before serving.

"Hash" is a catchall word for the odds and ends that go in the pot after the whole hog has been picked over. It is my family's (especially my aunt Louis's) pride and joy. True nose-to-tail eatin', this was a popular side dish among us, always served over rice. One year during our family reunion, the ever-popular and highly anticipated dish was somehow mistakenly left off our buffet table, tucked away inside the oven to stay warm. Most of us had just gotten settled with full plates after patiently waiting for food for hours when Louis suddenly noticed dozens of forlorn hashless paper plates. She hurriedly added the hash to the spread and made a big show of insisting every single one of us immediately stop eating and line back up at the buffet. Sure, we rolled our eyes and huffed, but truthfully, her hash was worth the commotion. This version doesn't include the whole hog but it's a good stand-in. A bowl of Charleston ice cream is my ideal landing spot for this hash. **Feeds 6 to 8**

LOUIS'S LINE-UP HASH

4 pounds bone-in pork butt

2 tablespoons kosher salt

2 yellow onions, diced

2 tablespoons freshly ground black pepper

¼ cup hot sauce

2 teaspoons red pepper flakes

1 cup apple cider vinegar

½ cup yellow mustard

Charleston Ice Cream (page 45), for serving

Set a smoker to medium (about 400°F).

Season the pork all over with the salt, then smoke for about 4 hours, or until a meat thermometer inserted into the pork registers 220°F.

In a medium stockpot, combine the smoked pork, onions, black pepper, hot sauce, red pepper flakes, vinegar, and 4 cups water. Bring to a boil over high heat. Reduce the heat to medium-low and simmer, stirring occasionally, until the pork is tender and falling off the bone, about 2 hours. Use tongs to transfer the pork to a cutting board to cool.

When the pork is cool enough to handle, pull off the meat, discarding the bone. Coarsely chop the pork, then return it to the pot and add 1 cup water and the mustard. Cook, stirring occasionally, until the hash thickens and appears red, 30 to 45 minutes more. Serve a spoonful of hash over some Charleston ice cream.

These dressing cakes represent Thanksgiving for me. My mom's oyster dressing, not one to hide inside the actual turkey, has always been far superior to the turkey it's sat next to on the table. We ate the turkey because we had to, but what we were all eyeing was that tasty, briny dressing. While this is a family recipe, there's a storied history of Brits stuffing poultry with oysters and bread to made a meal really stretch and feed the masses, which is one thing they have in common with Southerners. The following day would see the dressing pattied into these little cakes, beginning my fascination with the magic of leftovers. Flavors compounded and fully melded with the dressing's buttery richness, pronouncing the complexity even further. A sort of revival of the prior night's festivities is what it felt like. A "day after" dish like this was a hangover cure from the prior night's imbibing, a quick and easy meal, and a way to make space in the fridge. Every year, these are the reason I look forward to the day after Thanksgiving.

Instead of baking this dressing in a pan, then scooping it into patties the day after, we chill the dressing mix to give the flavors time to develop and then form it into patties to skip ahead to the best part. We typically dunk these in leftover turkey gravy, but for non-Thanksgiving meals, soubise swaps in nicely. This French onion sauce has the same luxuriously silky feel of a well-made gravy, and Parmesan and red onion bring out umami notes to match. **Feeds 4 to 6**

OYSTER DRESSING CAKES
WITH RED ONION SOUBISE

For the Dressing

Classic Cornbread (page 40), crumbled

2 teaspoons dried sage

1 teaspoon paprika

1 teaspoon celery salt

1 tablespoon plus 2 teaspoons neutral oil, such as canola or grapeseed

1 yellow onion, diced

2 celery stalks, diced

2 carrots, diced

2½ teaspoons kosher salt

8 ounces shucked raw oysters, drained (oyster liquor reserved) and finely chopped

A few dashes of hot sauce

5 large eggs, beaten

For the Soubise

1 tablespoon unsalted butter

1 teaspoon neutral oil, such as canola or grapeseed

1 large red onion, diced

Kosher salt

1 pint heavy cream

1 cup finely grated fresh Parmesan cheese

½ teaspoon red pepper flakes

½ teaspoon freshly grated nutmeg

Zest of 1 lemon

Freshly ground black pepper

Recipe continues

Make the dressing: In a large bowl, toss together the cornbread, sage, paprika, and celery salt.

In a medium skillet, heat 1 tablespoon of the oil over medium heat. Add the onion, celery, carrots, and salt. Cook, stirring occasionally, until the vegetables are soft and the onion is translucent, 7 to 8 minutes. Stir in the oysters and ½ cup of the reserved oyster liquor. Cover and cook over low heat until the oysters become plump and are fully cooked through, about 7 minutes. Remove from the heat, uncover, and let cool.

Add the hot sauce, eggs, and cooled vegetable-oyster mixture to the bowl with the cornbread. Stir to combine thoroughly, then chill in the refrigerator for at least 3 hours or up to overnight.

Make the soubise: In a medium pan, melt the butter over medium-low heat. Add the oil and onion and season with a generous pinch of salt. Cook, stirring often, until the onion is tender but not at all browned, 12 to 13 minutes.

In a separate medium saucepan, bring the cream to a boil over medium heat, then cook, stirring with a rubber spatula to prevent the cream from browning, for a full minute. Reduce the heat to low, add the Parmesan, and cook, stirring, until the cheese is incorporated into the cream, 2 to 3 minutes. Add the red pepper flakes, nutmeg, and lemon zest and season with salt and black pepper. Cook, stirring, until the cream thickens, 2 to 3 minutes more.

Pour the cream over the onions and bring the mixture to a simmer over low heat. Remove from the heat, give the soubise a good stir, and let it rest for 2 to 3 minutes. Taste and add more seasoning as needed.

Heat the remaining 2 teaspoons oil in a large cast-iron skillet over medium-low heat. Form the cornbread mixture into equal patties (you should have a dozen). When the oil shimmers, working in batches, add the patties and cook until golden brown on both sides, 4 to 5 minutes per side. Transfer to a plate.

Serve the oyster dressing cakes hot from the pan with a spoonful of the soubise over the top.

Slime, as a texture, isn't very popular in American cuisine. We have mucilage to thank for the slick, gooey texture of okra you either love (like I do) or hate. Even though the vegetable is a Southern staple with many health benefits, okra is deeply shamed for its mouthfeel. As for me, I'm into long-stewed okra that pulls from the bowl "to the ceiling," like I enjoyed during my time in Nairobi and Cameroon. But until you develop a slime-refined palate, this dish is a good start. Okra's vegetal, earthy flavors shine in several different approachable formats here: in a simple broth, and with the pickling of the seeds, which flips the typical slimy texture into something more luxurious and caviarlike. **Feeds 4**

CRISPY OKRA
WITH OKRA JUS AND OKRA SEED CAVIAR

1 pound okra

For the Okra Jus

1 tablespoon okra seed oil or grapeseed oil

½ yellow onion, cut in half

2 garlic cloves, peeled

1½ teaspoons freshly ground white pepper

1 teaspoon kosher salt

2 tablespoons apple cider vinegar

1 tablespoon unsalted butter

2 teaspoons tomato paste

For the Okra Seed Caviar

1 shallot, finely diced

2 teaspoons fresh lemon juice

1 teaspoon flaky salt

For the Crispy Okra

Neutral oil, such as canola or grapeseed, for frying

½ cup cassava flour or rice flour

½ teaspoon paprika

½ teaspoon ground ginger

½ teaspoon ground cumin

½ teaspoon ground coriander

1 teaspoon freshly ground white pepper

Kosher salt

Charleston Ice Cream (page 45), for serving

Preheat the oven to 300°F.

Cut off the tops of the okra pods and reserve, then cut a slit down the length of the pods, being careful to pierce only the flesh—not through the membrane. Using your fingers, gently open up the slit, exposing the membrane and seeds. Rake out the seeds and place them in a small bowl of water, setting the pods aside as you work. Rub the seeds to break them free of any leftover membrane and set aside to soak.

Make the okra jus: Place half the seeded okra pods and all the reserved tops on a baking sheet. Bake for

8 to 10 minutes, until toasty and aromatic. Remove from the oven.

Heat the okra seed oil in a medium saucepan over medium heat. When the pot is a bit smoky, add the toasted okra pods and tops and the onion and cook, stirring occasionally, until the onion begins to brown, 6 to 7 minutes.

Add the garlic, white pepper, and salt and cook, stirring, until fragrant, 1 minute more, then reduce the heat to medium-low and add 4 cups water. Cover the pot with the lid ajar and simmer the okra jus until the liquid takes on a rich green hue, about 20 minutes.

Recipe continues

Strain the jus, discarding the solids, then return the liquid to the pot. Whisk in the vinegar, butter, and tomato paste. Cook over low heat, uncovered, until reduced by two-thirds, about 10 minutes, then cover and keep warm over low heat.

Make the okra seed caviar: By now, the membrane should have risen to the top of the bowl of okra seeds, with the seeds remaining at the bottom. Using a spoon, skim off and discard the large pieces of membrane, then carefully pour off the remaining water and smaller bits of membrane. Rinse and drain the okra seeds.

Return the okra seeds to the bowl and add the shallot, lemon juice, and flaky salt. Stir to combine, then set the okra seed caviar aside.

Make the crispy okra: Fill a high-sided heavy-bottomed skillet with 1 inch of oil and clip a deep-fry thermometer to the side. Heat over medium heat to 350°F.

In a medium bowl, combine the flour, paprika, ginger, cumin, coriander, and white pepper. Thinly slice the remaining okra pods lengthwise, then add them to the bowl with the flour mixture and stir to coat. Working in batches, add the coated okra to the hot oil and cook until crispy, 7 to 8 minutes. Remove with a slotted spoon and transfer to a plate lined with paper towels. Immediately season with salt.

Spoon some rice into the center of each plate and ladle over a little jus. Top with some crispy okra and garnish with okra seed caviar.

Something I find inspiring within the cuisine of West Africa is the incredibly creative and effective use of natural thickeners for stews and soups. Throughout the Lowcountry, this tradition has clearly found its place: okra thickens soup, peanuts are crushed into velvety stews, and ground benne is used in both, similar to all-purpose flour. In this dish, creamy peanut butter serves as the thickener. It earns particularly nutty notes and creaminess from store-bought peanut butter. **Feeds 6 to 8**

STEWED PEANUT CHICKEN AND SHRIMP RICE

1 tablespoon garlic powder

1 tablespoon ground ginger

2 teaspoons smoked paprika

1 teaspoon freshly ground black pepper

1 teaspoon red pepper flakes

1 teaspoon ground cardamom

1 pound bone-in, skin-on chicken legs, thighs, or a mix

3 teaspoons kosher salt

2 teaspoons grapeseed oil

1 yellow onion, chopped

2 poblano peppers, seeded and chopped

1 cup long-grain rice, rinsed

1 tablespoon unsalted butter

1 cup full-fat coconut milk

1 cup chicken stock, homemade (page 41) or store-bought

3 tablespoons creamy peanut butter

1 pound shrimp, peeled and deveined

Juice of 1 lime, for serving

Torn fresh mint, for serving

¼ cup roasted unsalted peanuts, finely chopped, for serving

In a small bowl, combine the garlic powder, ginger, paprika, black pepper, red pepper flakes, and cardamom. Season the chicken evenly with half the spice mix and 2 teaspoons of the salt. (This step can be done a day ahead; store the chicken uncovered in the fridge.)

In a heavy-bottomed skillet or Dutch oven, heat the grapeseed oil over medium-high heat. When it shimmers, working in batches, add the chicken to the skillet and cook until the skin is crispy and golden brown on both sides, 3 to 4 minutes per side. Transfer the chicken to a plate.

Add the onion and poblanos to same skillet and cook, stirring occasionally, until lightly browned, about 4 minutes. Add the rice, butter, and remaining spice mix to the pan and toss to coat. Cook, stirring, until the rice is toasted and fragrant, 2 to 3 minutes. Add the coconut milk, stock, peanut butter, and remaining 1 teaspoon salt. Increase the heat to high and bring to a boil. Cook for 30 seconds, then reduce the heat to low.

Add the chicken, nestling it into the rice, and cover the pan. Cook for 15 minutes, then add the shrimp. Cover and cook until the chicken meat starts to pull away from the bone, the shrimp is no longer translucent, and the rice has mostly absorbed the liquid, 5 minutes more. Remove from the heat and stir.

Finish with a squeeze of lime juice, some torn mint, and chopped peanuts, then serve.

The Lowcountry is where I became enamored with rice. For some time, it was the only food I'd eat—maybe because Grandma Bearnie proudly fed us more grains of rice than there are granules of sand on the beach. It ran straight through her blood, and given its deep history in this place, it's easy to understand why. In her house, a pot of rice lived on the stove. It was served with eggs in the morning and as a side at supper. When there seemed to be more mouths to feed than food in the house, one-pot rice dishes like this one often fit the bill. Thankfully, I enjoyed eating Grandma Bearnie's pirloos as much as she enjoyed making them. For this, my favorite bean varieties to use are lady peas or crowder peas. **Feeds 6 to 8**

SPICED SHRIMP AND FIELD PEA PIRLOO

1 cup Carolina Gold rice

1 pound royal red shrimp, peeled and deveined

2 teaspoons kosher salt

½ teaspoon freshly ground black pepper

¼ teaspoon cayenne pepper

¼ teaspoon ground ginger

¼ teaspoon ground mustard

⅛ teaspoon smoked paprika

½ cup diced slab bacon

1 small yellow onion, diced

3 celery stalks, diced

1 red bell pepper, diced

4 garlic cloves, minced

½ habanero chile, seeded and minced

1 cup cooked field peas (see page 44), plus ½ cup bean liquid

1 tablespoon tomato paste

4 cups seafood stock or chicken stock, homemade (page 41) or store-bought

1 dried bay leaf

4 thyme sprigs, tied together with kitchen twine

2 tablespoons unsalted butter, cubed

½ cup chopped fresh parsley

¼ cup chopped fresh cilantro

A few dashes of Tabasco sauce

4 scallions, green tops only, very thinly sliced, for serving

Rinse the rice in a fine-mesh sieve under cool water, agitating it periodically until the water runs clear, 3 to 4 minutes.

Place the shrimp in a medium bowl and season with 1 teaspoon of the salt, the black pepper, cayenne, ginger, mustard, and paprika.

In a large Dutch oven, cook the bacon over medium-low heat, stirring occasionally, until the bacon begins to crisp and the fat is rendered, 10 to 12 minutes. Reduce the heat to low and add the onion, celery, and bell pepper. Cook, stirring occasionally, until the onion is translucent, about 7 minutes. Add the garlic and habanero. Cook until very

fragrant, 2 to 3 minutes more. Add the field peas with ½ cup of their likker, the rice, tomato paste, stock, bay leaf, thyme, and remaining 1 teaspoon salt. Increase the heat to high and bring the liquid to a boil. Reduce the heat to low, cover, and cook for 11 to 13 minutes, until most of the liquid has been absorbed.

Arrange the shrimp and butter over the rice in a single layer, cover, and cook until the shrimp is pink and opaque, 5 to 6 minutes. Remove from the heat and let rest for 1 to 2 minutes to ensure the residual heat fully cooks the shrimp; the shrimp should be curled. Uncover and stir in the parsley, cilantro, and hot sauce. Garnish with the scallions and serve.

You can find a version of escovitch—usually fish or meat cooked in a spicy, acidic sauce—in many regions of the world, but not typically in the Lowcountry. But I feel like it has a place here. I originally tried snapper escovitch in Jamaica; from the first bite, my mind was flooded with memories of Grandma Bearnie. The flavor profiles—hot, bright, and umami—mimic all the ways she cooked all the time. The ties between the African diaspora and the South run deep. In this version of the dish, I turned down the acid a bit (just like she would have) and paired it with a spiced-up rendition of her eggplant and tomatoes. I like to use small vermilion snappers from the coast of North Carolina, also known as beeliners, in this recipe; if you can't find those, feel free to swap them for two 2-pound red snappers. **Feeds 4**

RED SNAPPER ESCOVITCH
WITH SPICY TOMATOES AND EGGPLANT

For the Snapper

3½ teaspoons kosher salt

2 teaspoons smoked paprika

1½ teaspoons cayenne pepper

1½ teaspoons ground cumin

1½ teaspoons freshly ground white pepper

4 (1-pound) whole vermilion snappers (see headnote), gutted and scaled

Juice of 2 limes

Canola oil, for frying

1 Scotch bonnet or habanero chile, halved lengthwise and seeded, plus 1 teaspoon minced Scotch bonnet

1 red bell pepper, thinly sliced

1 yellow bell pepper, thinly sliced

1 white onion, thinly sliced

2 carrots, thinly sliced

2 garlic cloves, smashed

6 allspice berries

1 teaspoon juniper berries

1 teaspoon celery seeds

¼ cup distilled white vinegar

Freshly cracked green peppercorns

For the Spicy Tomatoes and Eggplant

1 pound baby eggplant, halved lengthwise

3 teaspoons kosher salt

3 tablespoons coconut oil

1 teaspoon red pepper flakes

1 teaspoon chili powder

1 teaspoon freshly ground black pepper

1 teaspoon cumin seeds

1 teaspoon coriander seeds

1 tablespoon tomato paste

2 teaspoons hot pepper vinegar

2 teaspoons distilled white vinegar

2 teaspoons dark brown sugar

4 Roma (plum) tomatoes, quartered

For Serving

4 scallions, thinly sliced

Leaves from 4 cilantro sprigs

Zest of 2 limes

Recipe continues

Prepare the snapper: In a small bowl, stir together 2½ teaspoons of the salt, the paprika, cayenne, cumin, and white pepper.

Place the fish on a large baking sheet. Using a paring knife, score both sides of the fillets by creating 3 cuts per side on an angle, slicing about midway between the flesh and the bone, just enough to slightly open the flesh. Rub the lime juice all over the fish, thoroughly rubbing inside each cavity as well. Evenly season the inside and outside of the fish using the spice mixture. Allow the fish to marinate at room temperature for 20 minutes.

Meanwhile, make the spicy tomatoes and eggplant: Line a rimmed baking sheet with parchment paper.

Using a paring knife, score the cut sides of the eggplant in a crosshatch pattern. Place the eggplant in a colander set over a large bowl and sprinkle with 2 teaspoons of the salt. Let stand for 45 minutes to 1 hour to drain. Gently pat the eggplant dry with paper towels, then coarsely chop it.

Preheat the oven to 400°F.

In a small skillet, melt the coconut oil over medium heat, then add the red pepper flakes, chili powder, black pepper, cumin, coriander, and remaining 1 teaspoon salt. Cook, stirring occasionally, until aromatic and bright, 2 to 3 minutes. Whisk in the tomato paste, hot pepper vinegar, white vinegar, and brown sugar. Cook until the brown sugar dissolves, 5 minutes more.

In a large bowl, combine the eggplant, tomatoes, and spice mixture. Toss to coat well. Spread evenly onto the prepared baking sheet and roast for 25 to 30 minutes, shaking the pan occasionally, until the eggplant is tender and the tomatoes are nice and blistered.

Meanwhile, fry the fish: Fill a very large skillet with ½ inch of oil and clip a deep-fry thermometer to the side. Heat over medium-high heat to 350°F. Working in batches, add the fish and a chile half to the hot oil and cook until the fish is golden brown and crispy on both sides, 8 to 10 minutes total, carefully flipping halfway through. Set the chile half aside and transfer the fish to a wire rack. Repeat with the remaining fish and chile half.

Carefully pour out and discard the hot frying oil. In the same skillet, combine the bell peppers, onion, carrots, garlic, allspice, juniper, celery seeds, minced chile, and the remaining 1 teaspoon salt. Cook over medium heat, stirring occasionally, until the vegetables begin to soften, 4 to 5 minutes. Add the vinegar and cook, stirring occasionally, until aromatic, 5 minutes more. Remove from the heat and stir in the green peppercorns.

Transfer the eggplant and tomatoes to a serving platter and lay the crispy fish over the top. Add the pickled vegetables and garnish with the scallions, cilantro, lime zest, and reserved chile halves.

I was lucky enough to grow up in a grits *and* rice household. My mom would often try her hand at a more boggy-style rice, mimicking the velvety corn porridges of her upbringing as she knew it. Dad's Geechee background gave him a penchant for "dry" rice, praising its maker for each identifiable grain. This combination of rice and gravy was the peacemaker. In the morning after she'd served dry rice for dinner, my mom would crisp up the leftovers in a cast-iron pan with a little something and drape her perfectly smooth gravy over it, creating a dish that straddled the line between wet and dry. While this oyster gravy can be had alone, pairing it with crab rice makes for a downright good marriage. **Feeds 4**

CRISPY CRAB RICE MIDDLINS AND OYSTER GRAVY

For the Gravy

4 tablespoons (½ stick) unsalted butter

¼ cup dry white wine

1 teaspoon kosher salt

12 raw oysters, freshly shucked, drained (oyster liquor reserved), and chopped

¼ cup all-purpose flour

2 cups chicken stock, homemade (page 41) or store-bought

2 dashes of hot sauce

1 bay leaf

1 teaspoon dried sage

1 teaspoon dried parsley

½ teaspoon cayenne pepper

½ teaspoon smoked paprika

½ teaspoon freshly ground black pepper

For the Rice

1 tablespoon bacon fat

1 medium onion, diced

2 celery stalks, diced

1 medium green bell pepper, chopped

2 garlic cloves, minced

1 teaspoon canola oil

1 pound jumbo lump crabmeat, picked over

2 cups Rice Middlins (page 46)

½ cup thinly sliced fresh chives

Kosher salt and freshly ground black pepper

Make the gravy: In a small saucepan, heat the butter, wine, and salt over medium heat. When the butter is melted, stir in the oysters and cook, stirring occasionally, until the oysters are cooked through and the liquid has reduced by two-thirds, 7 to 8 minutes. Add the flour and stir with a wooden spoon to combine. Cook, stirring continuously, until you have a medium golden brown roux, 5 to 6 minutes. Slowly stir in the stock and hot sauce. Add the bay leaf, sage, parsley, cayenne, paprika, and black pepper. Reduce the heat to low and cook, stirring frequently, until the gravy thickens, 10 to 15 minutes. If needed, cook for up to 7 minutes more to reach the desired consistency. Cover to keep warm and set aside.

Make the rice: In a medium Dutch oven, melt the bacon fat over medium-low heat. Add the onion, celery, bell pepper, and garlic. Cook, stirring occasionally, until the onion is soft and translucent, 7 to 8 minutes. Using a slotted spoon, transfer the mixture to a bowl.

Add the oil to the pot and heat over medium-high heat. When it shimmers, add the crab and cook, turning occasionally, until it begins to brown and become crispy around the edges, 5 to 6 minutes. Add the middlins and vegetable mixture, then stir in the chives. Season with salt and black pepper.

To serve, ladle the rice into bowls, then top each serving with a spoonful or two of the oyster gravy.

To me, cocktails are synonymous with cookouts, where a boozy gift is always met with open arms. This punch is as simple as the saying goes—1 part sour, 2 parts sweet, 3 parts strong, 4 parts weak. The math in this recipe doesn't exactly correspond to the saying, but I really like this punch with a little less lime juice. You came to party, but a sparkly punch bowl studded with berries will easily give the illusion that you put in the work. **Makes enough for about ½ dozen partiers**

RED RUM PUNCH

3 cups dark rum

4 cups apple cider

½ cup fresh lime juice

1 cup frozen raspberries

2 cups ginger ale

In a punch bowl, combine the rum, apple cider, lime juice, raspberries, and ginger ale. Ladle into glasses full of ice to serve.

I'm proud not to have fallen victim to the avocado toast fad—I was far too busy dreaming of this toast: the ultimate tropical seaside fantasy snack. Refreshing buttermilk meets its match in zingy lime, while bananas add nuance with their low, comforting hum. Cinnamon-sugar toast, specifically, is the essential vehicle for this magic. With all its quirks, I'm not sure this lime jam would be grandma-approved, but its versatility certainly deems it worthy of the labor of zesting and juicing a half dozen limes. Try it on baked goods, stir it into oatmeal, or add into yogurt. **Feeds 6**

CHARLESTON TOAST

For the Lime Jam

4 overripe bananas, mashed

¼ cup packed dark brown sugar

Zest and juice of 6 limes

For the Buttermilk Cheese

½ gallon whole milk

2 cups buttermilk

Zest and juice of 1 lime

1 teaspoon kosher salt

1 tablespoon distilled white vinegar

1 teaspoon ground cinnamon

2 teaspoons sugar

4 tablespoons (½ stick) unsalted butter, at room temperature

6 thick slices white bread, toasted

1 teaspoon flaky salt, for serving

1½ tablespoons benne seeds, toasted, for serving

Make the jam: In a medium pot, combine the bananas, brown sugar, lime zest, and lime juice. Cook over medium heat, stirring occasionally, until the mixture takes on the consistency of jam, about 30 minutes. Remove from the heat and let cool. (The jam can be stored in an airtight container in the refrigerator for up to a week. For long-term storage, use the Hot Water Bath Canning technique on page 39.)

Make the cheese: Clip a candy thermometer to the side of a medium saucepan. Combine the milk and buttermilk in the pan, then stir in the lime zest, lime juice, salt, and vinegar. Heat the mixture over medium heat, without stirring, until it reaches 125°F and the curds and whey begin separating, 7 to 8 minutes. Reduce the heat to low and simmer, stirring occasionally, for 3 minutes more, then remove from the heat.

Drape a few layers of dampened cheesecloth over a fine-mesh sieve and set the sieve over a large bowl. The curds should have formed at the top of the whey in a thick layer;

using a ladle, carefully scoop the curds out of the pot and into the cheesecloth-sieve setup so as to not break the large curds. Let the curds sit in the cheesecloth to drain for an hour or more. The cheese will still be wet to the touch but crumbly like goat cheese. Discard the whey or reserve it for another use (it will keep in an airtight container in the refrigerator for up to 5 days or in the freezer for up to 6 months; I typically use it to soak beans and grains for added protein and flavor).

Preheat the oven to 375°F.

In a small bowl, whisk together the cinnamon, sugar, and butter. Spread the butter mixture over the toast. Place the toast on a baking sheet and bake for 12 to 15 minutes, until golden brown. Let cool.

To serve, generously spread the jam over the toast, crumble some of the cheese on top, and sprinkle with flaky salt and toasted benne seeds.

Remember pudding? Or have you repressed the school-age memories of that foil-lined BPA-filled cup loaded with monotonous bites of smooth, aerated fat and sugar? Let this recipe serve to remind you that pudding is indeed delicious, especially when it's homemade. Imagine velvety, cool bites of caramelized sweet potatoes dancing across your tongue in gracefully orchestrated choreography, and not muddled by the fluff of your usual pecan and brown sugar streusel concoctions. All this dish needs for its performance is a straightforward whipped cream—it's that simple, and it's that good. A little shot of bourbon lends notes of caramel nuttiness. **Feeds 6**

DRUNKEN SWEET POTATO PUDDING

1 small sweet potato, scrubbed

½ cup packed dark brown sugar

½ teaspoon kosher salt

½ cup heavy cream

½ cup whole milk

½ cup plus 2 tablespoons granulated sugar

1 large egg, at room temperature

2 large egg yolks, at room temperature

2 tablespoons cornstarch

3 tablespoons unsalted butter

1 tablespoon bourbon

2 teaspoons pure vanilla extract

For the Whipped Cream

1 cup heavy cream

1 teaspoon confectioners' sugar

Preheat the oven to 400°F. Line a quarter baking sheet with parchment paper.

Using a fork, prick the sweet potato three or four times all over. Place on the prepared baking sheet and bake for 35 to 40 minutes, until fork-tender. Let cool, then run through a food mill to make a smooth puree. Set aside.

In a medium Dutch oven, stir together the brown sugar and salt. Cook over medium heat, undisturbed, allowing the sugar to melt, until the mixture caramelizes and appears dark brown in color, 10 to 12 minutes. Slowly and carefully whisk in the cream, milk, and granulated sugar. Increase the heat to medium-high and cook until the mixture liquefies again, 1 to 2 minutes more. Remove from the heat and cover to keep warm.

In a heatproof medium bowl, whisk together the egg, egg yolks, and cornstarch. Using a ladle, carefully scoop up 1 cup of the sugar mixture and very slowly drizzle

the mixture into the eggs, vigorously and continuously whisking so the eggs don't scramble. Pour that mixture into the pot with the remaining sugar mixture and return the pot to the heat over medium-high. Cook, whisking continuously, until the pudding thickens and begins a slow simmer, 1 to 2 minutes. Whisk in ½ cup of the sweet potato puree, the butter, bourbon, and vanilla, then remove from the heat.

Portion the pudding into small ramekins, cover each with plastic wrap, and refrigerate for 4 to 6 hours, until the pudding is set.

Make the whipped cream: In the chilled bowl of a stand mixer fitted with the whisk attachment, beat the cream and confectioners' sugar until soft peaks form.

Serve the pudding topped with a dollop of the whipped cream.

My memories and the yearning for the food of my childhood will be a constant itch I long to scratch. During the summer, we played "ice cream shop" by making our own version of the treat. We poured rice milk into plastic cups with fruit and jam, then plunged plastic spoons inside so they'd stick straight out the top after a few hours in the freezer. For me, even back then, the thrill was in the making. Here's a slightly more fanciful version you can also eat and enjoy; you don't need a begging child's permission to make this recipe. **Makes 8 pops**

BLUEBERRY RICESICLES

For the Rice Milk

2 cups short-grain rice

¼ cup sorghum molasses

For the Blueberry Syrup

1 cup blueberries

½ cup honey

Zest and juice of 2 lemons

Make the rice milk: In a small pot, bring 4 cups water to a boil over high heat. Place the rice in a heatproof ½-gallon container and pour the boiling water over the top. Set aside to soak for 2 to 3 hours; the starches from the rice will leach into the water, turning it milky white. Strain the liquid into a blender and add 1 cup of the soaked rice (save the remaining rice to cook for a separate dish or discard it). With the blender running, drizzle in the sorghum, then strain the mixture through a fine-mesh sieve placed over a bowl and discard the solids.

Make the syrup: Place the blueberries in a high-sided medium saucepan and cook over medium heat, stirring and smashing the berries with the back of a spoon until they burst, 3 to 4 minutes. Stir in 2 cups water, the honey, and the lemon zest and juice. Cook, stirring occasionally, until the sugar dissolves completely, 5 to 6 minutes. Remove from the heat and let cool.

Pour the strained rice mixture into ice pop molds, filling them two-thirds of the way. Carefully fill the remaining space with the blueberry syrup, taking care not to agitate the molds or mix the syrup and rice milk. Cover and freeze for at least 4 hours to set.

Serve, preferably in the warm sun, allowing the frozen pop to melt down to your elbows.

MIDL

ANDS

Here you'll meet my proud great-grandma Inez Miller of Mayesville, South Carolina, a railroad town where not much has changed since I first remember taking those trips, a comfortable resting point between Tidewater and Lowcountry. My cousins and I called her Geegee; others, Grandma Inez. The landscape changed as paved streets turned to dirt roads lined with plentiful stone-fruit orchards. Every person we passed gave a friendly wave or a tilt of the hat as we slowly drove over crater-like potholes. Known in town for her pristine garden and award-winning canning, Geegee held true to the culinary traditions of this land until her last breath. But is there such a thing as Midlands cuisine? The food identity of the region is rarely explored—is even unfairly hidden, in fact—so it's a fair question. What I know is that here the world's greatest stone fruits ripen just after the final watermelon has done its thing. You'll be hard-pressed to find a tomato, even a bad one, in December. A bite of put-up sweet corn brings summer warmth to the coldest winter's nights and revives memories of last year's canning parties; the best harvests of the season rest in wait in countless kitchens for just the right company. In these parts, "you didn't know it if you didn't grow it." With its bounty of produce that yields unique dishes, like Turtle Soup and Liver Nips, the obvious answer is yes, there is such a thing as Midlands cuisine. Geegee was a good representative of what this sort of cuisine was, and her community would say the same.

There is much to say about my great-grandma Inez, with her deep, piercing eyes, tightly coiled hair, and rich chocolate skin, but she'd want me to talk about her pickles. Thanks to her, this basic pickle recipe has won blue ribbons throughout the Midlands of South Carolina. It wouldn't take much of a walk through the town market to figure out her widely known talent. These pickles really are proofed for a fool: long after my grandma passed, this recipe fell into the hands of the men in the family, and even they couldn't possibly ruin it. **Makes one 1-gallon jar**

FOOLPROOF FRIDGE PICKLES

8 smaller firm cucumbers or summer squash, thinly sliced

2 white onions, thinly sliced

2 dill sprigs

2 garlic cloves

1 bay leaf

1½ tablespoons kosher salt

1 tablespoon sugar

1 teaspoon whole black peppercorns

1 teaspoon yellow mustard seeds

1½ cups distilled white vinegar

Pack the cucumbers, onions, dill, garlic, bay leaf, salt, sugar, peppercorns, and mustard seeds into a sterilized 1-gallon glass jar (or other nonreactive vessel with a tight-fitting lid). Pour the vinegar into the jar. Close the lid tightly and place the jar in the fridge, setting it upside down so it's resting on the lid. After 30 minutes, give the jar a good shake and turn it right-side up. Refrigerate for at least 45 minutes more; I find these pickles are at their best after about 6 hours, with a few shakes and flips every now and then. The salt will draw moisture from the vegetables, lending to your foolproof pickle brine.

They likely won't last this long, but you can store the pickles in the fridge for up to 30 days, as long as they remain fully submerged in their brine. (For long-term storage, use the Hot Water Bath Canning technique on page 39.)

The flavor profile of ham and cheddar combined is special to me. It has seen me through my adolescent picky-eating phase and even my Hot Pocket–only diet during freshman year of college. But way, way, way before me, this pairing dates back to the late 1800s and has, in some form, woven its way through just about every global cuisine imaginable. Midlands has a history of grape cultivation and is full of native species that are hearty enough to survive the heat and plentiful enough in sugar and pectin for jams and jellies like this simple one. You'll want to get a brick of cheddar and use a box grater to shred it by hand for this recipe to avoid the clumping that occurs with the cellulose-coated preshredded stuff. **Makes 12 biscuits**

HAM AND CHEDDAR DROP BISCUITS
WITH GRAPE JELLY

2 cups self-rising flour

1 teaspoon kosher salt

¼ teaspoon freshly ground black pepper

⅓ cup cold unsalted butter, diced

⅔ cup minced smoked country ham

⅔ cup shredded sharp cheddar cheese

1 to 1¼ cups buttermilk

1 large egg, beaten

Grape Jelly (recipe follows)

Preheat the oven to 400°F. Line a large baking sheet with parchment paper.

In a large bowl, whisk together the flour, salt, and black pepper. Add the cold butter and cut it in slowly, using a fork to combine, until pea-size pearls form. Fold in the ham and cheese. Add the buttermilk ½ cup at a time, stirring until the dough is still sticky but is soft and droppable

Drop the dough onto the prepared baking sheet by the heaping tablespoon, spacing the biscuits at least 1 inch apart. Let rest for 10 minutes. Using a pastry brush, brush some of the beaten egg over each biscuit, then bake for 12 to 15 minutes, until the biscuits begin to brown.

Serve the biscuits warm, spread with a generous amount of grape jelly.

Recipe continues

Grape Jelly

Makes 4 cups

    2 pounds seedless red grapes (preferably Concord)
    1½ cups sugar
    2 tablespoons fresh lemon juice
    ⅛ teaspoon kosher salt
    ½ teaspoon freshly ground black pepper

In a medium saucepan, combine the grapes and ½ cup water. Cover with the lid ajar and cook over low heat, stirring occasionally, until the fruit is soft, 8 to 9 minutes. Mash the grapes with a potato masher until fully crushed, then transfer the mixture to a fine-mesh sieve lined with three layers of damp cheesecloth set over a large heatproof bowl. Let the mixture drain, without pressing on the solids, until you have 2 cups of juice, about 45 minutes.

Clip a candy thermometer to a large heavy-bottomed pot. Transfer the collected juice to the pot and bring to a boil over high heat. Add the sugar, lemon juice, salt, and pepper. Return to a boil and cook, stirring frequently, for 8 to 10 minutes, until the temperature registers 220°F. To test if the jelly is done, dip a large metal spoon in, lift it horizontally above the pot, and let the jelly drip back into the pot. The jelly is done when it has thickened slightly and drops off the back of the spoon in a sheet. Using a spoon, skim off any foam from the top.

Ladle the jelly into a sterilized 1-quart jar (or other nonreactive heatproof vessel with a tight-fitting lid), leaving ¾ inch of headspace. Let cool completely, then seal. Store in the refrigerator for up to 30 days. (For long-term storage, use the Hot Water Bath Canning technique on page 39.)

This cornbread seems unassuming, masquerading as a peer among all the others, but she's different on the inside. You'll find her loaded with fatty, chewy bits of cracklin, that luscious fat adding texture and inner depth. With its roots extending back to colonial times, the method of adding cracklins to cornbread is found in many early books written on housewifery. This old-timey recipe feels luxurious and decadent, even with its humble ingredients. **Feeds 6 to 8**

CRACKLIN CORNBREAD

Unsalted butter, for greasing

1½ cups coarse yellow cornmeal

½ cup all-purpose flour

¾ cup pork cracklins, crushed

2 teaspoons baking powder

¼ teaspoon baking soda

1 cup buttermilk

2 large eggs, lightly beaten, at room temperature

3 tablespoons lard or shortening

Grease an 8-inch cast-iron skillet well with butter and place it in the oven. Preheat the oven to 375°F.

In a large bowl, combine the cornmeal, flour, cracklins, baking powder, and baking soda. In a separate small bowl, whisk together the buttermilk, eggs, and lard. Add the wet ingredients to the dry and mix until just combined; the batter should be thick.

Carefully remove the hot skillet from the oven and pour in the batter. Return the skillet to the oven and bake the cornbread for 25 to 30 minutes, until the top is golden brown and a toothpick inserted into the center comes out clean.

Remove the cornbread from the oven and let cool for 6 to 7 minutes before slicing and serving.

Pickled Beets and Onions

Cook beets. Remove skins and sl...
beets 1/4-inch thick, and measur...
slices, then slice thinly half ...
onions and add to beets. S...
lightly with salt. Heat to b...
enough sweetened vinegar (...
...ar as vinegar) t...
beets p...

I'm still in possession of many of my great-grandma Inez's handwritten recipes, and I follow them to a T, but the chef in me feels the need to make small tweaks when I imagine she isn't watching. Pickled vegetables were the driving force behind her pristine garden. These pickles are tangy, hot, and sweet—and so worth the stained fingers. **Makes one 1-quart jar**

PICKLED BEETS AND ONIONS

2 pounds red beets, trimmed and rinsed (don't pat dry)

4 cups apple cider vinegar

1 tablespoon mustard seeds

1 tablespoon celery seeds

1 tablespoon whole black peppercorns

½ cup sugar

2 teaspoons kosher salt

1 pound white onions, sliced

Preheat the oven to 400°F.

Tightly wrap each (still wet) beet individually in aluminum foil and place them on a rimmed baking sheet. Roast for 50 to 60 minutes until fork-tender, checking on the beets after 25 minutes; if they appear dry or are beginning to scorch, add 2 tablespoons water to the baking sheet to create steam. Remove them from the oven and let cool, still wrapped in the foil.

Meanwhile, when the beets are cool enough to handle, rub them using a kitchen towel you don't mind staining (this will get messy!). The skins should slide off easily. (If they don't, rewrap the beets and return them to the oven for 20 to 25 minutes more.)

In a medium saucepan, stir together 2 cups water, the vinegar, mustard seeds, celery seeds, peppercorns, sugar,

and salt. Bring to a boil over high heat. Boil for a full minute, then reduce the heat to low and simmer for 5 minutes.

Slice the peeled beets into ½-inch-thick rounds and place in a large bowl along with the onions. Toss to mix, then transfer to a sterilized 1-quart wide-mouthed glass jar (or other nonreactive heatproof vessel with a tight-fitting lid).

Remove the brine from the heat and pour enough hot brine over the beets and onions in the jar to fully submerge them. Let cool for 30 minutes, then tightly seal the jar and refrigerate overnight before serving. The pickled beets and onions will keep for up to 30 days, as long as they remain fully submerged in their brine. (For long-term storage, use the Hot Water Bath Canning technique on page 39.)

Every September, I try to find new and exciting ways to use up the season's heirloom tomatoes before they ever reach the refrigerator (putting them there would be a cardinal sin). During those few months when they're at their peak, we're inundated with tomatoes in the form of pies, sandwiches, and salads—and frankly it all starts to look the same by the middle of August. But then just like every year prior, I realize that tomatoes ain't broken and don't need fixing. So I make this tomato salad, and I'm proud that it's at least a *little* different than the others. **Feeds 4**

HERBY PEACH AND TOMATO SALAD
WITH PICKLED SHALLOTS

2 heirloom tomatoes, cored and cut into
   1-inch-thick slices

2 peaches, pitted and cut into wedges

1 tablespoon extra-virgin olive oil

Flaky salt

2 shallots, sliced into rounds

Leaves from 2 thyme sprigs

2 cups distilled white vinegar

2 tablespoons sugar

1 tablespoon kosher salt

Fresh parsley leaves, for serving

Fresh basil leaves, for serving

Fresh mint leaves, for serving

In a medium bowl, gently toss the tomatoes and peaches with olive oil and season with flaky salt.

In a small pot, combine the shallots, thyme, vinegar, sugar, and kosher salt. Bring to a boil over high heat. Boil for 1 minute, then reduce the heat to low and give the sugar and salt 3 to 4 minutes to dissolve. Remove from the heat and let cool.

On a large serving platter, arrange the tomato slices and peaches, then, using a slotted spoon, evenly layer the shallots over the top. Finish with torn parsley, basil, and mint and some more flaky salt before serving.

The sweetest fruit on Earth requires less fussing and more eating. For this one, be sure to pick the very best melons at the farmers' market. A ripened one should feel much heavier than it actually looks, and you'll be able to detect a slight melon fragrance on the outside of it. I particularly enjoy the cotton candy taste of a cantaloupe and the smooth, honey notes of a honeydew melon. Once you've taken your pick, you won't need to fuss much; I just add savory granola for intense crunch. **Feeds 8**

MELON SALAD
WITH PISTACHIO–MELON SEED GRANOLA

For the Melon

2 small melons (cantaloupe, honeydew, or
    canary melon)

1 tablespoon extra-virgin olive oil

Zest and juice of 2 limes

½ teaspoon flaky salt

For the Granola

½ cup rolled oats

½ cup unsalted shelled pistachios

½ cup honey

1 tablespoon red pepper flakes

1 tablespoon poppy seeds

1 tablespoon sesame seeds

½ teaspoon kosher salt

1 large egg white, beaten

Preheat the oven to 275°F. Line two baking sheets with parchment paper.

Prepare the melon: Slice ½ inch from the top and bottom of the melons so they can sit flat on your cutting board. Carefully cut around the skin and rind of each melon, exposing the flesh, then halve each lengthwise.

Using a spoon, scrape out the guts and seeds. Do the opposite of what you'd guess and do not discard them. Set the cut melons aside and place the guts and seeds in a small bowl. Using your fingers, carefully remove the seeds from the connective membrane and discard the membrane. Give the seeds a good rinse, then spread them evenly over one of the prepared baking sheets. Roast for about 20 minutes, until dried out. Remove from the oven and increase the oven temperature to 350°F.

Meanwhile, slice the melons into wedges and place in a large bowl. In a small bowl, whisk together the olive oil, lime zest, lime juice, and flaky salt. Pour the mixture over the melon wedges and toss to coat. Chill in the refrigerator while you make the granola.

Make the granola: In a large bowl, combine the toasted melon seeds, oats, pistachios, honey, red pepper flakes, poppy seeds, sesame seeds, and salt. Gently fold in the egg white. Spread the mixture evenly over the remaining prepared baking sheet. Bake for 20 to 25 minutes, stirring halfway through, until fragrant and toasted. Remove and let cool completely.

To serve, arrange the marinated melon on a platter and generously top with granola.

Carrot salad, the type that swims in thin mayo and is bedazzled with raisins, is a Southern staple. Still, even though it's a staple, it tends to get passed over at family reunions and church picnics the same way grape candy or orange drink does. But this is the carrot salad that changes all that. Crisp shaved carrots stand up well to this bright Dijon dressing, and the crunchy peanuts add another layer that makes this salad really stand out from the others. Now you can proudly walk into the church fellowship hall with your head held high and this carrot salad in your arms. **Feeds 4 to 6**

CARROT SALAD
WITH HONEYED PEANUTS

For the Carrot Salad

1 tablespoon plus 1 teaspoon kosher salt

1 pound carrots, shaved

2 tablespoons Duke's mayonnaise

1 tablespoon Dijon mustard

1 tablespoon extra-virgin olive oil

Juice of 1 lemon

1 teaspoon ground cumin

1 teaspoon ground coriander

For the Honeyed Peanuts

1 cup peanuts, roasted

½ cup (1 stick) unsalted butter

1 tablespoon honey

1 teaspoon kosher salt

Fresh parsley leaves, for serving

Make the salad: Fill a large pot with water and bring to a rolling boil over high heat. Fill a large bowl with ice and water and set it nearby. Add 1 tablespoon of the salt to the boiling water, then drop in half of the carrots and cook for 30 seconds. Using a slotted spoon, transfer the carrots to the ice bath to cool (agitate the water with your hand to encourage quicker cooling). Let the water return to a rolling boil, then repeat with the remaining carrots. When all the carrots have cooled, drain them and let dry on a plate lined with paper towels.

In a large bowl, whisk together the mayonnaise, mustard, olive oil, lemon juice, cumin, coriander, and the remaining 1 teaspoon salt. Add the carrots and toss to coat well.

Make the honeyed peanuts: Preheat the oven to 350°F. Line a baking sheet with parchment paper.

In a small high-sided saucepan, combine the peanuts, butter, honey, and salt. Set the pot over medium heat. As the butter melts, toss to coat the peanuts. Spread the coated peanuts on the prepared baking sheet and bake for 10 minutes, stirring once halfway through; the peanuts should be toasted and appear sticky. Remove from the oven and let cool, stirring the peanuts every few minutes to break them apart, then coarsely chop them. Add the peanuts to the carrot salad and stir to incorporate.

To serve, portion the salad into bowls and garnish with parsley.

The name of celery is blasphemed constantly. With its fresh, slightly sweet crunch and "I can be whoever you want me to be" attitude, I just don't get why it isn't better liked. Deeply caramelized or raw and simply dressed, celery is more versatile than we give it credit for. If you've got a source for locally grown celery, use it! If you're stuck buying the grocery-store stuff, be sure to pull away the outer stalks before diving into this dish: the bright, yellow center is where it gets good. **Feeds 4 to 6**

CUCUMBER AND CELERY HEART SALAD

For the Salad

2 English (hothouse) cucumbers, sliced

4 celery hearts, leaves and stalk thinly sliced

1 small red onion, thinly sliced

1 teaspoon kosher salt

2 tablespoons vinegar

For the Vinaigrette

2 celery stalks, cut into small dice

2 teaspoons lemon zest

3 tablespoons fresh lemon juice

1 tablespoon honey

1 teaspoon ground sumac

1 teaspoon celery seeds, lightly toasted

1 teaspoon kosher salt

3 tablespoons plain full-fat Greek yogurt

Extra-virgin olive oil, for serving

Flaky salt, for serving

Make the salad: In a medium bowl, toss together the cucumbers, celery hearts, onion, salt, and vinegar. Set aside for at least 20 minutes or up to 45 minutes.

Make the vinaigrette: In a large bowl, whisk together the celery, lemon zest, lemon juice, honey, sumac, celery seeds, salt, and yogurt. Drain any residual liquid off the cucumber mixture into the bowl and whisk the liquid into dressing.

Add the cucumber-celery mixture to the vinaigrette and toss to coat evenly.

To serve, arrange the mixture on a platter, drizzle generously with olive oil, and sprinkle with flaky salt to taste.

From a scientific perspective, this recipe works because lard is refined, meaning anything that could smoke or burn during heating has been removed. Lard maintains a high enough smoke point for frying chicken without imparting any off flavors. And from my perspective, frying chicken in lard tastes damn good. I'd eat this with Christmas Yeast Rolls (page 267) or soak up that chicken grease with a fresh slice of Malinda Russell's Salt-Rising Bread (page 65). This chicken is perfect at room temperature for a picnic with Tomato and Cornbread Panzanella (page 127). **Feeds 4 to 6**

LARD-FRIED CHICKEN

1 cup buttermilk

3 teaspoons kosher salt

1 teaspoon paprika

1 teaspoon cayenne pepper

1 teaspoon freshly ground black pepper

1 teaspoon garlic powder

1 teaspoon onion powder

5 pounds bone-in, skin-on chicken pieces (a mix of white and dark meat)

1½ cups all-purpose flour

½ cup cornstarch

1 tablespoon dried sage

Lard, for frying

In a large bowl, whisk together the buttermilk, 2 teaspoons of the salt, the paprika, cayenne, black pepper, garlic powder, and onion powder. Add the chicken and turn to coat. Cover and marinate in the refrigerator for at least 4 hours or up to 8 hours.

In a large bowl, combine the flour, cornstarch, sage, and the remaining 1 teaspoon salt. Remove the chicken from the marinade, allowing any excess to drip off. Dredge the chicken in the seasoned flour, turning and pressing gently to coat completely, then shake off any excess.

Fill a large high-sided cast-iron pan with 1 inch of lard and clip a deep-fry thermometer to the side. Heat over medium-high heat to 350°F. Working in batches, carefully add the dredged chicken to the hot lard, skin-side down, and cook for 5 to 6 minutes per side, until the chicken is crispy and golden brown, and a meat thermometer inserted into the chicken registers 165°F. Maintain an oil temperature of about 350°F as the chicken cooks and allow the oil to return to 350°F between batches.

Transfer the chicken to a wire rack and let cool for 7 to 8 minutes before serving.

In the Midlands, where some type of delicious fruit is wild and always ripe, a trip outside can easily satisfy any sweet tooth. But perhaps it's no surprise that here, fruit commonly turns up in savory settings, too: peaches are just as at home in Sunday's chicken bake as they are in a cobbler. A roulade might sound fancy, and it certainly looks it, but you'll find this dish to be a great and even simple way to introduce sweet and savory. But this dish is too good to restrict it to late summer, or whenever figs are in season where you are. So for the most consistent year-round results, I opt to use dried figs here, which have a more concentrated and mature flavor than fresh. **Feeds 4**

FIG AND GOAT CHEESE CHICKEN ROULADE

1 cup dried figs

2 ½ cups red wine vinegar

1 tablespoon light brown sugar

5 teaspoons kosher salt, plus more as needed

3 teaspoons freshly ground black pepper, plus more as needed

8 ounces goat cheese, at room temperature

1 teaspoon red pepper flakes

2 teaspoons fresh thyme leaves

1 teaspoon minced fresh rosemary leaves

1 teaspoon minced fresh sage

4 boneless, skin-on chicken breasts

8 fresh basil leaves

1 cup grated Havarti cheese

2 teaspoons extra-virgin olive oil

Juice of 1 lemon

1 tablespoon honey

2 teaspoons Dijon mustard

2 tablespoons unsalted butter

In a medium bowl, toss the figs with the vinegar, brown sugar, ¼ teaspoon of the salt, 1 teaspoon of the black pepper, and 2 tablespoons water. Set aside to allow the figs to rehydrate, stirring occasionally, for 6 to 7 minutes.

In a separate medium bowl, combine the goat cheese, ½ teaspoon of the salt, the remaining 2 teaspoons black pepper, the red pepper flakes, thyme, rosemary, and sage.

Preheat the oven to 375°F.

Trim the fat from each chicken breast; do not discard. Using a sharp knife, butterfly each chicken breast, slicing along the length of it, and, working parallel to the cutting board, continue slicing until nearly all the way through, but not completely, so that each breast opens like a book.

Place each butterflied chicken breast on a sheet of plastic wrap. Cover with another sheet of plastic wrap and, using a meat mallet, pound each breast to about a ¼-inch thickness. Remove the plastic and salt each piece of chicken on both sides with 1 teaspoon of the salt. Lay the chicken breasts flat and evenly spread goat cheese over one side of each piece. Next, lay 2 basil leaves per piece over the goat cheese. Strain the rehydrated figs and layer them on top of

Recipe continues

the basil in a single layer, leaving a ¼-inch border around the edges. Sprinkle each breast with Havarti.

Beginning with the long end closest to you, roll up each butterflied breast lengthwise, then wrap a reserved piece of chicken fat around each roulade and secure with kitchen twine at ¾-inch intervals. Season the chicken all over with salt and pepper and drizzle generously with olive oil.

Transfer the chicken to a roasting pan and roast until golden brown on the outside, about 20 minutes. Remove the chicken from the pan and let rest on a cutting board.

Meanwhile, strain the chicken drippings from the roasting pan into a small saucepan and set the pan over low heat. Stir in the lemon juice, honey, mustard, and remaining ¼ teaspoon salt—careful of the grease splatter! Simmer to warm through, about 2 minutes, then remove the pan from the heat and swirl in the butter, allowing the sauce to thicken as it melts.

To serve, slice the chicken into 1-inch-thick medallions, arrange them on a serving platter, and spoon the sauce over the top.

Growing up, I ate good. On any given Sunday, fragrant sauces simmered while some sort of meat cut was being pounded to death with a tenderizer. All this made for some of the greatest post-church eating I could dream of. When I entered the restaurant industry, though, I soon learned that a lot of the protein selections I grew up eating were considered scraps or subpar for diners at the restaurants I worked in. This revelation instilled in me an appreciation for technique and for the art of a great sauce. Suddenly my mom's obsession over a carefully tended roux and creamy, lump-free gravy made sense. These days, I'm occasionally tickled when some of the same cuts—like teres major and oxtail—that my former colleagues once turned up their noses at are now pricey and hard to find in stores due to their popularity. This dish is a really homey one for me. When I think of how the morning's leftover Folgers would meet the demands of dinner in the form of red-eye gravy, it warms my soul and makes me smile. **Feeds 4**

CUBE STEAK, RED-EYE GRAVY, BROCCOLI, AND CRISPY POTATOES

For the Potatoes

1 pound new potatoes, halved

1 teaspoon kosher salt

2 thyme sprigs

Olive oil

3 slices thick-cut bacon, diced

For the Broccoli

4 cups broccoli florets

1 tablespoon unsalted butter

1 teaspoon kosher salt

½ teaspoon red pepper flakes

For the Steaks

2 pounds cube steak

2 teaspoons kosher salt

2 teaspoons freshly ground black pepper

1 teaspoon ground mustard

1 teaspoon dried parsley

½ cup all-purpose flour

1 teaspoon neutral oil, such as canola or grapeseed

3 tablespoons unsalted butter

1 small yellow onion, sliced into thin rings

2 shallots, sliced into rings

1 garlic clove, minced

½ cup beef stock

½ cup brewed black coffee

1 tablespoon dark brown sugar

Chopped fresh parsley, for garnish

Recipe continues

Make the potatoes: Preheat the oven to 400°F.

In a large bowl, toss the potatoes, salt, thyme, and olive oil to coat. Transfer to a baking sheet, spread in an even layer, and roast for 45 to 50 minutes, stirring occasionally, until the potatoes are golden brown. Discard the thyme and transfer the potatoes to a serving bowl.

While potatoes roast, place the bacon in a cast-iron skillet and cook over medium-low heat, flipping occasionally, until the fat renders and the bacon is crispy, 7 to 9 minutes. Transfer the bacon to a plate lined with paper towels. Pour the bacon grease into a heatproof vessel and set aside.

Make the broccoli: In the same skillet, stir together the broccoli, butter, salt, and red pepper flakes. Cook, undisturbed, for 3 to 4 minutes, until the broccoli takes on a golden-brown hue, then stir and cook, undisturbed, for 2 to 3 minutes more, until the broccoli is browned all over. Remove the broccoli from the pan.

Make the steaks: Season the steaks all over with the salt, pepper, mustard, and dried parsley. Spread the flour in a shallow plate and dredge the steaks in the flour to coat both sides, shaking off any excess.

In the same skillet, heat the oil over medium-high heat. When the oil begins to smoke, add the steaks and cook until browned on the outside, about 2 minutes per side. Transfer the steaks to a plate.

Reduce the heat to medium and pour the reserved bacon grease back into the pan along with the butter. Add the onion and shallots. Cook until the onion is soft and beginning to brown, about 5 minutes. Add the garlic and sauté for 2 minutes more, until the garlic is aromatic. Add the stock and coffee and stir, scraping up any browned bits from the bottom of the pan with a wooden spoon. Stir in the brown sugar and reserved bacon, and reduce the heat to low. Return the steaks to the pan and cook, uncovered, until the gravy thickens, 7 to 8 minutes.

Transfer the steaks to a serving platter. Top with the onion-shallot mixture, then spoon all but ¼ cup of the gravy from the pan over the steaks. Top the steaks with fresh parsley.

Return the remaining gravy to medium heat. Add the broccoli, then cover and cook until fork-tender and warmed through, 3 to 4 minutes. Transfer to a serving bowl.

Serve the steak with the broccoli and potatoes alongside.

This recipe is for all the porch-sittin' Southerners who still take their mug of sipping buttermilk with a side of cornbread for dipping—that's to say, the OG milk & cookies. This "wet salad" pays mind to that ancient practice of front porch meditation combined with a few fresh bites to justify referring to it as a salad. The tang of buttermilk and sweetness of blueberries carry over nicely with the magic of cornbread and licorice-like fennel. **Feeds 6 to 8**

BUTTERMILK CORNBREAD SALAD
WITH FENNEL AND BLUEBERRIES

2 teaspoons apple cider vinegar

1 tablespoon extra-virgin olive oil, plus more for serving

2 teaspoons kosher salt

1 fennel bulb, thinly sliced

½ cup blueberries, halved

1 shallot, thinly sliced

1 tablespoon minced fresh parsley

1 teaspoon red pepper flakes

1 batch day-old Classic Cornbread (page 40)

½ cup buttermilk

Flaky salt, for serving

In a medium bowl, whisk together the vinegar, olive oil, and salt. Add the fennel, blueberries, shallot, parsley, and red pepper flakes. Toss to coat.

Arrange the cornbread on a serving platter, pour the buttermilk over the top to soak it, then spoon on the blueberry-fennel mixture. Drizzle some more olive oil on top and sprinkle with flaky salt to finish.

No matter the season, baked and stewed chicken dinners rarely lose in the Midlands. Ripe summer stone fruit gives this homey dish a lift as the sticky, sweet sugars from the plums melt into acidic punch. I'd recommend making this dish on a cool night with the windows open, letting the fruit aromas waft through the air and out into the neighborhood. Paired with a porch-pounding white wine as a reward for your hard work, you'll agree it was worth cranking up the oven. **Feeds 4 to 6**

CHICKEN THIGHS AND STEWED PLUMS

¼ cup cornstarch

3 teaspoons kosher salt

1 teaspoon freshly ground white pepper

¼ teaspoon ground cinnamon

¼ teaspoon ground allspice

⅛ teaspoon freshly grated nutmeg

⅛ teaspoon ground cloves

2 pounds bone-in, skin-on chicken thighs

2 ½ teaspoons canola oil

1 tablespoon unsalted butter

1 cup sliced leeks (white parts only), well washed

4 ripe medium plums, pitted and quartered

1 tablespoon dark brown sugar

3 (2-inch-long) strips of orange rind

1 teaspoon fennel seeds

½ teaspoon paprika

¼ cup dry white wine

½ cup chicken stock, homemade (page 41) or store-bought

On a shallow plate, combine the cornstarch, 2 teaspoons of the salt, white pepper, cinnamon, allspice, nutmeg, and cloves. Mix well. Dredge the chicken in the mixture, turning to coat and pressing to adhere. Shake off any excess.

Heat a large heavy-bottomed skillet over medium heat. Add the oil to the pan. When the pan just begins to smoke, add the chicken and cook until a golden crust forms on the outside, 4 to 5 minutes per side. Transfer the chicken to a plate.

Add the butter and leeks to the pan and cook, stirring occasionally, until the leeks begin to soften, 5 to 6 minutes. Stir in the plums, brown sugar, orange rind, fennel seeds, and paprika. Cook, stirring occasionally, until the plums are soft and syrupy, about 6 minutes more. Add the wine, reduce the heat to low, and cook for 1 to 2 minutes, using a wooden spoon to scrape up any browned bits from the bottom of the pan. Stir in the stock and remaining 1 teaspoon salt. Return the chicken and any collected juices to the pan and cook, uncovered, until the sauce reduces by one-third, 7 to 9 minutes more.

Serve the chicken family-style, spooning plenty of sauce over the top as you plate it.

There once was a Southern grandma who couldn't be bothered with pulling out a pot for boiling hot water to prepare oversteeped, bitter tea that needed to then be cooled for hours. Instead, she saw the magic in the fierce heat of midday sunlight to accomplish the very same job, and she exercised the notion that caffeine would ward off bacteria. Thanks to her (and the sun), the secret to a slowly brewed and mild summer iced tea was unlocked. If you put this tea up against other, newly developed methods that shun heat, even the sun-kissed variety, I think it would stack up nicely—and so I will stick to my old-school methods. **Makes 3 quarts**

FRONT PORCH SUN TEA

6 black tea bags

Simple syrup and lemon wedges, for serving
  (optional)

On a warm afternoon, combine the tea bags and 12 cups cool water in a 1-gallon glass pitcher. Loosely cover the top with cheesecloth or muslin. Depending on the desired strength, let the tea brew in direct sunlight for 3 to 6 hours, ensuring the temperature of the tea doesn't exceed 165°F. (I find 4½ hours is great for medium-strength tea.)

Remove the tea bags, squeezing out the excess liquid into the pitcher, and discard.

Serve over ice with simple syrup and lemon wedges, if desired.

My taste typically skews on the side of savory; I've never had much of a sweet tooth. But in the Midlands, the land of summer fruits, that all changes. Bushy strawberry patches are everywhere, studded with petite, white blooms readying themselves to offer up fragrant, sweet red berries. This rice custard brûlée is the collaboration summer's ripest berries scream for, and its crisp seared top adds a welcome crunch. This recipe takes the fruit-driven, custardy rice pudding I know and love and adds a classic French twist. **Feeds 12**

RICE CUSTARD BRÛLÉE
WITH STRAWBERRIES

For the Strawberries

¾ cup small-diced strawberries

½ teaspoon kosher salt

2 teaspoons granulated sugar

For the Rice Custard

3 cups whole milk

2 cinnamon sticks

4 green cardamom pods, crushed

2 (1-inch) strips of orange peel

1 vanilla bean, split lengthwise

Neutral oil, such as canola or grapeseed, for greasing

1 large egg

3 large egg yolks

½ cup packed light brown sugar

2½ cups cooked white rice

1 teaspoon kosher salt

Granulated sugar, for topping

Make the strawberries: In a small bowl, combine the strawberries, salt, and granulated sugar. Set aside to macerate for at least 20 minutes and up to 1 hour.

Make the rice custard: Pour the milk into a small saucepan and add the cinnamon sticks, cardamom pods, and orange peel. Using the tip of a paring knife, scrape the vanilla seeds into the milk. Bring to a simmer over medium-low heat, then cook, stirring occasionally, until the mixture is aromatic and the vanilla seeds are evenly combined, 5 to 6 minutes. Cover and remove from the heat. Let stand for at least 5 minutes and up to 15 minutes. Strain the milk, discarding the solids.

Preheat the oven to 350°F. Grease twelve 6-ounce ramekins with oil.

In a large bowl, whisk together the egg, egg yolks, and brown sugar. While whisking the egg mixture vigorously, slowly pour in the milk. Fold in the rice and salt, then stir well until everything is combined and the mixture is free of lumps.

Ladle the rice mixture into the prepared ramekins. Place the ramekins in a large baking pan and fill the pan with water until it reaches halfway up the sides of the ramekins. Bake for 30 to 35 minutes, until the pudding is browned around the edges and set but still has a slight jiggle when shaken. Carefully remove the ramekins from the water bath and let cool.

Sprinkle the tops of the puddings with a thin layer of granulated sugar. Gently pass the flame of a kitchen torch over the surface of the pudding in smooth, slow, even strokes, until the sugar has melted and caramelized. (Alternatively, if you don't have a torch, set the ramekins under the broiler for 1 to 2 minutes, watching them carefully so they do not burn.)

Serve warm, with a spoonful of macerated strawberries on top. Crack the brûléed top with the back of a spoon and enjoy.

Whenever I am tasked with making dessert, you can be certain it will be rustic and simple. Travis, the very first pastry chef I worked with, tried to convince me that perfecting his art would give me the finesse I lacked as a young, clumsy cook. My head was usually too far deep into the gelato freezer (for quality assurance, of course) to hear him, but some simple things stuck: the fact that cooking spray makes parchment paper stick to a sheet pan effortlessly; the unintuitive power of a pinch of salt in a world of sweet; and, best of all, this easy, free-form pastry that relies on ripe fruit, frangipane, and imperfection. **Feeds 12**

SUMMER FRUIT GALETTE
WITH BROWN SUGAR

For the Crust

1½ cups all-purpose flour

½ cup packed light brown sugar

¼ teaspoon kosher salt

10 tablespoons (1¼ sticks) unsalted butter, cubed and chilled

¼ cup ice-cold water

For the Frangipane

4½ tablespoons unsalted butter, at room temperature

½ cup packed light brown sugar

1 large egg, at room temperature

1 cup ground almonds

For the Filling

1 pound ripe stone fruit, pitted (pits reserved) and thinly sliced

Juice of 1 lemon

2 teaspoons packed light brown sugar

½ teaspoon pure vanilla extract

1 large egg, beaten

¼ cup brown sugar

Vanilla ice cream, for serving

Make the crust: In a large bowl, combine the flour, brown sugar, and salt. Add the butter and use your fingertips to rub it into the flour until the mixture has the texture of large breadcrumbs. Add the ice water and mix with your hands to bring the dough together. Turn the dough out onto a clean surface, knead it a few times, then shape it into a ball. Wrap the dough in plastic wrap and refrigerate for 1 to 2 hours.

Make the frangipane: In a medium bowl, beat together the butter and brown sugar until light and fluffy. Add the egg and mix to combine. Fold in the almonds.

Make the filling: In a large bowl, stir together the stone fruit, lemon juice, brown sugar, and vanilla.

Preheat the oven to 350°F.

On a large piece of parchment paper, roll out the chilled dough into a large round, about 12 inches in diameter.

If it becomes too soft, return it to the fridge for about 10 minutes to make it easier to work with. Spread the frangipane over the dough, leaving a 1-inch border. Carefully arrange the fruit filling on top. Fold the edges of the dough in toward the center to cover some of the fruit, then brush the dough with the beaten egg. Use the parchment to transfer the galette to a baking sheet. Bake for 35 to 40 minutes, until golden brown.

Meanwhile, in a small saucepan, combine the reserved stone fruit pits, the brown sugar, and ½ cup water. Bring to a simmer over low heat, then cook until thickened, 25 to 30 minutes. Strain the syrup and let cool.

Let the galette cool slightly, then generously brush the fruit with the syrup. Slice and serve warm, with vanilla ice cream on top.

Shortcake is the ultimate dessert. I love the way the juices of whatever fruit you're using kindly leach into the cake, and when the lightly sweetened cream melds into the spongy crumb. It's a soggy, tasty, heavenly mess. Here, I'm renewing a classic by swapping out strawberries for ripe, juicy peaches, both fresh and processed into the vanilla-bean-spiked peach butter of your dreams. Maybe it's because I was born in Georgia and absorbed the state's ambient peach obsession fresh out the womb, but I'm incredibly fond of the fruit: its honeylike flesh, its almost meaty texture, its pleasantly bitter center. The best I've had are from Sumter County, South Carolina, and I make sure to stop at any and every roadside peach stand I see whenever I drive through. For this recipe, ripe summer peaches are a must. The best ones give off a floral aroma at the stem. Stick your thumb into the divot at the stem and check for a slight, tennis ball–like give. **Feeds 12**

PEACH SHORTCAKE

For the Peach Butter

3 ripe peaches

Zest and juice of 2 lemons

¼ cup packed light brown sugar

1 vanilla bean, split lengthwise

For the Cake

1½ cups (3 sticks) unsalted butter, at room temperature, plus more for greasing

3 cups cake flour, sifted, plus more for dusting

8 ounces cream cheese, at room temperature

2 tablespoons lard

⅛ teaspoon kosher salt

6 large eggs, at room temperature

3 cups granulated sugar

1½ cups heavy cream

¼ cup confectioners' sugar

4 ripe peaches, pitted and sliced into thin wedges

4 fresh basil leaves, thinly sliced, for garnish

Zest of 1 lemon, for garnish

Make the peach butter: Bring a large pot of water to a boil over high heat. Fill a large bowl with ice and water and set it nearby. Using a paring knife, score the skin of the peaches with a small X at their bases. Add the peaches to the boiling water and cook for 1 full minute, then use a slotted spoon to remove them and immediately transfer them to the ice bath. Let them cool for 1 minute, then remove them from the ice bath and, using your hands, gently peel the peach skin off the flesh.

Pit the peaches and place the flesh in a small high-sided saucepan, discarding the skin and pits. Add the lemon zest, lemon juice, brown sugar, and vanilla bean and cook over low heat, stirring occasionally, until the peaches begin to break down, 20 minutes. Remove the pan from the heat.

Meanwhile, make the cake: Preheat the oven to 350°F. Grease a standard 9-inch tube pan with butter and dust it with flour, tapping out any excess.

In a stand mixer fitted with the paddle attachment, combine the butter, cream cheese, lard, and salt. Beat on medium-high speed until smooth, 2 minutes. Add the eggs one at a time, mixing until incorporated. Reduce the mixer speed to medium and add the granulated sugar 1 cup at a time, mixing until just incorporated. Repeat with the flour. This will only take a couple of minutes total—do not overmix.

Pour the batter into the prepared pan. Bake for about 1 hour, or until a toothpick inserted into the center of the cake comes out clean. Remove from the oven and let cool in the pan for

10 to 15 minutes; the residual heat will continue to set the cake. Carefully turn the cake out onto a wire rack to cool completely, about 1 hour.

To assemble, in the chilled bowl of a stand mixer fitted with the whisk attachment, beat the cream and confectioners' sugar until stiff peaks form.

Using a serrated knife, gently halve the cooled cake crosswise at its equator. Remove the top half. Spread half the whipped cream over the bottom half of the cake, then layer half of the fresh peach slices over the whipped cream. Top the peach slices with half of the peach butter, then gently replace the top half of the cake. Top with the remaining whipped cream, then the remaining peach butter, and finish with the remaining fresh peach slices. Garnish with the basil and lemon zest before slicing and serving. It'll keep in the refrigerator, covered, for up to 1 day.

I don't know if this is a bragging right exactly, but the fact that I could effortlessly prepare most classic cocktails before I could even see over a bar is pretty impressive. As an only child in the home of very social parents, I got my fill of fun as the cutest cocktail waitress in town. Cracking open a beer for Uncle Jerrod and pouring Uncle Bo's gin and tonic the way he liked without missing a beat earned me a constant ear to the grown-up gossip I so craved. Years later, I'd find myself doing some form of so-called bartending at a chain restaurant (complete with a salad bar and walls of flair). For whatever reason, these experiences have made me the family expert on all things food- and beverage-related—a magician who can make something out of nothing. When I cook at home, I often feel like I'm a contestant on an episode of Food Network's *Chopped*. One night at a family reunion in Mayesville, South Carolina, with just a paltry stocked bar and some forgotten odds and ends, I created this punch, a crowd-pleaser that's now a forever tradition. **Makes enough for a dozen partiers**

FAMILY REUNION WATERMELON PUNCH

4 ears corn, shucked, husks reserved

2 cups sugar

1 small watermelon

2 cups fresh lime juice (from 12 to 16 limes)

3 cups gin

1 cup vodka

Cut the corncobs in half. In a medium stockpot, combine the corncobs, reserved husks, sugar, and 4 cups water. Bring to a boil over high heat, then reduce the heat to low and simmer for 15 minutes. Let the corn mixture cool, then strain through a fine-mesh sieve. Discard the solids and set the corncob simple syrup aside.

Halve the watermelon crosswise at its equator and scoop out the flesh using a large, metal serving spoon. (Reserve the watermelon rind for another use, such as the pickled watermelon rind on page 263.) Place the watermelon flesh, seeds and all, in a blender along with the lime juice and puree until smooth. Transfer the pureed watermelon to a fine-mesh sieve placed over a large pitcher or punch bowl to strain the juice; you should have about 4 cups juice. Discard the solids.

To the pitcher or punch bowl, add the corncob simple syrup, gin, and vodka. Chill in the refrigerator for at least 1 hour before serving. Serve over ice and plan to have a good time.

LOWI

ANDS

While all regions in this book hold a place in my heart and feel like home in some way, the Lowlands—Tidewater, Virginia, to be specific—is where I grew up. This is home: open-fire beach cooking, oyster roasts, and steamed crab legs. Home is also the nuanced food my mom put on the table to tell her story, honor my dad's rich diasporic lineage, and please a child who preferred hoop cheese and saltines. This is where I got my start in restaurants, first at a small Italian restaurant in town and then at a touristy seafood shack on the beach. The military bases in the surrounding area diversified the cuisine, so I ate new-to-me things like Filipino pancit and lumpia at friends' houses and Korean bibimbap or Greek moussaka on the weekends at some of our favorite restaurants.

But the Black food history of the Lowlands is easily the richest in all of the South. Realizing that I had chosen to spend my formative years on a deep dive into kitchens that largely weren't expressive of who I was as a chef, my mom's friend urged me to take a look at her friend Michael Twitty's blog, Afroculinaria. So I did, and his blog changed my views toward foods that had sometimes been bastardized in my upbringing. More than that, it changed my world: before this, I knew little of the powerful, redemptive history surrounding the foodways of my own backyard.

Little did I know then that I would meet and befriend Mr. Twitty myself nearly a decade later, eventually embarking on a culinary pilgrimage of sorts to Cameroon with him and several others, where I connected to my roots on an even deeper level.

I've made versions of these crispy, delicate little fried cabbage pancakes at restaurants and in my very own home, where they are a breakfast staple. I've often watched my mom bulk them up with canned salmon and loads of the week's forgotten vegetables. We'd eat them over bowls of hot grits or rice. To me, they are reminiscent of okonomiyaki (loosely translated as "grilled as you like it"), a popular savory pancake from southern Japan. I like to drizzle Spicy Sorghum-Miso Mustard (page 110) over them. **Makes 4 pancakes**

CABBAGE AND MUSHROOM PANCAKES

¾ cup all-purpose flour

1 cup fine yellow cornmeal

1 teaspoon sugar

1 teaspoon baking powder

2 large eggs

2 tablespoons white miso paste

2 cups buttermilk

1 cup shredded green cabbage

1 cup shredded red cabbage

1 cup thinly sliced shiitake mushrooms

4 tablespoons grapeseed oil

For Serving

Honey

Chopped scallions

Toasted benne seeds

Flaky salt

In a small bowl, stir together the flour, cornmeal, sugar, and baking powder. In a large bowl, vigorously beat the eggs and miso into the buttermilk. Pour the dry ingredients into the wet and whisk to combine evenly. Add the green and red cabbages and the mushrooms and toss to incorporate.

Preheat the oven to 275°F.

In a small nonstick skillet, heat 1 tablespoon of the grapeseed oil over medium heat. When the oil shimmers, add 1 cup of the cabbage pancake batter and carefully press down to ensure the pancake makes contact with the bottom of the skillet all the way to its outer edges. Cook, undisturbed, until the bottom is gold brown,

5 to 6 minutes, then give the pan a wiggle to release the pancake. Now hold your breath as you attempt to flip the pancake: hold the pan's handle with both hands, tilt the pan forward, and quickly flick your wrists in an upward motion to toss the pancake up and over (or simply use a spatula to flip it if this all sounds too intense). Cook on the second side until it's golden brown, about 5 minutes more, then slide the pancake onto an oven-safe plate and place it in the oven. Repeat with the remaining oil and batter to make four pancakes total.

Serve the pancakes hot, drizzled with honey and topped with scallions, toasted benne seeds, and flaky salt.

Peanuts are a state treasure in Virginia. The greatest, truest boiled peanuts begin with green peanuts, picked fresh and stored in the refrigerator. My granddad was a peanut farmer, which meant in my family, peanuts were had in many forms; for other folks, finding fresh ones was rough unless you knew someone. We know this dish to be one of the many "gathering pots" of our culture, a "watering hole of the South" so to speak, just like cauldrons of stew or communal crab boils and fish fries that encouraged the people to gather around. Indeed, peanuts held that power, too. Your best bet to find these today is to scoop them out from slow cookers into Styrofoam cups at Southern gas stations, where you'll typically find them alongside jars of red-tinged pickled eggs and deviled pig's feet. This is a nearly obsolete delicacy, but it's worth making if you can find fresh peanuts, usually at roadside farmstands or little country stores. **Feeds 10 to 12**

HOT BOILED PEANUTS

1 pound in-shell green Virginia peanuts

1½ cups kosher salt

5 garlic cloves

3 tablespoons apple cider vinegar

2 teaspoons red pepper flakes

3 bay leaves

Wash the peanuts in cool water until the water runs clear, then place them in a large bowl and add cool water to cover. Set aside for 1 hour to rehydrate and loosen any remaining dirt, changing the water halfway through the soaking time. Drain and rinse the peanuts one more time.

Transfer the peanuts to a large stockpot and add the salt, garlic, vinegar, red pepper flakes, bay leaves, and 6 quarts water. Stir well and weigh down the peanuts with a heatproof plate to keep them submerged. Bring to a rolling boil over high heat, then cover and reduce the heat to medium-low to maintain a simmer. Cook for 1½ hours, then test for doneness: once shelled, the peanuts should hold their shape but be tender to the bite. If they are still al dente, cook for 30 minutes to 1 hour more, adding more water as needed to keep them submerged.

Enjoy hot or at room temperature. Store the peanuts in their cooking liquid in an airtight container in the refrigerator for up to 5 days.

Once during a food festival, a renowned chef from up north showed up at my tent and made me fight to call salmon croquettes a Southern food. Sure, salmon isn't swimming in our Southern coastal waters, but croquettes of many types have made their way onto our tables throughout time, and salmon—in canned form—was often a main ingredient. I'm not sure why anyone would ever think these aren't Southern. Its poached flesh as bright pink as the can's loud outer label, salmon was always available and affordable, though it was the rare instance in which we didn't know exactly where the seafood on the table came from. This old-school recipe gets an obvious upgrade by using salmon fillets, which lend a nice flakiness to each bite. Now that my restaurant, Good Hot Fish, has me thinking about sourcing all the time, my advice is to use king (Chinook) salmon, which is rich, buttery, and sustainably managed. Frozen is fine; just make sure it's fully thawed before using. **Feeds 6**

SALMON CROQUETTES
WITH BUTTERMILK TARTAR SAUCE

For the Croquettes

2 tablespoons kosher salt

4 dried bay leaves

1 pound skinless salmon fillets

1 sleeve Ritz crackers
   (about 32 crackers), crushed

1 bunch scallions, green parts only,
   minced

4 garlic cloves, minced

¼ cup Duke's mayonnaise

1 large egg, lightly beaten

2 tablespoons yellow mustard

1 teaspoon fish sauce

1 teaspoon kosher salt

½ teaspoon paprika

½ teaspoon garlic powder

½ teaspoon onion powder

1 bunch parsley, minced

2 tablespoons vegetable oil

For the Tartar Sauce

2 cups Duke's mayonnaise

¼ cup buttermilk

¼ cup chopped Foolproof Fridge
   Pickles (page 157), plus 2 teaspoons
   brine from the jar

¼ cup fresh parsley, chopped

3 garlic cloves, grated

¼ teaspoon freshly ground white pepper

⅛ teaspoon cayenne pepper

Make the croquettes: Bring a medium pot of water to a boil over high heat. Add the salt and bay leaves. Reduce the heat to medium, maintaining a hard simmer. Place the fillets in the water and poach until cooked through, 7 to 8 minutes, depending on thickness. Remove the salmon from the water and transfer to a plate to cool slightly. When the salmon is cool enough to handle, flake it into a large bowl, then fold in the crackers, scallions, garlic, mayo, egg, mustard, fish sauce, salt, paprika, garlic powder, onion powder, and parsley until completely combined. Using your hands, form the mixture into 6 equal patties and place on a plate. Cover and refrigerate for at least 1 hour or up to overnight.

Heat the oil in a large cast-iron skillet over medium-high heat. Working in batches as needed, add the patties and cook until both sides are golden brown, 3 to 4 minutes per side.

Make the tartar sauce: In a small bowl, whisk together the mayo, buttermilk, pickles, pickle brine, parsley, garlic, white pepper, and cayenne.

Serve the croquettes with the tartar sauce alongside.

The backstory of these crabs doesn't go much deeper than some creative folks in a restaurant kitchen using up leftover batter. The batter is still an anomaly in some places, but you'll see many a family cookout on my mom's side in which leftover batter from a fish fry is thinned out with a little light beer, then crab-dunking commences. What follows are crabs fried until that firetruck-red shell screams through the batter, waiting to be torn apart. A feasting after-party of sorts commences: bodies posed at near 90-degree angles over grease-soaked newspapers, eager hands tearing into crispy batter and ripping apart crab legs to dip them in red sauce. It's almost a race to consume it all before the last crab can make its way out of the hot oil. **Feeds 6 to 8**

DEEP-FRIED HARD-SHELL CRABS
WITH GOOD HOT RED SAUCE

For the Crabs

½ bushel live male blue crabs

6 cups self-rising flour

1 tablespoon garlic powder

1 tablespoon onion powder

1 tablespoon paprika

2 teaspoons kosher salt

2 teaspoons freshly ground black pepper

2 teaspoons cayenne pepper

3 large eggs, lightly beaten

3 (12-ounce) cans lager beer

Peanut oil, for frying

For the Sauce

½ cup (1 stick) unsalted butter

1 cup Stewed Tomatoes (page 38) or canned stewed tomatoes

1 tablespoon prepared horseradish

2 tablespoons fresh lemon juice

2 tablespoons packed light brown sugar

½ cup hot sauce

¼ cup yellow mustard

Make the crabs: To ensure the crabs stay calm and collected while you're rudely dipping them in batter, keep them in your refrigerator until the moment you need them. Start with the batter: In a large bowl, combine the flour, garlic powder, onion powder, paprika, salt, black pepper, and cayenne. Slowly whisk in the eggs and then the beer. Let the batter rest in the refrigerator for 10 to 15 minutes.

Fill a large stockpot one-third of the way with oil and clip a deep-fry thermometer to the side. Heat over medium heat to 350°F.

Working in batches of 6 crabs at a time, dip the crabs into the batter and allow any excess to drip off. Carefully drop the crabs into the oil and cook until the crust is golden brown and you can see the red shell peeking through, 3 to 5 minutes. Hold each crab over the pot for about

5 seconds and give it a gentle shake to let excess oil drip off, then transfer it to a wire rack or a tray lined with paper towels. Repeat to fry the remaining crabs, letting the oil return to 350°F between batches.

Meanwhile, make the sauce: In a small high-sided saucepan, combine the butter, tomatoes, horseradish, lemon juice, brown sugar, hot sauce, and mustard. Cook over medium heat, stirring continuously to combine and melt the butter, until the mixture just begins to form tiny bubbles around the edges, 5 to 6 minutes. Reduce the heat to low, cover, and simmer for about 15 minutes. Remove from the heat and use an immersion blender to puree until smooth.

Serve the crabs hot with the dipping sauce alongside, picking them as usual, but also enjoying crispy bits of fried batter.

Every place in the South called Brunswick lays claim to some form of this rich tomato-based stew, traditionally laden with a variety of game meats. Like every territorial culinary war, they all claim theirs to be the best of the best, or at least the OG. Historical evidence leads me to believe we have the great Jimmy Matthews—an enslaved black man from Brunswick County, Virginia—to thank for this timeless dish, having originated around the 1820s. My version uses rabbit, browned at the start to help develop those rich, intense flavors. I do enjoy preparing mine over an open fire on a cold winter night, but a stockpot on the stove is good, too. I typically pair this stew with Classic Cornbread (page 40). **Feeds 8 to 10**

VIRGINIA BRUNSWICK STEW

6 rabbit hind legs

2 tablespoons kosher salt

2 teaspoons freshly ground black pepper, plus more for serving

2 tablespoons lard

2 yellow onions, diced

8 ounces smoked country ham, diced

3 bay leaves

4 cups Stewed Tomatoes (page 38) or canned stewed tomatoes

2 tablespoons tomato paste

1 tablespoon dried parsley

1 tablespoon dried sage

1 tablespoon cayenne pepper

2 cups fresh corn kernels (cut from about 2½ cobs)

2 pounds frozen butter beans or lima beans

½ pound okra, thinly sliced

3 tablespoons unsalted butter

Season the rabbit with 1 tablespoon of the salt and the pepper. In a large stockpot or Dutch oven, melt the lard over medium heat. Add the rabbit and cook until browned on the outside, 3 to 4 minutes per side. Transfer to a large plate.

To the same pot, add the onions and cook, stirring, until soft and translucent, 7 to 8 minutes. Return the rabbit to the pot along with any collected juices and add the ham and bay leaves. Add enough water to cover the rabbit by about an inch. Increase the heat to high and bring to a boil, then reduce the heat to low, cover, and simmer for about 90 minutes; foam will rise to the top of the pot and the rabbit will become tender. Using a spoon, skim the

foam off the surface. Turn off the heat, then use tongs to carefully transfer the rabbit to a cutting board or baking sheet. Once cool enough to handle, pick the rabbit meat from the bones; discard the bones. Return the meat to the pot, and turn the heat to low.

Stir in the remaining 1 tablespoon salt, the tomatoes, tomato paste, parsley, sage, and cayenne. Cook for about 45 minutes, then add the corn, butter beans, and okra. Cook, stirring occasionally, until fully incorporated, 30 minutes more. Stir in the butter to melt.

Ladle the stew into bowls and finish with more cracked black pepper to taste.

I grew up eating "cream of" soups from red-and-white cans on busy weeknights, but also drinking hot, simmered-for-hours potlikker during cold winters. Here I take some collagen-rich potlikker left over from making collards and introduce heavy cream, sherry vinegar, and sweet potatoes. It takes the few things I love about the idea of those store-bought soups—rich creaminess, nostalgia, and simplicity—and what I know about the power of really good potlikker to make a soup that's worth the hours you'll spend on it. **Feeds 6 to 8**

COLLARD AND SWEET POTATO CHOWDER

1 bunch collard greens

1 smoked turkey leg

¼ cup sherry vinegar

1 teaspoon red pepper flakes

2 tablespoons unsalted butter

1 yellow onion, diced

2 celery stalks, diced

3 garlic cloves, minced

4 cups heavy cream

2 large sweet potatoes, peeled and cut into ½-inch cubes

2½ teaspoons kosher salt

1 teaspoon freshly ground black pepper

1 teaspoon freshly grated nutmeg

1 tablespoon extra-virgin olive oil

To stem the collards, hold the stem of one leaf in one hand and, with your other hand, grab and pull the leaf off the center rib. Reserve 8 nice leaves for garnish and finely chop the remaining leaves.

In a large pot, combine the smoked turkey, chopped collards, vinegar, red pepper flakes, and 6 cups water. Bring to a boil over high heat, then cover and reduce the heat to low to maintain a simmer. Cook, stirring occasionally and keeping the collards submerged, until the turkey and collards are fork-tender, about 30 minutes. Remove from the heat and let cool. When the turkey is cool enough to handle, use two slotted spoons to transfer it to a baking sheet or large plate. Using your hands, pull the meat from the bones and return it to the pot; discard the bones.

In a Dutch oven or other heavy-bottomed pot, melt the butter over medium-low heat. Add the onion and celery and cook, stirring, until soft and translucent, 5 to 6 minutes. Add the garlic and cook until fragrant and beginning to brown, 2 minutes more. Add the cream. Stir in the boiled collards with their potlikker, then add the sweet potatoes. Reduce the heat to low and stir in 2 teaspoons of the salt, the pepper, and the nutmeg. Cover and simmer until the sweet potatoes are tender, about 1 hour.

Meanwhile, preheat the oven to 325°F.

Stem the remaining whole collards and tear the leaves into 2- to 3-inch pieces. In a small bowl, toss with the olive oil and remaining ½ teaspoon salt. Spread the collards evenly over a baking sheet and bake until crispy but not browned, about 15 minutes.

To serve, ladle the hot soup into bowls and top generously with the crispy collards.

Our part of Virginia has sandy soil that's ideal for peanut growing. Being the nation's top peanut producer is a title we wear proudly, right alongside our salty pork pride. Boiled peanuts are more than good enough to snack on straight, but when you make an entire batch of that Southern caviar, it's worthy of a dish that highlights its beauty. This dish requires a reasonable amount of patience while you work to shell a pound of boiled peanuts, but by the end, you'll respect and feel proud of the effort that went into making this mighty little legume a star. **Feeds 4 to 6**

BOILED PEANUT AND VIRGINIA HAM SOUP

4 ounces smoked country ham (preferably Lady Edison), chopped, plus 4 thinly shaved slices for garnish

1 yellow onion, chopped

2 cups chicken stock, homemade (page 41) or store-bought

1 pound Hot Boiled Peanuts (page 200), shelled, plus 1 cup of their cooking liquid

½ cup heavy cream

1 teaspoon kosher salt

Cracked black pepper

1 teaspoon extra-virgin olive oil

In a Dutch oven, combine the chopped ham, onion, and stock. Bring to a boil over high heat, then reduce the heat to low, cover, and cook for 40 minutes, until the ham and onion are tender.

Add half the boiled peanuts and the 1 cup cooking liquid to the pot. Cook until the peanuts begin to loosen from their skins and the broth has reduced by ⅔ cup, 20 to 25 minutes.

Meanwhile, coarsely chop the remaining peanuts.

Remove the soup from the heat and puree with an immersion blender until smooth. Add the chopped peanuts to the pot along with the cream, salt, and pepper to taste. Return the pot to medium heat and cook, stirring occasionally, until the flavors are melded, about 10 minutes more.

Meanwhile, in a medium saucepan, heat the olive oil over medium-low heat. When the oil is just smoking, add the ham slices. Cook, flipping the ham occasionally, until crispy, 3 to 4 minutes.

Ladle the soup into bowls and garnish with some cracked black pepper and the crispy ham crumbled over the tops.

I don't know how, but vintage bowls have made their way through the hands of decades of women into my home without any evidence of the years of use. I am now the caretaker of some of these bowls that hold as many memories as they have had side dishes over the years. They've housed simple vegetables way less elevated than CorningWare's depictions of "L'Echalote" and "Le Romarin." With my stockpot ever present on the stove, streaked with salt residue from being unattended, I knew exactly what would fill those bowls— buttery turnips, kissed with pats of butter that made me forget I wasn't supposed to like vegetables. I smash the creamy, starchy veg onto my plate with the back of a spoon, their crystallized jackets forming a seal to protect a sweet, fluffy center. Works like a charm for rutabagas and potatoes, too. Just a few ingredients make sheer magic. **Feeds 4 to 6**

SALT TURNIPS

½ cup kosher salt

2 pounds large turnips, tops trimmed

3 bay leaves

A few pats of unsalted butter

Cracked black pepper

Fill a large stockpot with water and whisk in the salt. Add the turnips and bay leaves. Bring to a boil over high heat, then reduce the heat to low and cook until the turnips are fork-tender, about 45 minutes. Drain the turnips and transfer to a baking sheet to cool slightly; a salty crust will form a seal on the skin of the turnips.

Use a knife to quarter each turnip and place on a serving platter. Finish with pats of butter scattered all over. Stir, allowing the butter to melt, then sprinkle with pepper and serve.

Using low-cost meats and other unlikely proteins to make a sauce stretch isn't a new idea. Italians, for instance, famously save their meat-rich sauces for indulgent weekends, getting by during the week with delicious, cost-friendly ragùs. In Hillsville, we referred to this type of eating as a "necessity mess," a name and concept that, as far as I know, stretches back to home-cooking "receipt books" from the Depression era. There's no real recipe in particular for necessity mess—it's more like a blueprint for affordable sustenance. On our table, popular versions usually saw potatoes or elbow macaroni as the starch, a host of use-them-up-quick vegetables that were no longer fresh, leftover fatty pork, sometimes beans, and often tomatoes, and that's what I've shared here. **Feeds 8 to 10**

NECESSITY MESS

1 pound fatback, diced (see Note)

½ pound country sausage

1 yellow onion, diced

2 carrots, diced

1 celery heart, diced

1 teaspoon dried parsley

1 teaspoon cayenne pepper

1 tablespoon fish sauce

1 cup Stewed Tomatoes (page 38) or canned stewed tomatoes

1 teaspoon plus 1 tablespoon kosher salt

2 cups frozen butter beans or lima beans

8 ounces elbow macaroni

Freshly ground black pepper

Heat a large skillet over medium-low heat. Add the fatback and sausage to the pan and cook, stirring occasionally, until the fatback and sausage are golden brown and beginning to crisp, 10 to 12 minutes. Using a slotted spoon, transfer the fatback and sausage to a plate lined with paper towels. Pour off all but 1 tablespoon of the fat from the skillet, saving the remainder for a later use.

Add the onion, carrots, celery, parsley, and cayenne to the skillet with the melted fat. Cook over medium heat, stirring, until the onion is soft and translucent, 6 to 7 minutes.

Add the fish sauce and tomatoes and use a wooden spoon to scrape up any browned bits stuck to the bottom of the pan. Stir in 1 teaspoon of the salt and crisped fatback and sausage. Reduce the heat to low, cover, and cook, stirring occasionally, until the flavors are melded and the sauce is slightly reduced, 30 to 35 minutes.

Stir in the butter beans and cook, covered, until warmed through, about 10 minutes more.

Meanwhile, fill a large stockpot with water and bring to a boil over high heat. Add the remaining 1 tablespoon salt and the macaroni and cook until al dente according to the package instructions. Drain the macaroni, reserving ½ cup of the pasta cooking water, and add the pasta to the tomato sauce. Toss the pasta continuously in the sauce, adding a few tablespoons of the reserved pasta water at a time, until the pasta is well coated, 1 to 2 minutes.

Spoon the mess into bowls and serve topped with a few twists of black pepper.

Note: Fatback is easier to slice after it's been left in the freezer for about 45 minutes.

With the strong military presence in my hometown, global cuisine was commonplace. My mom was a frequent flyer at the local international grocery stores and stocked the pantry with the soy sauces and vinegars that caught her eye. It's a habit that I've picked up as an adult, and the way I cook now is heavily influenced by the diverse foodways of my home region, from Westernized Chinese restaurants to the home cooking of Filipino neighbors. Stir-fries like this one made it to our table often. We weren't experts on Asian culture by any means, but I always loved how this style felt like a break from monotony, showing me that there were whole worlds of cuisines to explore. **Feeds 4 to 6**

STIR-FRIED FARRO
WITH CRISPY PORK BELLY

1 pound skin-on pork belly

3 teaspoons kosher salt

1 cup farro

1 tablespoon neutral oil, such as canola or grapeseed

1 cup diced carrots

1 cup sliced green beans

1 cup sliced mushrooms, such as shiitakes or chanterelles

1 cup sliced scallions

3 garlic cloves, grated

1 (2-inch) knob fresh ginger, peeled and grated

2 teaspoons rice vinegar

1 tablespoon light brown sugar

½ cup tamari

½ teaspoon red pepper flakes

½ teaspoon ground mustard

1½ tablespoons untoasted sesame oil

Preheat the oven to 425°F.

Using a knife, score the pork belly skin with diagonal cuts spaced 1 inch apart, being taking care not to pierce the flesh. Season the belly with 1 teaspoon of the salt, rubbing it into the scored skin. Pat the belly dry using paper towels, then place it on a rack, skin-side up, and set the rack in a roasting pan. Roast for 30 minutes, until the fat begins to render, then turn the oven to broil. Broil the pork for 8 to 10 minutes, watching closely. When the skin is bubbling and golden, remove the pork from the oven and let rest for 5 to 6 minutes. If you want to double-check on the temperature, the interior of the pork should register 160°F on an instant-read thermometer.

Meanwhile, in a medium pot, combine 3 cups water and the remaining 2 teaspoons salt. Bring to a boil over high heat, add the farro, cover, and cook for 9 minutes, until the grains turn plump and tender to the bite and the water has been more or less absorbed. Drain the farro and spread over a baking sheet to cool.

Meanwhile, in a large sauté pan, heat the neutral oil over medium heat. When the oil shimmers, add the carrots, green beans, and mushrooms. Cook, stirring occasionally, until the mushrooms have softened, 3 to 4 minutes. Add the scallions, garlic, and ginger and cook, stirring constantly, until fragrant, about 1 minute more. Stir in the vinegar, brown sugar, tamari, red pepper flakes, mustard, and sesame oil. Stir in the farro. Cook, stirring continuously, until the sauce reduces to one-quarter of its original volume, 2 minutes more.

Transfer the farro and vegetables to a serving bowl. Thinly slice the pork belly and lay it on top, then serve.

This special dish is time-consuming to make, since you have to ensure the oxtail fat is rendered and its meat is tender enough to melt in your mouth. Even still, it was commonplace but still special for me growing up. Because of its laboriousness, it showed up only on weekends, amplifying its novelty. I didn't realize just how meaningful it would be to others until I decided to put it on Benne on Eagle's menu. After that, we were running through 50 pounds of oxtail every weekend, and it became our most popular entrée. From the oxtail's ridiculously decadent sauce to the creamy, melt-in-your-mouth black-eyed peas, this is the most inviting dish on earth. I tear into the oxtails and scoop up forkfuls of middlins, dunking into the sauce and scooping up the beans as I go. **Feeds 4 to 6**

BEER-BRAISED OXTAIL, BLACK-EYED PEAS, AND RICE MIDDLINS

3 pounds oxtails (each about 3 inches thick)

1 tablespoon kosher salt

4 tablespoons extra-virgin olive oil

4 celery stalks, chopped

4 carrots, chopped

1 yellow onion, chopped

1 garlic head, halved crosswise

2 bay leaves

2 thyme sprigs

4 juniper berries

1 tablespoon whole black peppercorns

1 tablespoon tomato paste

1 (12-ounce) bottle dark stout

4 cups chicken stock, homemade (page 41) or store-bought

1 tablespoon cold unsalted butter

Cooked black-eyed peas (see page 44)

Rice Middlins (page 46)

Season the oxtails with the salt; place them on a baking sheet or platter in a single layer and refrigerate, uncovered, for at least 4 hours or up to overnight.

Preheat the oven to 325°F.

Heat 2 tablespoons of the oil in a Dutch oven over medium-high heat. When the oil shimmers, add half of the oxtails and cook until browned on the outside, 2 to 3 minutes per side. Transfer to a large plate. Repeat with the remaining oil and oxtails.

Using ultrafine cheesecloth, wrap the celery, carrots, onions, garlic, bay leaves, thyme, juniper, and peppercorns into a bundle and tie with kitchen twine to make a sachet. Add the sachet to the empty pot, then add the tomato paste and stout and cook over low heat, using a wooden spoon to scrape up any browned bits from the bottom of

the pot. Add the stock and bring to a boil over high heat. Return the oxtails to the pot along with any collected juices and cover tightly. Transfer to the oven and cook until the oxtails are fork-tender, 3½ to 4 hours.

Drain the oxtails, reserving the cooking liquid and discarding the sachet. Cover the oxtails to keep warm.

Carefully skim off and discard the top layer of fat from the cooking liquid and pour the liquid into a medium saucepan. Bring to a rolling boil over high heat for 30 seconds, then reduce the heat to medium-low and simmer until the liquid has reduced by a third, about 15 minutes. Remove from the heat and whisk in the butter to melt.

To serve, pile the black-eyed peas onto a serving platter. Place the oxtails on top and ladle some of the sauce over them. Serve with a warm bowl of middlins alongside.

In terms of proteins, words like "candied" and "glazed" make me think of Southern BBQ. Caramelized burnt ends of pork or glossy, sticky sauces hanging on to fatty meat for dear life are what draw me to mouthwatering methods such as this. Fatty meats like short ribs love this treatment the most, with their gelatinous generosity making it tough for sauce to say no. You won't need to fire up a smoker for this, but you'll still yield a nice sticky sauce that will have you licking your fingers and throwing your head back. **Feeds 4 to 6**

CANDIED SHORT RIBS
WITH SKILLET RED CABBAGE

2 garlic cloves, minced

1 teaspoon ground ginger

1 tablespoon fish sauce (I prefer Squid brand or Red Boat)

1 teaspoon freshly ground white pepper

2 tablespoons packed dark brown sugar

2 pounds bone-in short ribs

¾ cup coconut water

1 cup chicken stock, homemade (page 41) or store-bought

3 tablespoons unsalted butter

1 small head red cabbage, cored and thinly sliced

2 teaspoons kosher salt

2 teaspoons freshly ground black pepper

1 teaspoon red pepper flakes

1 tablespoon sorghum molasses

2 tablespoons apple cider vinegar

In a large bowl or zip-top bag, combine the garlic, ginger, fish sauce, white pepper, and 1 tablespoon of the brown sugar. Add the short ribs, turn to coat, and allow them to marinate at room temperature for at least 10 minutes or up to 30 minutes.

Heat a large skillet over medium heat. Add the short ribs and cook until browned all over, 3 to 4 minutes per side. Transfer to a plate; reserve the skillet.

In a high-sided medium saucepan, heat the remaining 1 tablespoon brown sugar over medium-low heat, stirring often to prevent burning, until dark amber in color, 4 to 5 minutes. Reduce the heat to low, then very carefully add the coconut water and stock, being careful of splatter.

Cook, stirring, until the mixture coats the back of a metal spoon, 2 to 3 minutes. Add the browned short ribs and any collected liquid, cover, and cook until the short ribs are fork-tender, about 1 hour.

Meanwhile, in the skillet you used for the short ribs, melt the butter over medium-low heat. Add the cabbage and toss to coat. Cooking, stirring occasionally, until the cabbage begins to soften and turn bright purple, 7 to 9 minutes. Add the salt, black pepper, red pepper flakes, sorghum, and vinegar and stir with a wooden spoon, scraping up any browned bits from the bottom of the pan.

Serve the short ribs with a helping of braised cabbage alongside.

For some reason, in the '90s home cooks stuffed everything, from portobello mushrooms to bell peppers to all types of squash. Results were mixed. Nevertheless, my mom nailed it when she whipped up these eggplants, and therefore, I will forever consider the fad a worthwhile one. Kissed with a West African–inspired sauce, this is the best version of a stuffed vegetable you'll ever have—far better than any sad, shriveled old stuffed pepper. **Feeds 4**

SAUSAGE AND RICE STUFFED EGGPLANT
WITH TOMATO-PEANUT GRAVY

For the Eggplant

2 medium eggplants

2 teaspoons kosher salt, plus more as needed

1 (12-ounce) can diced tomatoes

3 garlic cloves, minced

1 chicken bouillon cube

1 tablespoon tomato paste

4 ounces country sausage

1 cup long-grain white rice

1 tablespoon unsalted butter

1 teaspoon paprika

1 teaspoon ground allspice

1 teaspoon freshly ground black pepper

1 bunch parsley, finely chopped

2 teaspoons extra-virgin olive oil

For the Gravy

2 teaspoons extra-virgin olive oil

¼ cup chunky peanut butter

1 tablespoon tahini

2 teaspoons tomato paste

Kosher salt

Make the eggplant: Preheat the oven to 400°F. Set a wire rack over a baking sheet.

Slice each eggplant in half lengthwise. Using a spoon, scoop out the center of each eggplant half, leaving a ½-inch border of flesh attached to the skin; save eggplant flesh for another use. Sprinkle the flesh side of the eggplant halves evenly with the salt. Place flesh-side down on the prepared rack to drain and set aside.

In a high-sided medium saucepan, combine the tomatoes, garlic, bouillon, and 1 cup water. Bring to a boil over high heat, then reduce the heat to low and whisk in the tomato paste. Cover and simmer until the bouillon has dissolved and the sauce is aromatic, about 20 minutes.

In a large heavy-bottomed skillet, cook the sausage over medium-high heat, stirring occasionally, until crisp and browned, 6 to 7 minutes. Add the rice and cook, stirring frequently, until the rice is toasted, 2 minutes. Ladle in 1½ cups of the tomato sauce and stir. Reduce the heat to low. Cover and cook for 10 to 12 minutes, until most of the liquid has been absorbed. Remove the skillet from the heat. Add the butter, paprika, allspice, pepper, and parsley. Stir until the butter has melted. Season with salt to taste.

Pat the flesh side of the eggplant halves dry with a paper towel. Drizzle the eggplants, inside and out, with the olive oil. Place on a baking sheet, flesh-side up, and bake for 7 to 8 minutes, until the eggplant skin starts to brown at the edges and the remaining liquid leaches out. Remove

Recipe continues

from the oven and let cool slightly. When the eggplant is cool enough to handle, generously stuff the cavity of each eggplant half with the sausage-rice mixture.

Pour the remaining tomato sauce into the bottom of a large Dutch oven. Arrange the stuffed eggplants in the sauce, rice-side up. Bake for 10 to 12 minutes, until the eggplants become incredibly tender to the touch. Remove from the oven and transfer the eggplants to a serving platter, reserving the sauce in the pot.

Make the gravy: Place the Dutch oven over medium-low heat and add the olive oil. When the oil starts to smoke, whisk in the peanut butter, tahini, and tomato paste. Cook until the tomato paste transforms from bright red to brick red, 2 to 3 minutes, then reduce the heat to low. Add about 2 tablespoons water to loosen the mixture to the consistency of a thin gravy and use a wooden spoon to scrape up anything that's sticking to the bottom of the pot. Cook for 10 minutes more, then remove from the heat. Season with salt to taste.

Drizzle the tomato-peanut gravy over the eggplants and serve.

Whether pancit, ramen, spaghetti, or pad thai, noodles made their way to our table in many forms, giving us a respite from the otherwise heavy rotation of rice and grits. They served as a solid vehicle for almost anything we could find in the corners of the pantry, giving my mom a good justification for collecting a myriad of bottled sauces from the Asian markets in our town, sometimes saucing up noodles with our usual flavors. At the time it felt like we were all yearning for a break from Down South, and we did that through food. Green chickpeas are harvested young and can be eaten fresh; find them in the produce section at Asian markets. **Feeds 4**

BUCKWHEAT NOODLE BOWLS

1 pound bone-in, skin-on chicken thighs

1 teaspoon kosher salt

1 teaspoon curry powder

¼ cup plus 1 tablespoon neutral oil, such as canola or grapeseed

1 tablespoon extra-virgin olive oil

1 (1-inch) piece fresh ginger, peeled and chopped

8 garlic cloves: 3 kept whole, 5 thinly sliced or shaved on a mandoline

1 jalapeño, halved and seeded, plus additional slices for garnish

½ cup fresh cilantro leaves

1 cup coconut milk

1 cup chicken stock, homemade (page 41) or store-bought

1 lemongrass stalk, sliced lengthwise

1 cup shelled green chickpeas

1 tablespoon fish sauce

4 lime wedges

1 (8-ounce) package soba noodles

4 cilantro sprigs, for garnish

Season the chicken thighs all over with the salt and curry powder.

Heat a Dutch oven over medium-high heat, then add 1 tablespoon of the neutral oil. When the oil is shimmering, add the chicken and cook until golden brown on the outside, 5 to 6 minutes, flipping hallway through.

Meanwhile, in a blender, combine the olive oil, ginger, whole garlic cloves, jalapeño, cilantro, and coconut milk and puree until smooth.

Increase the heat under the chicken to high and add the coconut milk mixture, stock, and lemongrass. Bring to a boil, then reduce the heat to low. Partially cover and simmer until the chicken is cooked through and the liquid has reduced by half and thickened slightly, about 45 minutes. Remove the pot from the heat.

Remove and discard the lemongrass. Remove the chicken from the pot and let cool slightly. When cool enough to handle, remove the meat from the bones, discarding the bones and skin.

Return the chicken to the pot and add the green chickpeas and fish sauce. Cover and cook over low heat until the chicken is tender, about 10 minutes, then remove the pot from the heat.

Meanwhile, heat the remaining ¼ cup neutral oil in a small saucepan over medium heat. When the oil just begins to smoke, add the sliced garlic and cook, continuously stirring, flipping, and agitating it, until the garlic is an even golden brown color, about 2 minutes. Carefully use a slotted spoon to transfer the garlic chips to a plate lined with paper towels.

Discard all but 1 teaspoon of the hot oil in the pan. Heat the oil over medium-high heat. When it shimmers, add the

lime wedges, flesh-side down, carefully pressing to ensure the flesh makes full contact with the pan. Cook until they begin to brown, 4 to 5 minutes, then use tongs to remove them from the pan.

Bring a medium pot of water to a boil over high heat. Add the noodles and cook according to the package instructions. Drain the noodles in a colander, then run them under cool water to stop the cooking.

Divide the noodles evenly among four bowls. Spoon the chicken, chickpeas, and coconut broth over the noodles. Top each bowl with crunchy garlic chips and jalapeño slices. Garnish with cilantro and a charred lime wedge before serving.

Feather-n-Fin, Chic-a-Sea, and Captain D's, the sites of post-cheer-practice meals, my parents' first date, and my first job, respectively, are likely where my obsession with fried fish began. I, and many coastal folks, have a deep appreciation for the simple, obligatory fried-fish plate. Several of my great-aunts saw themselves as the neighborhood "fish plug," frying and selling fish from tents as fast as their husbands could catch them. I was always in awe of these women, who rapidly gutted and filleted perch, catfish, and whatever else with the dullest knives I'd ever seen, looking gloriously fierce with shining fish scales in their hair. Their fold-out tables were filled with chafing dishes of green beans, collards, fried okra, and soup beans and colorful bottles of condiments and sauces. Brown, grease-seeped paper bags filled their arms while they yelled "Good hot fish!" to bystanders whose mouths would water at the words. This was the genesis for my first restaurant, Good Hot Fish, a fish camp–style counter-service restaurant. This recipe, which I feature as a plate special when the mood strikes me, is marked by a crispy cornmeal exterior speckled with spices that encases tender, flaky white fish, its steam begging to escape. To complement, a tartar sauce spiked with trout roe accompanies the fish. **Feeds 4**

CORNMEAL FRIED CATFISH
WITH TROUT ROE TARTAR SAUCE

For the Fish

2 pounds catfish fillets

2 teaspoons kosher salt

2 teaspoons freshly ground black pepper

1 cup fine yellow cornmeal

½ cup all-purpose flour

1 tablespoon celery salt

1 teaspoon onion powder

1 teaspoon garlic powder

1 teaspoon ground sage

1 teaspoon dried parsley

1 teaspoon cayenne pepper

1 teaspoon paprika

Canola oil, for frying

For the Tartar Sauce

1 cup Duke's mayonnaise

¼ cup Foolproof Fridge Pickles (page 157), chopped

Zest of 1 lemon

2 tablespoons fresh lemon juice

2 tablespoons minced fresh chives

8 ounces trout roe

Make the catfish: Season the fillets all over with salt and black pepper. In a shallow dish, combine the cornmeal, flour, celery salt, onion powder, garlic powder, sage, parsley, cayenne, and paprika. Dredge each fillet in the cornmeal mixture, gently pressing it to adhere to the fish, then shake off any excess.

Fill a deep fryer or 10-inch cast-iron skillet with ½ inch of oil and clip a deep-fry thermometer to the side. Warm over medium heat to 350°F. Set a wire rack over a baking sheet.

Working in batches, add the catfish to the hot oil and cook until golden brown and crispy, 3 to 4 minutes. Transfer the fish to the rack and repeat with the remaining catfish. Allow the oil to return to 350°F between batches.

Make the tartar sauce: In a small bowl, combine the mayo, pickles, lemon zest, lemon juice, and chives. Fold in the trout roe and refrigerate until ready to serve.

Serve the catfish hot, with the tartar sauce alongside.

Eating Cornish hens provides an instinctual, carnivorous thrill that I enjoy, and I will never stop liking the sensation of ripping right into them with my hands. Having an entire mini bird all to myself is an interactive tableside dream, and one my family indulged in every Christmas. We'd sit together after a long hard day of snacking on pecan-crusted cheese balls and cooking, humming over the rich, herbaceous stuffing that had absorbed all the savory juices of the roasted birds. You can eat this dish with a fork and knife, but I recommend you forgo the utensils and dig right in. **Feeds 4**

WILD RICE AND SAUSAGE STUFFED CORNISH HENS

For the Stuffing

¾ cup chopped walnuts

3 cups chicken stock, homemade (page 41) or store-bought

1½ cups wild rice

½ teaspoon kosher salt

½ teaspoon freshly ground black pepper

2 tablespoons canola oil

1 large onion, diced

1 pound pork sausage, casings removed if using links

¼ cup whiskey

1½ teaspoons dark brown sugar

4 thyme sprigs

For the Herb Butter

½ cup (1 stick) unsalted butter, at room temperature

¼ cup fresh parsley, chopped

2 teaspoons kosher salt

½ teaspoon freshly ground black pepper

4 Cornish hens

1 teaspoon kosher salt

Make the stuffing: In a small skillet, toast the walnuts over medium heat, stirring continuously, until fragrant and toasty brown, 4 to 5 minutes. Remove from the skillet and let cool.

In a medium saucepan, combine 2 cups of the stock, the rice, salt, and pepper. Bring to a boil, then reduce the heat to low, cover, and cook until the liquid has been absorbed and the rice is tender, about 20 minutes.

Preheat the oven to 400°F.

Heat a large skillet over medium heat. Add the oil, onion, and sausage. Cook, stirring often, until the sausage is browned, 6 to 8 minutes. Add the whiskey and use a wooden spoon to scrape up any browned bits from the bottom of the pan, then stir in the remaining 1 cup stock,

the brown sugar, and the thyme. Stir well, reduce the heat to low, and bring to a simmer. Cook until the mixture is aromatic and the sugar has dissolved, about 5 minutes. Remove and discard the thyme sprigs. Add the cooked rice and toasted walnuts and stir well to combine. Remove from the heat and let cool.

Make the herb butter: In a small bowl, combine the butter, parsley, salt, and pepper and mix well.

Stuff each hen evenly with the rice mixture. Using your fingers, separate the breast skin from the flesh and spread the herb butter under the skin. Season the outside of each hen with the salt and place in a large roasting pan. Roast for 1 hour, until golden brown, using a spoon to baste them with their drippings halfway through. Remove from the oven, baste once more, then serve.

This dish, which we ate some mornings, never really had a name. According to my mom, she simply "made it up," following the whims of a Virginian's natural love for all things ham-related. A true country breakfast, this dish is a harmony of comforting Southern sensations: ham seared in smoky bacon fat, voluptuous gravy, and white bread grilled in plenty of butter. And yet it had no name—until I tried chipped beef in college. Away for a weekend on a snowboarding trip, a friend made a broke version of it with jarred beef gravy and frozen Steak-umms. The gears in my head turned as I remembered my mom's breakfasts and I thought, *Chipped country ham!* **Feeds 8**

CHIPPED VIRGINIA HAM BREAKFAST TOAST
WITH SAWMILL GRAVY

8 paper-thin slices smoked country ham, cut into long, skinny strips

2 tablespoons bacon fat

2 tablespoons all-purpose flour

1 cup whole milk

1½ teaspoons kosher salt

2 teaspoons freshly ground black pepper

3 tablespoons unsalted butter

4 thick slices white bread

4 large eggs

Red pepper flakes

In a heavy-bottomed skillet, cook the country ham and bacon fat over medium heat, stirring occasionally, until the ham begins to crisp just slightly but not brown, 2 to 3 minutes. Whisk in the flour and cook, stirring, until the roux takes on a golden hue, 2 to 3 minutes more. Whisk in the milk, reduce the heat to medium-low, and simmer, stirring occasionally, until thickened, 10 to 15 minutes. Stir in 1 teaspoon of the salt and 1½ teaspoons of the pepper.

Meanwhile, melt 1 tablespoon of the butter in a 12-inch sauté pan over medium-low heat. Add the bread and toast until buttery and golden brown, 2 to 3 minutes per side. Transfer to a plate.

Melt the remaining 2 tablespoons butter in the same pan over medium heat. Crack the eggs into the pan carefully, keeping the yolks intact. Cook until the egg whites are just set, about 3 minutes. Season with the remaining ½ teaspoon each salt and pepper and remove the pan from the heat.

To serve, place a slice of toast on each plate and smother with some of the ham and gravy. Using a spatula, carefully transfer an egg onto each toast slice. Sprinkle with a few red pepper flakes and serve.

Like with a lot of my recipes, this is the part where I tell you this one isn't traditional. With the words "COTTAGE CHEESE" probably screaming at you from the ingredient list, it doesn't take an immersive experience in Rome to figure that out. I don't know how or when ricotta translated to cottage cheese to us Southerners, but with our "use what you got" attitude, it was bound to happen. I won't pretend this dish isn't an abomination of traditional Italian cookery, but it's just so tasty . . . can't both be true? To my picky childhood self, this lasagna was shout-and-dance-worthy; little did I know that my mom used the cloak of cheese and pasta to sneak an entire salad's worth of vegetables into my diet. I still burst through the door of my childhood home in Virginia and expect to turn that kitchen corner and find a Pyrex dish of oozy, rich, curd-filled lasagna, always there no matter the hour I show up. And when it does, I say, "Hallelujah!" I do draw the line at that green shaker can of powdered knockoff "Parmesan" (at least *now* I do), so this recipe calls for freshly grated Parmesan. **Feeds 8 to 10**

HALLELUJAH LASAGNA

2 tablespoons extra-virgin olive oil, plus more for greasing

2 large yellow onions, diced

3 celery stalks, diced

3 carrots, diced

2 green bell peppers, diced

1 cup sliced cremini mushrooms

2 teaspoons kosher salt, plus more for the pasta water

2 teaspoons freshly ground black pepper

1 teaspoon dried sage

Leaves from 2 oregano sprigs, minced

1 pound mild Italian sausage, casings removed if using links

3 garlic cloves, minced

3 cups Stewed Tomatoes (page 38) or canned stewed tomatoes

1 pound dried lasagna noodles

2 cups full-fat cottage cheese

1 egg, lightly beaten

1 teaspoon red pepper flakes

1 cup minced fresh parsley

1 cup freshly grated Parmesan cheese

1 pound shredded low-moisture mozzarella cheese

In a large skillet, heat the olive oil over medium-high heat. When it shimmers, add the onions, celery, carrots, bell peppers, and mushrooms and cook, stirring, until the vegetables begin to soften, 5 to 6 minutes. Stir in the salt, pepper, sage, oregano, and sausage. Cook, stirring occasionally with a wooden spoon and breaking up the meat, until it begins to brown, 6 to 7 minutes. Add the garlic and cook until fragrant, 3 to 4 minutes more. Stir in the tomatoes, reduce the heat to low, and cook until the sauce thickens, 35 to 40 minutes.

Recipe continues

Meanwhile, fill a large stockpot with water, add salt, and bring to a boil over high heat. Add the lasagna and cook until al dente according to the package instructions. Drain.

Preheat the oven to 400°F. Grease a 3-inch-deep 9 × 13-inch casserole dish with olive oil.

In a medium bowl, stir together the cottage cheese, egg, red pepper flakes, parsley, and ½ cup of the Parmesan.

Add a few tablespoons of the sauce to the bottom of the prepared dish to coat. Place some lasagna noodles in an even layer at the bottom of dish, overlapping to cover completely. Add ½ cup of the cottage cheese mixture on top of the noodles and use a spatula to spread it evenly. Scatter around ¼ cup of the mozzarella on top. Then add ½ cup of sauce, and follow with another layer of overlapping noodles. Repeat the layers twice more, ending with a thin layer of sauce. Top the final layer of sauce with the remaining ¼ cup mozzarella and the remaining ½ cup Parmesan.

Cover the baking dish tightly with aluminum foil and bake for 30 minutes. Remove the foil and bake for 10 minutes more, until the top forms a golden brown crust.

Remove the lasagna from the oven, then wait: the best lasagna has time to settle before you eat it. When it comes out of the oven, it might seem like it's a sloshy mess, but 45 minutes later (mine is always still very hot, but you might need less time in a cold kitchen) it will be glorious—the excess moisture gets absorbed into the noodles and filling, and the lasagna will be ready for a relatively clean slice.

Coming up, there were no cartoons or screen time for me. If the weather wasn't conducive to an outdoor foraging exploration in the woods, I'd turn to my other favorite pastime: reading. I did a lot of that. I'd sit by my bedroom window and dust off a stack of my mom's old *Ebony*, *Jet*, and *Essence* magazines, scouring them for anything food-related. If I was lucky, I'd land on a column by Dr. Jessica B. Harris, and I'd read it from top to bottom and then over again. I'd find articles about the top Black hotel chefs in America—mostly men in toques, but that didn't deter me. The recipes on these pages beckoned me, and I came running. I distinctly remember landing on Vernette Walker's Beef with Beer and Brandy Sauce recipe in a December '84 issue of *Ebony*. We had all the ingredients in the house, so I begged my mom to let me play chef for our dinner guests that night. And she did. I remember our family friends' *oohs* and *aahs* with every flick of my ten-year-old wrist. This memory lives in my head rent-free, and this recipe is an updated version of the clipping I still have tucked away in my knife roll. I'd serve this decadent beef with Classic Cornbread (page 40), Salt Turnips (page 212), and Charleston Ice Cream (page 45) alongside, for a company-worthy feast. **Feeds 6 to 8**

BEEF CHEEKS
WITH BEER AND BRANDY SAUCE

2 tablespoons rice flour

2 ½ teaspoons kosher salt

2 teaspoons freshly ground black pepper

4 pounds beef cheeks, ½ inch of the fat cap removed

1 tablespoon unsalted butter

1 tablespoon grapeseed oil

2 shallots, diced

2 leeks, white parts only, well washed and thinly sliced

2 carrots, diced

2 celery stalks, diced

2 garlic cloves, smashed

1 tablespoon tomato paste

¼ cup brandy

1 (12-ounce) can dark beer

1 cup chicken stock, homemade (page 41) or store-bought

1 tablespoon fresh thyme leaves

1 tablespoon minced fresh parsley

In a large bowl, combine the flour, salt, and pepper. Add the beef cheeks and toss to coat.

Heat a large skillet over medium-high heat. Add the butter and grapeseed oil. When the oil begins to smoke a bit, add the beef, working in batches as needed, and cook until browned all over, 2 to 3 minutes per side. Transfer to a plate.

To the same pan, add the shallots, leeks, carrots, and celery. Cook over medium-low heat, stirring, until the shallots are soft and translucent, 5 to 6 minutes. Add the garlic and cook until fragrant, 2 to 3 minutes more. Stir in the tomato paste and cook for 1 to 2 minutes, until incorporated.

Pour in the brandy, beer, and stock and use a wooden spoon to scrape up any browned bits from the bottom of the pan. Bring to a simmer, then reduce the heat to low. Return the beef to the pan along with any juices from the plate. Cover and cook for 3 hours, then stir in the thyme and parsley and check if the beef is fork-tender; if not, cook for up to an hour more, if needed.

Serve the beef with the pan sauce spooned over the top and a well-thought-out vehicle for sopping alongside.

Despite my parents' best intentions, I grew up a rebel. That sounds cool on paper, but what that actually looked like was me skipping my high school club meetings to sneak into our guest room and watch Emeril or Rachael Ray—which was where I learned that rémoulade was decidedly *not* the pink slurry I'd been making at beachside restaurants to pair with fried calamari. I was shocked to see stuff like shaved fennel—vegetables!—going into their takes. This version really changed how I approached the complexity of food, and I think its refreshing, cooling notes add so much to barbecued meats. **Feeds 4 to 6**

BAKED BBQ CHICKEN
WITH SWEET POTATO CELERY RÉMOULADE

For the Rémoulade

2 teaspoons fresh lemon juice

1 small celeriac

1 small sweet potato, peeled

¾ cup Duke's mayonnaise

2 teaspoons Dijon mustard

3 tablespoons chopped fresh parsley

1 teaspoon kosher salt

Freshly ground black pepper

For the Chicken

1 tablespoon kosher salt

3 tablespoons packed dark brown sugar

2 tablespoons smoked paprika

½ teaspoon garlic powder

½ teaspoon onion powder

1 teaspoon coarsely ground black pepper

3 pounds bone-in, skin-on chicken pieces (a mix of light and dark meat)

1 tablespoon honey

1 teaspoon apple cider vinegar

Make the rémoulade: In a large bowl, stir together 1½ teaspoons of the lemon juice and 1 cup water. Peel the celeriac, then thinly slice using a mandoline. Cut into thin matchsticks, adding the celeriac to the lemon water as you go. Repeat with the sweet potato, adding it to the same bowl.

In another large bowl, stir together the mayonnaise, mustard, parsley, and remaining ½ teaspoon lemon juice.

Drain the celeriac and sweet potato and shake off any excess water. Add to the mayonnaise mixture, season with the salt and pepper, and toss to coat. Cover and refrigerate for at least 1 hour or up to 3 hours. Taste the sauce before serving and adjust the seasoning if needed.

Make the chicken: In a medium bowl, combine the salt, brown sugar, paprika, garlic powder, onion powder, and pepper. Add the chicken and toss to coat. Cover and marinate in the fridge for at least 2 hours or up to 5 hours.

Preheat the oven to 325°F. Line a baking sheet with parchment paper and place the chicken on it to come to room temperature.

Cover the chicken with aluminum foil and bake until it registers 155°F on a meat thermometer, about 45 minutes. Uncover the chicken, turn on the broiler, and broil for 2 to 3 minutes, until the skin is crisp, watching carefully to make sure it doesn't burn. Remove from the oven. Pour the pan juices into a small high-sided saucepan and let the chicken rest on the baking sheet.

Add the honey to the pot with the pan juices and bring to a boil over medium-high heat. Cook, stirring, until thickened and syrupy, 6 to 7 minutes. Remove from the heat and whisk in the vinegar. Brush the glaze generously over the chicken. Transfer the chicken to a plate and serve with a side of the rémoulade.

Shrimp-eating mullet, also called whiting, is found in shores among muddy waters. It's an oily, fatty fish variety, best eaten fresh. The richness of mullet stands up well to this simple dinner-in-a-pouch. The only thing that's not so simple about it is that the mullet is full of bones, so you'll need to be ready for some solid fish pickin'. **Feeds 4**

MULLET DINNER IN PARCHMENT

12 fingerling potatoes

4 teaspoons kosher salt

½ cup extra-virgin olive oil

2 teaspoons fresh lemon juice

1 shallot, thinly sliced

2 garlic cloves, thinly sliced

2 teaspoons minced fresh oregano

2 teaspoons minced fresh parsley

1 teaspoon ground cumin

1 teaspoon Aleppo pepper

½ teaspoon dark chile powder

4 whole mullet (or sea bream or sea bass), gutted

1 teaspoon freshly ground white pepper

1 teaspoon paprika

1 lemon, thinly sliced

½ cup cherry tomatoes

½ cup pitted Castelvetrano olives

Preheat the oven to 400°F.

Place the potatoes in a medium pot and add 2 teaspoons of the salt and water to cover. Bring to a boil over high heat, then reduce the heat to medium-low and cook until the potatoes are fork-tender, 6 to 7 minutes. Use a slotted spoon to transfer the potatoes to a baking sheet to cool.

Meanwhile, in a small bowl, whisk together the olive oil, lemon juice, shallot, garlic, oregano, parsley, cumin, Aleppo pepper, and chile powder.

Season the fish liberally, including inside the cavities, with the remaining 2 teaspoons salt, the white pepper, and the paprika.

Tear off four sheets of parchment paper, each about 20 inches long. Fold the parchment pieces in half crosswise to mark the center, then unfold.

To assemble the pouches, place one piece of fish lengthwise below the crease of one sheet of parchment. Add a couple slices of lemon to the cavity of the fish. Spoon a quarter of the olive oil mixture over the fish, then add some tomatoes, olives, and 3 fingerling potatoes. Fold the parchment over the fish, then seal the pouch by rolling the edges together and folding shut. Place the pouch on a baking sheet. Repeat with the remaining ingredients.

Roast for 10 to 12 minutes. Transfer each packet to a plate and serve, opening the pouches tableside using a fork, taking care to avoid the hot steam.

Before the ramen movement gained speed here in the South, there was yock. In Virginia, we know this noodle dish to be the product of Chinese restaurants landing in Black communities in Tidewater due to immigration. New Orleanians have yaka mein, a noodle soup that jumped from Cantonese restaurants to Creole street vendors during the nineteenth century. Over two centuries of culinary call-and-response, the latter adapted the dish into a brothy hangover staple in a Styrofoam cup that is just barely, only kind of Asian. A box of Virginia yock is less soupy and more gravy-like, with hot, tomato-based, soy-sauce-spiked noodles piled into a Chinese takeout container. To Westernize it even further, by "tomato-based" I mean *ketchup*, and by "noodles" I mean *spaghetti*. I've tried many times to refine the dish, but there simply is no other way to make yock: ketchup and spaghetti are the way, the truth, and the light. This super-regional, nearly extinct dish deserves a place on the Ark of Food. A few Chinese spots throughout the 757 still have it, and if you're lucky, you may be able to find it via word of mouth at Black church fundraisers and some underground spots I promised not to share. But since you're unlikely to come across it on your own, I will share my secrets to making a solid version. It will never be exactly right, but it's always fun to try. **Feeds 6 to 8**

VIRGINIA YOCK

2 teaspoons kosher salt, plus more for the pasta water

2 teaspoons freshly ground white pepper

2 teaspoons paprika

2 teaspoons ground sage

1 teaspoon ground coriander

1 teaspoon ground mustard

1 pound medium (41/50) white shrimp, peeled and deveined

1 tablespoon canola oil

1 teaspoon toasted sesame oil

5 scallions, green parts only, thinly sliced

1 green bell pepper, diced

2 celery stalks, diced

2 hot link sausages, diced

3 garlic cloves, minced

3 cups chicken stock, homemade (page 41) or store-bought

1 cinnamon stick

2 star anise pods

1 dried bay leaf

1 tablespoon white miso paste

1 tablespoon dark brown sugar

2 teaspoons fish sauce

¼ cup soy sauce

¼ cup ketchup

1 pound spaghetti

For Serving

Diced white onion

Thinly sliced hard-boiled eggs

Hot sauce

Cayenne pepper

In a small bowl, combine the salt, white pepper, paprika, sage, coriander, and mustard. Add the shrimp, toss to coat, and set aside to marinate at room temperature.

In a Dutch oven, heat the canola and sesame oils over medium-low heat. When the oil is just smoking, add the scallions, bell pepper, and celery. Cook, stirring, until the vegetables are softened, 5 to 6 minutes. Add the sausage and the garlic and cook, stirring frequently, until the garlic is fragrant, 3 to 4 minutes. Pour in the chicken stock, then add the cinnamon stick, star anise, and bay leaf. Whisk in the miso, brown sugar, fish sauce, soy sauce, and, yes, the only ketchup you'll find in these pages. Simmer proudly until the flavors are melded, about 20 minutes. Carefully fish out and discard the cinnamon stick, anise pods, and bay leaf.

Meanwhile, fill a large stockpot with water and bring to a boil over high heat. When the water is boiling, season with enough salt until its taste mimics the ocean. Add the spaghetti and cook to al dente according to the package instructions. Drain the pasta and set aside, reserving ¼ cup of the cooking water.

Reduce the heat under the simmering broth to low. Drop in the marinated shrimp, cover, and cook until the shrimp is pink and opaque, 3 to 4 minutes. Add the cooked spaghetti and the reserved ¼ cup pasta cooking water. Cook, stirring, until the mixture emulsifies and thickens, 3 to 4 minutes more.

To serve, divide the shrimp and noodles into bowls, scooping up any reduced broth that remains. Top with chopped onion, sliced eggs, and/or your favorite vinegar-forward hot sauce. Virginian iterations of yock are not complete without a little dusting of cayenne before serving.

Somewhere between her postdoctoral studies and a promotion, my mom put a full stop on making banana pudding from scratch, introducing a secret shortcut—Jell-O pudding—into the mix. I was in my early teens then, so my palate wasn't refined enough to really notice how artificial-tasting and gritty it was. Imagine my shock when I visited home during college and spotted the telltale boxes hidden in the pantry. My world was shaken; but truthfully, the spoon-licking memories trump technical matters like whether the pudding came from a box or not. But I do still make my version from scratch, and I encourage you to do the same, because try as you might, you will never get the voluptuous, rich texture of homemade pudding from a box. **Feeds 4 to 6**

BANANA PUDDING

For the Pudding

1 cup sugar

¼ cup cornstarch

½ teaspoon kosher salt

6 large egg yolks, lightly beaten

3½ cups whole milk

2 tablespoons unsalted butter, cubed

1 tablespoon pure vanilla extract

1 box Nilla wafers (about 50 cookies)

4 large ripe bananas, thinly sliced

For the Whipped Cream

½ cup heavy cream

2 teaspoons sugar

Make the pudding: In a large saucepan, whisk together the sugar, cornstarch, salt, and egg yolks. Drizzle in the milk, whisking vigorously. Place the pan over medium heat and bring to a simmer. Cook, stirring, until the pudding thickens slightly, 4 to 7 minutes. Remove from the heat, then whisk in the butter and vanilla. Pour the pudding into a bowl and cover with plastic wrap, pressing it gently against the surface of the pudding to prevent a skin from forming. Refrigerate for at least 4 hours or up to overnight to thicken.

Line the bottom of a trifle dish evenly with cookies, breaking them to fit as needed. Add about a third of the pudding, then top with a layer of bananas. Repeat twice with more cookies, pudding, and bananas.

Make the whipped cream: In the chilled bowl of a stand mixer fitted with the whisk attachment, whip the cream with the sugar until soft peaks form, 2 to 3 minutes.

Dollop the trifle with whipped cream and chill in the refrigerator until ready to serve.

You might think politics can be plenty divisive in the South, but few debates rile people up as much as the question of whether sugar belongs in cornbread. Neither side of my family puts even a speck of sugar in their cornbread, but I'm gonna throw a stick of dynamite into the works and just say it: I'm okay with sweet cornbread. Part of the reason is because I learned that sweet cornbread was a luxury for many impoverished Black Southerners in the post-slavery era, who saw sugar and butter as something worth celebrating if they got their hands on them. Putting sugar into cornbread was a rare indulgence for them, and this dessert-worthy version pays tribute to that feeling. **Feeds 6**

BUTTERMILK-MOLASSES CORNBREAD CAKE

1 cup buttermilk

¼ cup crème fraîche

4 tablespoons (½ stick) unsalted butter, melted, plus more for greasing

3 large eggs, at room temperature

1 cup whole milk

1 cup sugar

1½ tablespoons honey

1 cup all-purpose flour

1 cup fine white cornmeal

1 teaspoon kosher salt

1 tablespoon baking powder

6 tablespoons sorghum molasses

In a small bowl, whisk together the buttermilk and crème fraîche until evenly combined. The mixture should be fairly loose. Chill in the refrigerator while you make the cornbread.

Place a rack in the center of the oven and preheat the oven to 350°F. Grease a 9-inch cast-iron skillet with butter and place it in the oven to preheat as well.

In a large bowl, whisk together the eggs, milk, sugar, and honey. Slowly whisk in the flour and cornmeal, alternating ½ cup at a time. Whisk in the salt and baking powder, then the melted butter.

Carefully remove the skillet from the oven and the pour in the batter. Return the skillet to the oven and bake for 25 to 30 minutes, until the top is golden brown and a toothpick inserted into the center comes out clean. Remove from the oven and let cool for 10 minutes.

To serve, slice the cornbread into 6 wedges. Plate each wedge on a plate. Pour the buttermilk mixture over each piece, then slowly and evenly drizzle a thin stream of sorghum over the tops.

HOME

LAND

This chapter represents a culmination of the food that describes who I am and where I've been—it's a distillation of what it looks like to cook while Black where and how I live today in Asheville. In these recipes, you'll find influences of my culture, my studies, other chefs, and, of course, restaurants. Working in restaurants was my first and is my forever job. I've worked at nearly as many restaurants as I've spent years in this industry: bartending years before I could even buy myself a beer; enduring midservice yelling from coke- and alcohol-addicted chefs; being the prep cook, line cook, expediter, and dishwasher all in one day; diving headfirst into wine; swiftly pivoting to catering; learning that professional kitchens weren't filled with the Southern hospitality I'd grown up accustomed to. Whether in Baltimore or West Texas, it was all the same for me, and it was rough. None of my stories are surprising, unfortunately. Instead, they mimic those of so many other Black chefs, woman chefs, and queer chefs. Harassing, ass-grabbing, gaslighting, discriminating . . . this environment wasn't something I would have ever chosen for my seventeen-year-old self. I learned, or I assumed, this is what professional cooking was. What it had to be.

But I found myself grappling endlessly with this disconnect between the warmth my younger self craved in kitchen chaos and the professional life I'd set out to create. After years of the line-cook grind, I got the itch to do something for me. It helped that, as far back as I could remember, my family had stories of the women and their entrepreneurship. Whether working at a fundraising fish fry, volunteering a church bake sale, making a quilt, or putting up produce to sell, they knew how to make a buck from their skills. I had a vision of myself, much like them, feeding the masses and connecting with my community while making a little money.

Finding out that Malinda Russell did the same thing more than a century before me added much-needed fuel to my fire. Like my own, Russell's travels and life experiences inspired the food she made. So here, I'm sharing all the knowledge I picked up on my journey so far, including the Kenyan art of using all the parts of okra, the delights of Cameroonian soya, and the homestyle cooking of my Mexican-German wife.

This simple recipe turns sweet potatoes into stunners at a very low cost—hence the name. This relish-y chutney of sorts is warm and bracing. I recommend featuring it on a cheese plate, slathering it on sandwiches, or using it to top summer red links. **Makes 8 cups**

SWEET POTATO BARGAIN

1 pound sweet potatoes, peeled and shredded

1 shallot, thinly sliced

1 cup apple cider vinegar

2 tablespoons sorghum molasses

1 teaspoon celery seeds

1 teaspoon mustard seeds

½ teaspoon red pepper flakes

½ teaspoon kosher salt

½ teaspoon coriander seeds, toasted and crushed

½ teaspoon ground turmeric

In a high-sided medium saucepan, combine the sweet potatoes, shallot, vinegar, sorghum, celery seeds, mustard seeds, red pepper flakes, salt, coriander, and turmeric. Cook over medium heat, stirring occasionally, until the liquid has been mostly absorbed, about 20 minutes. Remove from the heat and let cool. Store in an airtight container in the refrigerator for up to 2 weeks.

Hot, cheesy dips are my love language. Coupled with warm, freshly fried saltines (a great vehicle for pretty much anything), this dip exists just to bring that sorry, ever-popular spinach artichoke dip to its knees. Briny oysters sautéed in butter swim in harmony with creamy collards hit with just the right amount of acidity. **Feeds 8 to 10**

HOT COLLARD AND OYSTER DIP
WITH FRIED SALTINES

1 teaspoon kosher salt, plus more as needed

4 cups packed chopped collard leaves

1 tablespoon unsalted butter, plus more for greasing

12 ounces shucked raw oysters, drained

4 ounces cream cheese, at room temperature

½ cup Duke's mayonnaise

½ cup sour cream

1 teaspoon fresh lemon juice

4 scallions, thinly sliced

¼ cup freshly grated Parmesan cheese

2 teaspoons Worcestershire sauce

1 teaspoon garlic powder

1 teaspoon onion powder

1 teaspoon freshly ground black pepper

5 dashes of Tabasco sauce

Smoked paprika

Neutral oil, such as canola or grapeseed

1 sleeve of saltines (about 40 crackers)

Fill a 2-quart pot with 6 cups water and bring to a boil over high heat. Fill a medium bowl with ice and water and set it nearby. When the water comes to a boil, season with salt until its taste mimics the ocean. Add the collards and stir so all the pieces are submerged. Boil for 30 seconds, then use a spider to pull out the collards and dunk them into the ice bath. Swirl the collards in the ice water to cool them off quickly, then drain them and lay them on a plate lined with a tea towel. Hold the towel over the sink and twist to squeeze out excess water. Set the collards aside.

Preheat the oven to 400°F. Lightly grease a 9 × 13-inch casserole dish with butter.

In a medium skillet, melt the butter over medium heat. Increase the heat to medium-high, add the oysters, and cook until they plump up and become firmer, 2 to 3 minutes. Remove the oysters from the skillet and chop any large ones in half.

In a large bowl, combine the cream cheese, mayonnaise, sour cream, and lemon juice with a spoon (or use a handheld mixer) until evenly combined and smooth. Add the scallions, Parmesan, Worcestershire, garlic powder, onion powder, 1 teaspoon salt, the black pepper, and the Tabasco. Fold in the oysters and collards. Transfer the mixture to the prepared casserole dish. Bake for 18 to 20 minutes, until bubbling. Remove from the oven and sprinkle with paprika.

Meanwhile, fill a Dutch oven with 1 inch of oil and clip a deep-fry thermometer to the side. Heat over medium-high heat to 350°F. Working in batches to avoid crowding, carefully drop the saltines into the hot oil and cook until both sides are golden and toasty, 3 to 4 minutes, flipping them with a slotted spoon halfway through the cooking time. Transfer the saltines to a plate lined with paper towels.

Serve the dip hot, with the fried saltines alongside.

Ham salad isn't a new concept: its bright pink presence is a misleadingly dazzling staple at many church functions, sometimes with cheddar or sometimes with spring peas. It might attract the eye, but its one-note flavor is usually anything but dazzling. I do like the idea behind it, though, and I think it deserves more than to be halfheartedly spooned onto a plate, only to be left behind at the end of dinner. My version is straightforward, but I amped up the flavor with more spice and acid and stuffed it into charred okra because I think ham salad works so much better as a condiment. Stuffed okra is popular globally but still fairly unseen in the South. This recipe removes the seeds and membrane for the slime-sensitive. (But don't toss those seeds—instead, try pickling them following the instructions on page 157.) Note that you'll need a piping bag for this recipe, though a big zip-top bag with one corner snipped will do in a pinch. **Feeds 8 to 10**

HAM SALAD—STUFFED OKRA

1 pound cooked honey-baked ham, chopped

¼ cup chopped Foolproof Fridge Pickles (page 157)

1½ teaspoons freshly ground black pepper

1½ teaspoons paprika

1 tablespoon yellow mustard

½ cup Duke's mayonnaise

½ pound okra, sliced lengthwise

Juice of ½ lemon

1 teaspoon kosher salt

In a food processor, pulse together the ham, pickles, pepper, paprika, and mustard until the mixture begins to form a paste, then transfer to a medium bowl. Fold in the mayonnaise and stir until completely combined. Scoop the salad into a piping bag and chill it in the refrigerator.

Heat a charcoal or gas grill to medium (400°F) or heat a grill pan over medium heat.

Use tweezers or a small spoon and your fingers to free the seeds and membrane from the okra. (Reserve the okra seeds for another use.) Place the okra over direct heat and cook, watching carefully and flipping regularly, until grill marks form on the bottom, 3 to 4 minutes. The okra should still be firm and maintain its structure. Transfer the okra to a baking sheet. Drizzle with the lemon juice and sprinkle with the salt, then let cool slightly.

When the okra is cool enough to handle, remove the ham salad from the fridge. Cut about ½ inch off the tip of the piping bag and fill each piece of okra with ham salad. Arrange on a platter and serve.

I have a thing for road trips that are made complete by gas station snacks. I've crossed three lanes of traffic for "the best pepperoni rolls" and survived a cross-country ride almost exclusively on assorted Haribo gummies. My most memorable stock-up was at a major grocer in Cameroon, Africa. With a three-hour drive ahead of me, the aisle that captivated my hard-to-get attention was the one filled with ground nuts, each proudly wearing its own distinct candylike coating. The wardrobe ranged from powdered cocoa to spicy corn to banana and strawberry. Some even had little cookies and peanut butter puffs sprinkled within. My favorites were spiced ground nuts and cookie-coated peanuts, easily putting Chex Mix to shame. Back home, desperate for these store-bought sensations, I got into the kitchen and made these right before a road trip. The feeling's not quite the same when you don't pull off a highway to stock up, but I recommend it just the same. **Feeds 6 to 8**

SUMAC-COATED BACON FAT PEANUTS

For the Syrup

1 tablespoon fresh lime juice

1 tablespoon fish sauce

1 cup sugar

For the Spiced Nuts

2 teaspoons kosher salt

2 teaspoons ground sumac, plus more
  as needed

1 teaspoon cayenne pepper

¾ cup bacon fat, melted

4 cups raw peanuts

Preheat the oven to 350°F.

Make the syrup: In a small saucepan, combine the lime juice, fish sauce, and sugar. Place over medium heat and cook, stirring frequently, until the sugar begins to bubble and melt, 2 to 3 minutes. Remove from the heat and let cool.

Make the coating: Line a baking sheet with a silicone baking mat or parchment paper.

In a small bowl, mix together 1 teaspoon of the salt, the sumac, and the cayenne.

In a medium bowl, combine the peanuts and 3 tablespoons of the cooled syrup, tossing quickly to coat. Add the spice mixture and melted bacon fat and toss again to coat evenly.

Spread the coated nuts over the prepared baking sheet. Bake for 6 to 7 minutes, until the nuts are toasted. Immediately sprinkle with more sumac to taste and the remaining 1 teaspoon salt, toss to coat, and enjoy, or let cool and store in an airtight container at room temperature for up to 5 days.

Before Lawry's, there was kitchen pepper. I often describe it as that spice blend every old Black Southerner with any kitchen acumen leans on. Like many culinary truths out there, there are a lot of versions: no two recipes are the same. Kitchen pepper is my "all seasoning," and I keep it on me like Beyoncé does hot sauce in her purse. The warm spice blend works with everything—and I really mean everything—including grilled proteins, baked goods, and, perhaps most especially, these unassuming crispy chicken wings. Let's consider kitchen pepper wings the older, more mature cousin of lemon pepper wings. **Feeds 6 to 8 (depending on everyone's self-control)**

KITCHEN PEPPER CHICKEN WINGS

For the Kitchen Pepper

2 tablespoons ground sumac

2 teaspoons coarsely ground black pepper

2 teaspoons ground ginger

2 teaspoons ground allspice

2 teaspoons ground cinnamon

2 teaspoons freshly grated nutmeg

2 teaspoons ground cloves

For the Wings

3 to 4 pounds chicken wings

1 tablespoon kosher salt

For the Glaze

4 tablespoons (½ stick) unsalted butter

¼ cup sorghum molasses

1 tablespoon fresh lemon juice

Preheat the oven to 425°F. Set a wire rack over a baking sheet.

Make the kitchen pepper: In a small bowl, combine the sumac, pepper, ginger, allspice, cinnamon, nutmeg, and cloves. Stir to combine well. (The kitchen pepper will keep in an airtight container in a cool, dry place for up to 3 months.)

Make the wings: Place the chicken wings in a large bowl, add the salt and 2 tablespoons of the kitchen pepper, and toss to coat. Arrange the wings on the prepared rack. Roast for 45 to 50 minutes, flipping the wings halfway through, until the skin is golden brown.

Meanwhile, make the glaze: In a medium saucepan, melt the butter over low heat. Whisk in another tablespoon of the kitchen pepper, the sorghum, and the lemon juice. Pour the glaze into the biggest bowl you have.

Remove the wings from oven and use tongs to transfer them to the bowl with the glaze. Toss to coat well, then transfer the wings to a serving platter (if you wanna be fancy) and watch the people flock.

Soya on the streets of Cameroon, yakitori in Japan, or something unrecognizable and deep fried at the state fair . . . there's just something about food on a stick that really gets me going. It's everywhere, and many cultures lay claim to their version of skewering, following it up with open-fire cooking. Well, *my* version is a simple but flavor-packed bite. It's great with a little soy sauce or White BBQ Sauce (page 280) for dipping. **Feeds 5**

GRILLED SORGHUM CHICKEN ON A STICK

2 tablespoons soy sauce

1 tablespoon untoasted sesame oil

1 tablespoon grapeseed oil

3 garlic cloves, minced

3 tablespoons sorghum molasses

2 tablespoons dry white wine

1 tablespoon rice vinegar

½ teaspoon ground ginger

½ teaspoon ground allspice

½ teaspoon paprika

½ teaspoon freshly ground black pepper

5 boneless, skinless chicken thighs, cut into 2-inch pieces

1 bunch scallions, white parts only, cut into 1-inch pieces

Neutral oil, such as canola or grapeseed, for the grill grates

In a large bowl, whisk together the soy sauce, sesame oil, grapeseed oil, garlic, sorghum, wine, vinegar, ginger, allspice, paprika, and black pepper. Pour ¼ cup of the marinade into a separate bowl and reserve for basting. Add the chicken to the rest of the marinade in the large bowl and toss to coat. Cover and marinate in the refrigerator for at least 1 hour or up to 6 hours.

At least 30 minutes before you plan to grill, soak five wooden skewers in water to prevent them from burning; drain them before using.

Heat a gas or charcoal grill to medium (400°F) or heat a grill pan over medium heat.

Thread the chicken and scallions onto the skewers, using 4 pieces of chicken and 4 pieces of scallion for each skewer and alternating them as you go. Discard the marinade.

Brush the grill grates with oil. Place the skewers on the grill and cook for 4 minutes. Baste with the reserved marinade, then flip the skewers and cook for 3 minutes more, until the chicken is cooked through and slightly charred. Remove from the grill and baste generously with the remaining marinade, then arrange on a platter and serve.

Deep research and a love for fried snacks are how I was first introduced to akara, or Nigerian bean fritters. This falafel-like snack sees black-eyed peas soaked and tediously hulled from their little jackets, then blended and fried into light airiness. In this recipe, I also draw on memories of fried corn snacks in the Backcountry and merge the two together, with the marriage made complete by a nontraditional dipping sauce. **Feeds 8 to 10**

BLACK-EYED PEA HOMINY FRITTERS
WITH BROWN BUTTER MAYONNAISE

For the Mayonnaise

1½ cups (3 sticks) unsalted butter

2 large egg yolks

2 tablespoons Dijon mustard

1 tablespoon apple cider vinegar

2 teaspoons kosher salt, plus more as needed

For the Fritters

½ cup black-eyed peas, soaked in water overnight and drained

1 (12-ounce) can white hominy, drained

2 eggs, separated

1 tablespoon minced jalapeño

1 tablespoon kosher salt, plus more as needed

Neutral oil, such as canola or grapeseed, for frying

Make the mayonnaise: In a small high-sided saucepan, melt the butter over medium-low heat. Cook, stirring occasionally, until foamy and fragrant (it will have a nutty aroma) and the milk solids are beginning to brown and caramelize, about 8 minutes. Remove from the heat and let cool.

In a blender, combine the egg yolks, mustard, vinegar, and salt. Blend on medium speed until combined, about 20 seconds. With the blender running on medium speed, slowly pour in the cooled brown butter in a thin stream and blend until smooth.

Make the fritters: Working in batches, roll a small handful of soaked black-eyed peas between your palms to separate the hulls from the peas; discard the hulls and drop the peas into a food processor as you go.

Add the hominy and egg yolks to the food processor and pulse about five times to combine. Transfer the hominy

mixture to a large bowl, add the jalapeño and salt, and stir to mix well.

In a small bowl, vigorously whisk the egg whites until they form soft peaks, 4 to 5 minutes. Fold the egg whites into the hominy mixture.

Fill a large high-sided cast-iron skillet or Dutch oven with 1 inch of oil and clip a deep-fry thermometer to the side. Heat over medium heat to 350°F. Working in batches, scoop up 2-tablespoon portions of the hominy batter and lower into the hot oil, being sure not to crowd the pan. Cook until golden brown on one side, 2 to 3 minutes, then flip and fry for 2 minutes more. Transfer to a plate lined with paper towels and immediately season with salt. Repeat with the remaining batter, allowing the oil to return to 350°F between batches.

Serve the fritters on a platter with a sidecar of the brown butter mayonnaise.

Before my wife, Meaghan, and I were married, we spent some time dating long-distance. One afternoon when she was visiting me during this era of our relationship, she was craving shrimp cocktail and whipped up this ceviche-like version. Shortly after that, she uprooted herself from her home in Texas and moved in with me, so I give this dish a bit of credit for our lingering summer romance turned marriage. Fittingly, its name is a tribute to "U-Haul-ing," self-deprecating slang for the phenomenon of lesbians falling in love and moving in together at lightning speed. It's a stereotype, but Meaghan and I said our first hellos one hot summer night at a dive bar in Texas and found ourselves cohabitating in just under a year. Now this dish is what I always think of when I hear "shrimp cocktail." Meaghan's family serves this alongside the traditional saladitas—very tasty saltine crackers. At home, we amp up the shrimpy flavor and use round prawn crackers to chase our cocktail. You can easily find them at your local Asian market. **Feeds 6 to 8**

U-HAUL SHRIMP COCKTAIL
WITH PRAWN CRACKERS

2 tablespoons kosher salt

2 pounds small to medium white shrimp, peeled and deveined

1 cup fresh lime juice

1 cup clam juice

5 Roma (plum) tomatoes, cored and quartered

3 garlic cloves

1 bunch cilantro, coarsely chopped

3 Mexican oregano sprigs, coarsely chopped

1 teaspoon celery seeds, toasted

1 red onion, diced

1 cup diced celery

2 jalapeños, thinly sliced

4 avocados, diced

1 (4-ounce) bag uncooked prawn crackers or bagged shrimp chips

Neutral oil, such as canola or grapeseed, for frying

In a medium stockpot, bring 4 quarts water to a rolling boil. Fill a large bowl with ice and water and set it nearby. Add the salt to the boiling water, then add the shrimp and cook until pink and opaque, about 1 minute. Immediately transfer to the ice bath to cool. Drain, transfer to a large nonreactive bowl, and add the lime juice. Cover and refrigerate for 1 to 2 hours.

In a blender, combine the clam juice, tomatoes, garlic, cilantro, oregano, and celery seeds and pulse just a few times so the mixture remains chunky.

Add the onion to the shrimp, stir, and let mellow for 2 to 3 minutes. Pour the tomato mixture over the shrimp. Add the celery, jalapeños, and avocados. Stir gently so as

not to smash the avocados. Refrigerate until chilled, up to 4 hours.

If using prawn crackers, fill a Dutch oven or heavy-bottomed stockpot with 2 inches of oil and clip a deep-fry thermometer to the side. Heat over medium-high heat to 350°F. Set a wire rack over a baking sheet. Drop 3 or 4 crackers into the hot oil, leaving room for them to expand, and cook until they puff up, about 15 seconds. Using a slotted spoon, transfer the crackers to the rack. Repeat with the remaining crackers, letting the oil return to 350°F between batches.

Transfer the shrimp to a serving bowl and serve chilled, with the prawn crackers alongside for dipping . . . or just eat the shrimp straight from the bowl.

Picture this: After a successful service slinging fried seafood for hours into the night, the mood was up, and we had enough roe left over to do celebratory caviar bumps—a common post-shift ritual. In the midst of all this, I remembered in a flash a dreamy *Condé Nast Traveler* article I'd rested my eyes on decades earlier. The issue highlighted Italy, and in one unforgettable photo, sturgeon caviar was lasciviously displayed resting delicately on the rim of a Peroni can. That night, as cans of Miller Lite made their way to our hands, a hillbilly version of what I'd often dreamed of was born. **Feeds up to 6**

TROUT ROE BEER

1 ounce trout roe

1 (6-pack) lager beer

Add a generous spoonful of caviar to the rim of each beer, just to the side of the can's mouth.

Immediately find some comfy chairs in the shade, preferably seaside, crack open a beer, and pound it, enjoying little bits of trout roe in each sip along the way.

I'm a strong advocate for the johnnycake as a workhorse party-bite vessel. It can stand up to the heartiest sauces and dips and is way more impressive and wow-inducing than your standard chips. Plus, they sit well at room temperature, so you can prepare them hours in advance and finish them as your guests trickle in. I find myself frying these up at events and food festivals to carry pretty much anything you could imagine. This recipe fully embraces the "make ahead" ethos with toppings that you can prepare far, far ahead of time: smoked trout, brown butter–coated sunflower seeds, and pickled watermelon rind. Together, they add up to all the flavors I find essential for appetizers: umami, saltiness, acidity, and sweetness. **Feeds 10 to 12**

SMOKED TROUT, SUNFLOWER SEEDS, AND WATERMELON RIND
ON A JOHNNYCAKE

For the Trout

½ cup kosher salt

½ cup packed light brown sugar

1 tablespoon red pepper flakes

8 (6- to 8-ounce) skin-on rainbow trout fillets

For the Pickled Watermelon Rind

3 cups apple cider vinegar

1 (3-inch) piece fresh ginger, peeled and halved

1 (2-inch) strip of orange rind

1 tablespoon coriander seeds

1 cinnamon stick

4 whole cloves

2 star anise pods

2½ cups granulated sugar

2 teaspoons kosher salt

Rind from 1 small watermelon, peeled and thinly sliced into 1 by 3-inch strips

For the Sunflower Seeds

½ cup sunflower seeds

½ cup (1 stick) unsalted butter

1 teaspoon kosher salt

Classic Johnnycakes (page 114), for serving

Make the trout: In a large nonreactive container, combine the salt, brown sugar, and red pepper flakes with 1 gallon of cool water and stir until the salt and sugar have dissolved. Add the trout fillets, being sure they are submerged, then allow them to brine in the refrigerator for 2 to 3 hours—any longer, and they'll get too salty.

Heat a smoker to 225°F.

Remove the fish from the brine and pat dry. Place the fish directly on the grill grates, skin-side down. Close the lid and smoke for 90 minutes to 2 hours, depending on the thickness of the fish, until the fish is opaque, tender, and easily flakes.

Meanwhile, make the pickled watermelon rind: In a Dutch oven set over medium-high heat, combine 2 cups water, the vinegar, ginger, orange rind, coriander, cinnamon stick, cloves, star anise, granulated sugar, and salt.

Recipe continues

Cover and bring to a boil, then reduce the heat to low and simmer for about 10 minutes. Add the watermelon rinds and continue to simmer, covered, until the rinds begin to turn translucent, about 45 minutes. Take care not to reduce the pickling liquid to the point of browning; if needed, add ½ cup more water and continue cooking. Use a slotted spoon to transfer 24 rind pieces to a baking sheet and let cool. Transfer the remaining rind and its pickling liquid to a glass jar and store in the fridge for up to 1 week. (For long-term storage, use the Hot Water Bath Canning technique on page 39.)

Make the sunflower seeds: In a medium skillet, cook the seeds over medium heat, stirring continuously, until golden brown and toasted, 3 to 4 minutes. Transfer the seeds to a cutting board and coarsely chop. In the same pan, add the butter and cook over medium heat, swirling the pan occasionally, until the butter is golden brown and smells nutty, 8 to 9 minutes. Remove the pan from the heat and stir in the salt and chopped seeds.

To assemble, flake the smoked trout on top of the johnnycakes. Add a few pieces of the pickled watermelon rind and spoon some brown butter sunflower seeds over the top. Arrange on a platter and serve.

These are easy, make-ahead dinner rolls that have saved me on many holidays. I've shown up to dinners last minute—late, even—with these in tow and have been deemed a savior. I've sent them off with a boss in a major Christmas crunch and likely hung on to my job a little longer for that very reason. Soft, simple, perfection. I suggest serving these with Country Ham Ramp Butter (page 65), apple butter mustard (see page 92), and Grape Jelly (page 160), but straight butter is great, too. **Makes 24 rolls**

CHRISTMAS YEAST ROLLS

2 cups whole milk

½ cup lukewarm water

3 tablespoons unsalted butter, at room temperature

2 tablespoons sugar

1 tablespoon kosher salt

2½ tablespoons instant yeast

6 cups all-purpose flour

Neutral oil, such as canola or grapeseed, for greasing

Clip a candy thermometer to the side of a small saucepan. Warm the milk over medium-low heat to 100° to 110°F. Transfer the warm milk to a stand mixer fitted with the paddle attachment and add the water, butter, sugar, salt, and yeast. Beat on low just to combine, about 1 minute, then let the mixture rest to activate the yeast. The mixture should become foamy and bubble in 7 to 8 minutes.

Add 5 cups of the flour to the mixture and beat on low just until a shaggy dough begins to form, 1 to 2 minutes. With the mixer running on medium-low, add the remaining flour, ¼ cup at a time, until a smooth dough ball forms, 6 to 7 minutes. The dough should appear smooth but feel sticky to the touch.

Lightly grease a medium bowl with oil and transfer the dough to it. Cover with a damp tea towel and set aside in a warm spot to rise for 20 minutes.

Deflate the puffed dough with a gentle fist and turn it out onto a clean work surface. Stretch the dough into a rough 8 by 12-inch rectangle. Divide the dough lengthwise into 4 even pieces. Using your hands, divide each portion into 6 equal pieces, for a total of 24 pieces.

Line a baking sheet with parchment paper. Grease your hands with a little bit of oil. Place one dough piece in the palm of one hand. With the pointer finger and thumb of your other hand, pinch the edges of the dough toward the center to tighten it into a ball shape. Seal the seam together with your fingers, then deftly place the ball seam-side down on the prepared baking sheet. Cover the ball with a tea towel and repeat with the rest of the dough pieces. Let the balls of dough rise for 20 minutes.

Preheat the oven to 375°F.

Bake the rolls for 20 to 25 minutes, until golden brown. Serve hot.

In culinary school, French technique was the be-all and end-all of cuisine, my education a whirlwind tour of béchamel, pâté, mille-feuille, and lots of other words I worked hard to pronounce correctly. Afterward, at home, with a renewed sense of culinary confidence, I was determined to show what those hard-earned dollars had been spent on. I'd suit up, apron crisp and knives sharp, ready to show off something professional and "real"—not Southern. Once, when I decided to fillet a whole salmon, my parents watched in sheer horror as I cleared the body of its skin with a clean *zzzzippppp*—off went the head, along with the carcass and tail, all skillfully intact. When I looked up, I didn't see the doting expression I'd expected. "Where the hell's the rest of the fish?" my dad shrieked in a way that was more confused than discouraging. My mom's refrains of "That's not how I taught you" and "Why are you doing it like that?" taught me that even with professional training and learned technique, I could never forget my roots—and that set me free. I started to think that, maybe, I could find a way to bridge the two worlds. In that vein, this sweet potato consommé recipe is that middle ground that I've come to embrace. **Feeds 4 to 6**

SWEET POTATO CONSOMMÉ

4 whole sweet potatoes

1 cinnamon stick

2 teaspoons whole cloves

2 teaspoons kosher salt

Freshly grated nutmeg, for serving

Preheat the oven to 400°F. Line a baking sheet with parchment paper.

Arrange the sweet potatoes on the prepared baking sheet and roast for 45 to 50 minutes, until fork-tender.

Transfer the roasted sweet potatoes to a large heavy-bottomed saucepan and add the cinnamon stick and cloves. Add enough water to just cover the potatoes. Slowly bring to a simmer over low heat, then cook, undisturbed,

until the liquid is a nice, clarified caramel color, about 1 hour. Remove the pot from the heat and carefully strain through a fine-mesh sieve set over a large bowl. Reserve the cooked sweet potatoes for another use (such as the Drunken Sweet Potato Pudding on page 148).

Stir the salt into the consommé. Ladle into bowls and finish with nutmeg before serving.

As a know-it-all seventeen-year-old, I felt I was destined to travel the world, exploring other cultures—and I did just that as soon as I got a chance, spending a gap year in Nairobi, Kenya, with other know-it-all, recently graduated teenagers. After some time there, the excitement over a new cultural experience waned, and I longed for the home I'd thought I'd never look back at again. Each night, I stuck to the hip of Gift, the cook in the home where I was staying, and we reveled in the unexpected connections we had in our ways of cooking and eating. In the American South, we season our greens and beans with cured meat; in Kenya, they use dried fish for the same purpose. One particular example threw me for a loop: in true Kenyan fashion, she once surprised me by physically—hand to mouth—feeding me kachumbari, a tomato salad that felt so much like home. I'll always remember that sudden intimacy, which made me feel so included in a place so far away. This version of that dish includes vodka and coconut milk, which combine in a rich, creamy sauce that's also punchy and bracing. **Feeds 6 to 8**

EGGPLANT VODKA KACHUMBARI

4 small eggplants, sliced into 1-inch-thick rounds

2 teaspoons kosher salt, plus more as needed

1 white onion, thinly sliced

Zest and juice of 1 lime

2 ounces vodka

2 teaspoons canola oil

¼ cup extra-virgin olive oil

½ cup full-fat coconut milk

4 Roma (plum) tomatoes, quartered

1 jalapeño, thinly sliced

2 ripe avocados, diced

1 English (hothouse) cucumber, thinly sliced

Flaky salt, for serving

Season the eggplant slices generously with salt, then place them in a colander. Set the colander in the sink to drain for about 45 minutes.

In a small bowl, combine the onion, the 2 teaspoons salt, lime zest, lime juice, and vodka.

Heat a grill to medium (400°F) or heat a grill pan over medium heat.

Pat the eggplant slices with a paper towel. Transfer them to a large bowl, add the canola oil, and toss to coat. Grill the eggplant over direct heat until blackened and charred in some spots, 3 to 4 minutes, flipping the eggplant halfway through. Return the eggplant to the bowl and let cool, then dice.

In a large bowl, whisk together the olive oil and coconut milk. Gently fold in the eggplant, tomatoes, jalapeño, avocados, and cucumber. Stir in the onion mixture. Divide the salad among plates and spoon the remaining vinaigrette over each. Finish with flaky salt and serve.

When it comes to food, I am all about the funk. The funk I'm referring to has nothing to do with George Clinton and everything to do with the pleasant yet slightly sour and cheesy smell of successful fermentation. This salad in particular provides an approachable level of funk from sprouted grains along with the nutty crunch of a salsa made from just about every seed in your cupboard. A bright, herbaceous chermoula brings them together to make a textural dream salad. Sprouting might seem daunting at first, but it's a simple process that takes only a few days and will lend umami to balance this dish and classify it as gut-healthy. **Feeds 4 to 6**

SPROUTED SORGHUM SALAD
WITH ALL-SEED SALSA

For the Sorghum Sprouts

2 cups whole-grain sorghum berries, soaked in water overnight

For the All-Seed Salsa

2 tablespoons mustard seeds

2 tablespoons sunflower seeds

2 tablespoons pumpkin seeds

2 tablespoons benne seeds

2 tablespoons fennel seeds

2 tablespoons poppy seeds

1 chile de árbol, crushed

½ cup chili oil

For the Chermoula

½ teaspoon coriander seeds, toasted and crushed

½ teaspoon cumin seeds, toasted and crushed

1 teaspoon black peppercorns, coarsely ground

½ cup packed fresh cilantro, minced

½ cup packed fresh parsley, minced

½ cup packed fresh mint leaves, minced

½ teaspoon freshly grated ginger

2 teaspoons lemon zest

2 teaspoons fresh lemon juice

1 teaspoon kosher salt

¼ cup extra-virgin olive oil

1 teaspoon red pepper flakes

2 cups chopped asparagus

Flaky salt, for serving

Make the sprouts: Drain the soaked sorghum and place in a sterilized ½-gallon jar with cool water to cover. Soak again overnight. Drain the grains, then transfer to a piece of cheesecloth and tie it closed with kitchen twine. Hang the satchel over a jar set on a plate and let stand in a warm spot, out of direct sunlight, until the sorghum begins to sprout, 4 to 5 days. Pour a few tablespoons of room-temperature water over the sorghum each day to prevent the grains from drying out. When the sprouts are about ½ inch long, remove them from the cheesecloth. Gently transfer to a fine-mesh sieve and rinse. Store in a paper towel–lined container in the fridge for up to 5 days.

Make the salsa: In a large skillet, combine the mustard seeds, sunflower seeds, pumpkin seeds, benne seeds, fennel seeds, and poppy seeds. Cook over medium-high heat, stirring continuously, until toasted and aromatic, 4 to 5 minutes. Remove from the heat and let cool. Stir in the chile de árbol. Add the chili oil and stir to coat.

Make the chermoula: In a small bowl, whisk together the coriander, cumin, black pepper, cilantro, parsley, mint, ginger, lemon zest, lemon juice, salt, olive oil, and red pepper flakes.

Working in batches, cook the asparagus in a large cast-iron skillet over medium-high heat, turning, until charred and blistered on all sides, 7 to 8 minutes. Transfer to a large bowl.

Add the sprouts and ¾ teaspoon of the chermoula and toss to coat well. Add more chermoula, if desired. Transfer the sprout mixture to a plate. Give the all-seed salsa a good stir, then drizzle it over the sprout mixture. Finish with flaky salt before serving.

With colder months come stews and hours-long braised meats. The dregs of the darkest season never seem to spell bright and fresh meals for the dinner table, but this salad does, and that's why it deserves some space. Just like the fruit and vegetables we get excited about in the warm months, winter's produce—sweetened by frost and housed in rich, cakey soil—is a miracle in itself. Winter spells crisp brassicas, flavorful root vegetables, and hearty fruits, and they deserve just as much love. This salad is white in appearance, but it's anything but bland. Pops of acid and crisp bites of pear stand up well to the fresh nuttiness of crunchy cauliflower, fennel, and radish. **Feeds 4 to 6**

WINTER WHITE SALAD

1 small head cauliflower, quartered and shaved on a mandoline

2 Asian pears, shaved on a mandoline

1 fennel bulb, shaved on a mandoline, fronds reserved for serving

1 cup shaved radish (use a mandoline)

1 cup extra-virgin olive oil

¼ cup white wine vinegar

2½ tablespoons Dijon mustard

2 tablespoons honey

2 teaspoons kosher salt

½ teaspoon freshly ground white pepper

In a large bowl, combine the cauliflower, pears, fennel, and radish. In a separate small bowl, whisk together the olive oil, vinegar, mustard, honey, salt, and white pepper. Pour the vinaigrette over the cauliflower mixture and toss to coat.

Divide the salad among bowls and garnish with the fennel fronds before serving.

I have my two-year stint on garde-manger duty at Cinghiale in Baltimore to thank for my stellar salad-making. Though I really wanted to master the grill or sauté station, the management there had a different path in mind for me, the greenest line cook. After I spent an entire service picking pickled pig's feet as a penalty for calling them "feet" and not "trotters," I realized their goal was to teach me to keep my head down and shut up. And so that's what I did, zeroing in on the slight gaps between the slippery skin, fat, cartilage, and membranes in the feet to free every wisp of meat with gloved fingers. Even without the feet, this labor-intensive salad involves cleaning wild fruit, preparing the lettuce and the dressing, and making fresh buttermilk cheese. But once you start eating it, this one-of-a-kind salad will clearly justify all the elbow grease. **Feeds 4 to 6**

WARM RADICCHIO SALAD
WITH PICKLED PIG'S FEET

For the Pig's Feet

2 cups distilled white vinegar

2 tablespoons Tabasco sauce

1 teaspoon mustard seeds

1 teaspoon celery seeds

1 teaspoon whole black peppercorns

2 tablespoons kosher salt

2 tablespoons sugar

4 pig's feet

2 bay leaves

For the Buttermilk Cheese

2 cups cultured buttermilk

4 cups whole milk

Zest and juice of 1 lemon

2 teaspoons kosher salt

2 teaspoons freshly cracked black pepper

For the Dressing

¼ cup Duke's mayonnaise

¼ cup red wine vinegar

1 tablespoon honey

¼ cup crushed walnuts, lightly toasted

2 teaspoons dried parsley

¼ teaspoon kosher salt

1 teaspoon freshly ground black pepper

½ cup extra-virgin olive oil

For Serving

2 heads radicchio, cored and quartered

1 cup blackberries, halved lengthwise

Freshly ground black pepper

Thinly sliced fresh chives

Pickle the pig's feet: In a large bowl, whisk together the vinegar, Tabasco, mustard seeds, celery seeds, peppercorns, salt, and sugar. Add the pig's feet. Cover and refrigerate for at least 2 days and up to 5 days; the longer they pickle, the more intense the briny flavor will become.

Remove the pig's feet from the brine and place them in a large stockpot along with the bay leaves. Add enough water to cover. Bring to a boil over high heat, then reduce the heat to medium-low and cook until tender, about 2 hours. Use a spoon to skim off and

reserve 2 tablespoons of fat from the top in a medium bowl, then use tongs to transfer the pig's feet to a large bowl of hot water. This will allow any excess fat to float to the top. Using a slotted spoon, skim any excess fat and discard. Drain and rinse the pig's feet and let cool slightly, then, when cool enough to handle, pick the meat from the feet. Place the meat on a plate and tent with aluminum foil to keep warm.

Make the cheese: Clip a candy thermometer to the side of a medium saucepan. Combine the buttermilk and milk in the pan over medium heat, and stir in the lemon zest, lemon juice, salt, and pepper. Heat the mixture to 125°F, without stirring, until the curds and whey begin separating, 7 to 8 minutes. Reduce the heat to low and simmer, undisturbed, until curds begin to form at the surface, about 3 minutes more. Remove from the heat.

Line a fine-mesh sieve with several layers of cheesecloth and set it over a large bowl. Using a ladle, begin to scoop the large curds into the strainer, letting the whey catch underneath. When the large curds have been removed, slowly pour the remaining whey with smaller curds into the strainer, taking care not to break the large curds. Let the cheese strain for 4 to 6 hours. Discard or reserve the whey for a later use.

Make the dressing: In the medium bowl with the reserved pork fat, add the mayonnaise, vinegar, honey, walnuts, dried parsley, salt, and pepper. Whisk to combine. Steady your bowl by placing a kitchen towel underneath it, and while whisking with one hand, slowly drizzle in the olive oil with the other, until the dressing thickens and emulsifies.

In a serving bowl, toss together the warm pig's feet meat, radicchio, and dressing. Gently fold in the blackberries and crumbled buttermilk cheese. Finish with black pepper and chives before serving.

Furikake is one of those condiments that makes your food come alive. It's a seaweed-sugar-sesame mixture that originated in Japan, and its use can be likened to the way we utilize salt and pepper in the United States. It enhances the flavor of and adds interest to whatever you sprinkle it on. Versions I've found in Asian grocers have included freeze-dried egg, miso, and even varieties of dried fish. Deeply inspired, I've made my own combinations that have included dried shrimp, dried collards, and—as this recipe does—crispy chicken skin. Here, it levels up the root vegetables, and I encourage you to use it generously and liberally. **Feeds 6 to 8**

ROASTED ROOT VEGETABLES
WITH CHICKEN SKIN FURIKAKE

For the Root Vegetables

6 cups chopped root vegetables (such as sweet potatoes, purple carrots, and/or parsnips)

2 yellow onions, chopped

1 teaspoon kosher salt

2 teaspoons canola oil

For the Chicken Skin Furikake

1 tablespoon benne seeds, toasted and lightly ground

1 teaspoon kosher salt

½ teaspoon sugar

¼ teaspoon paprika

⅛ teaspoon red pepper flakes

Raw chicken skin (pulled from a few breasts and/or thighs)

Make the root vegetables: Arrange racks in the upper and lower thirds of the oven. Preheat the oven to 450°F.

In a large bowl, toss the root vegetables and onions with the salt and oil to coat well. Arrange the vegetables on a baking sheet in an even layer. Place on the bottom rack and bake for 45 to 50 minutes, until golden brown and fork-tender.

Meanwhile, make the furikake: In a small bowl, stir together the benne seeds, salt, sugar, paprika, and red pepper flakes. Using a paper towel, pat the chicken skins dry. Place them on a baking sheet and sprinkle with the seasoning mixture. Place the baking sheet on the top rack and bake for 12 to 15 minutes, until golden and crispy. Remove from the oven and let cool. Place the chicken skins on a cutting board and coarsely chop. Transfer to a medium bowl.

To serve, transfer the vegetables to a serving bowl, sprinkle with the chicken skin furikake, and toss to coat well.

Now, don't get me wrong: I don't know much about Alabama barbecue, though a random stop at Archibald & Woodrow's BBQ in Tuscaloosa turned me into a lifelong fan of white BBQ sauce. Sure, my style hangs closer to the Carolinas between Lexington Dip and Carolina Gold, but this one snatched from Alabama shows major versatility. Here, my version of the classic tangy, peppery sauce is slathered all over ultra-crunchy, crispy, caramelized sweet potatoes. Acidic, juicy bites of beet chow chow turn up the volume on this dish. I eat a lot of sweet potatoes, and I can't imagine any better way to cook them.

Makes 10 pieces

LOADED TWICE-BAKED SWEET POTATOES WITH SPICY BEET CHOW CHOW AND WHITE BBQ SAUCE

For the Sweet Potatoes

6 medium sweet potatoes

2 teaspoons neutral oil, such as canola or grapeseed

½ cup plain full-fat Greek yogurt

2 tablespoons tahini

½ teaspoon ground sumac

½ teaspoon ground cinnamon

1 teaspoon kosher salt

½ teaspoon freshly ground black pepper

For the White BBQ Sauce

½ cup Duke's mayonnaise

2 teaspoons distilled white vinegar

2 teaspoons light brown sugar

1 tablespoon yellow mustard

½ teaspoon fresh lemon juice

2 teaspoons prepared horseradish

1 teaspoon kosher salt

1 teaspoon freshly ground black pepper

¼ teaspoon paprika

⅛ teaspoon cayenne pepper

1 cup Spicy Beet Chow Chow (page 54)

Thinly sliced fresh chives, for garnish

Make the sweet potatoes: Preheat the oven to 400°F. Line a baking sheet with parchment paper.

Toss the sweet potatoes with the oil and place on the prepared baking sheet. Roast for 45 to 50 minutes, until fork-tender. Remove from the oven and let cool; leave the oven on.

Use a paring knife to split the sweet potatoes and scoop the flesh from two halves into a medium bowl, removing all the flesh and discarding the skins. Scoop the flesh from the remaining halves, but leave some attached to the skins; reserve the skins. Add the yogurt, tahini, sumac, cinnamon, salt, and pepper to the bowl with the sweet

potato flesh and use a potato masher or ricer to combine until smooth.

Generously stuff the 10 potato skins with the yogurt mixture, heaping it in, and return them to the baking sheet. Bake for about 15 minutes, until the stuffing begins to brown.

Meanwhile, make the BBQ sauce: In a small bowl, whisk together the mayo, vinegar, brown sugar, mustard, lemon juice, horseradish, salt, black pepper, paprika, and cayenne until smooth.

To serve, top the potatoes with a generous helping of chow chow and a drizzle of white BBQ sauce. Garnish with chives.

I grew up eating grits more than any other food. I'd seen them soaked overnight, slowly cooked in a double boiler, made in a pressure cooker, and oftentimes blasted in a microwave. Never about looks or glam, this was the go-to, stick-to-your ribs breakfast we relied on. Before I even had a sense of the term "Southern food," I knew grits as our breakfast. But maybe, like me, you've grown to crave more variety in your life. This sort of set-it-and-forget-it version, in which I swap out grits for rolled oats, is full of all one might find on a Southerner's morning table. They're swimming with greens, likely from the night before, and chock-full of hard-boiled eggs. Sausage-studded white gravy (an obscure type found only in the Deep South) adds depth and creaminess. **Feeds 8 to 10**

BAKED SAVORY OATS
WITH SAUSAGE AND EGG GRAVY

For the Oats

5 large eggs

2 teaspoons kosher salt

1 tablespoon extra-virgin olive oil

3 tablespoons unsalted butter

1 yellow onion, minced

2 garlic cloves, minced

1½ teaspoons freshly ground black pepper

1 bunch kale, leaves stemmed and finely chopped

1 cup whole milk

1 cup heavy cream

½ cup freshly grated Parmesan cheese

2 cups rolled oats

For the Gravy

4 ounces pork sausage, casings removed if using links

1 tablespoon unsalted butter

1 tablespoon all-purpose flour

1½ cups whole milk

¼ teaspoon kosher salt

½ teaspoon freshly cracked black pepper, plus more for serving

Tabasco sauce, for serving

Make the oats: Preheat the oven to 350°F.

Fill a large bowl with ice and water and set it near the stove. Place the eggs in a small pot of water with 1 teaspoon of the salt, then bring to a boil over high heat. When the water comes to a boil, turn off the heat and cover, then set a timer for 9 minutes. Remove the eggs with a slotted spoon and transfer to the ice bath to cool.

When the eggs are cool enough to handle, peel them and set one aside for garnish. Chop the remaining 4 eggs and set aside for the gravy.

Heat the olive oil and 1 tablespoon of the butter in a Dutch oven over medium heat. When the oil is just smoking, add the onion and cook, stirring occasionally, until slightly softened, 3 to 4 minutes. Add the garlic

Recipe continues

and cook until fragrant, about 1 minute more. Stir in the remaining 1 teaspoon salt and the pepper. Working in batches, add the kale and cook, stirring to wilt, for 5 to 6 minutes. Stir in the milk, cream, Parmesan, oats, and remaining 2 tablespoons butter.

Transfer the pot to the oven and bake, uncovered, for 20 to 30 minutes, until the oats have set and thickened.

Meanwhile, make the gravy: In a large cast-iron skillet, cook the sausage over medium heat, crumbling with a wooden spoon, until the meat is cooked through and the fat is completely rendered, 10 to 12 minutes. Do not drain the fat from the skillet.

Add the butter and flour to the skillet with the sausage and cook, stirring, until a roux forms and the flour becomes golden and toasty, about 2 minutes. Whisk in the milk, scraping up any browned bits from the bottom of the pan. Reduce the heat to low and simmer, stirring, until the gravy thickens, about 10 minutes. Season the gravy with the salt and pepper, then gently fold in the reserved chopped eggs.

Remove the pot from the oven. Slice the reserved hard-boiled egg. Top the oats with the gravy and garnish with the sliced egg, then serve. Set Tabasco and a pepper mill on the table for folks to season their own plates.

By now you've gauged the importance of the magical potion that is potlikker; if so, you can be considered a Southern culinary–literate cook. Potlikker is said to be healing, with the thought that the green color of the liquid is made up of nutrient richness and minerals removed from the cooking process. My great-aunts allegedly snuck potlikker into my baby bottle despite my mom's skepticism of its benefits. The science isn't conclusive, but would aunties lie? In any case, this broody green goodness serves as the foundation of my cooking. To me, it is what master stock is to a chef in China, or, even more so, what demi-glace is to a French chef de cuisine. Its flavor-packed goodness can serve as a stock substitute and simplifies the making of flavorful gravies, which this recipe will readily prove. **Feeds 6 to 8**

TURKEY WINGS
WITH POTLIKKER GRAVY

For the Wings

6 whole turkey wings (about 5 pounds total), or 7 turkey wings without the tips

2 teaspoons canola oil

2 teaspoons kosher salt

For the Potlikker

1 teaspoon canola oil

1 pound smoked turkey seasoning meat (necks, tails, etc.)

1 cup packed chopped stemmed collards or kale leaves

1 yellow onion, halved

3 garlic cloves

2 teaspoons mustard seeds

2 teaspoons whole black peppercorns

1 bay leaf

1 tablespoon apple cider vinegar

For the Gravy

3 tablespoons all-purpose flour

1 teaspoon kosher salt

1 teaspoon freshly ground black pepper

Make the wings: Preheat the oven to 300°F.

Using a paring knife, separate each turkey wing into 3 segments: the drumette, the flat, and the tip. Set aside the tips. Place the drumettes and flats in a roasting pan, add the canola oil and salt, and toss to coat evenly. Arrange skin-side up, cover, and roast for 2 hours, until tender and cooked through.

Meanwhile, make the potlikker: Heat the oil in a Dutch oven over medium-high heat. Add the reserved wing tips and cook, turning until golden brown all over, 5 to 6 minutes. Add the turkey seasoning meat, greens, onion, garlic, mustard seeds, peppercorns, bay leaf, vinegar, and 4 cups water. Give it a stir, being sure everything is submerged. Increase the heat to high and bring to a boil, then reduce the heat to low and partially cover the pot. Cook for 45 minutes, until the seasoning meat is

Recipe continues

tender and easily breaks apart. (If it doesn't, cover and simmer for 10 minutes more, then check again.)

Strain the potlikker through a fine-mesh sieve into a large bowl and discard the solids. Measure out and reserve 3 cups of the potlikker; discard or save any remaining potlikker for another use (such as the chowder on page 121).

Set a wire rack over a rimmed baking sheet. Remove the turkey wings from the oven and turn the temperature to broil. Pour 3 tablespoons of the drippings from the pan into a medium saucepan and set aside. Transfer the wings to the prepared rack and broil until crispy and browned, 4 to 5 minutes, checking often to make sure the wings don't burn. Remove from the oven.

Make the gravy: Add the flour to the reserved drippings in the saucepan and cook over medium-low heat, whisking continuously, until the mixture develops a blond color, 2 to 3 minutes. Whisk in the reserved potlikker, 1 cup at a time, then stir in the salt and pepper. Cook over low heat, stirring occasionally, until the gravy thickens, 7 to 8 minutes.

Transfer the wings to a platter, spoon the gravy over the top, and serve.

I do have a thing for brassicas, never needing to be told to eat more of them. I could enjoy any member of that family of vegetables raw in a salad, but roasting them until caramelized, lifting their natural sugars, is my favorite method. They are readily available everywhere, but there are still nuances; ideally, find some from a local farm once they've been hit by the season's frost, which converts their natural starches into sugar. Cauliflower, nutty and earthy, holds up well to many cooking methods. Roasting it as in this recipe keeps the center tender and allows the outside to develop a nice caramelization. Acidic, sweet, and herbaceous gremolata makes this already fine dish even better. **Feeds 4**

SPICE-ROASTED CAULIFLOWER
WITH GREEN OLIVE–GOLDEN RAISIN GREMOLATA

For the Cauliflower

1 large head cauliflower, quartered through the core

2 teaspoons extra-virgin olive oil

2 teaspoons kosher salt

1 teaspoon ground turmeric

½ teaspoon ground cumin

½ teaspoon ground coriander

For the Gremolata

¼ cup extra-virgin olive oil

½ cup minced fresh parsley

1 shallot, minced

3 tablespoons brined capers, drained and minced

Zest and juice of 1 orange

½ cup golden raisins, minced

¼ cup pine nuts, toasted and chopped

½ cup Castelvetrano olives, pitted and minced

½ cup Cerignola olives, pitted and minced

Make the cauliflower: Preheat the oven to 450°F. Line a baking sheet with parchment paper.

In a large bowl, toss the cauliflower with the olive oil, salt, turmeric, cumin, and coriander. Spread in a single layer on the prepared baking sheet. Roast for 40 to 45 minutes, until golden brown.

Meanwhile, make the gremolata: In a medium bowl, combine the olive oil, parsley, shallot, capers, orange zest and juice, raisins, pine nuts, and all the olives. Stir to mix well.

Plate the cauliflower, drizzle each with the gremolata, and serve.

Fun to hook and even better to eat, flounder is a great catch in Virginia waters. With a sweet and clean taste, this staple is best prepared in pretty simple ways. Even as a child, I noticed the irresistible flavors that resulted when my flounder picked up the sticky syrup of the sweet potatoes on my plate and swam with the potlikker from my greens. This recipe makes the most of that magic combination. With that, you've no need for fancy sides—I'd go for rice (see page 45) or a bright, green salad. **Feeds 4**

HAM HOCK—GLAZED FLOUNDER

For the Glaze

1 ham hock

1 (1-inch) knob fresh ginger, peeled and
   chopped

½ teaspoon whole cloves

1 teaspoon whole white peppercorns

1 garlic clove

½ cup fresh orange juice

3 tablespoons packed dark brown sugar

½ cup sorghum molasses

2 tablespoons Dijon mustard

1 tablespoon fresh lemon juice

For the Fish

1 (1- to 1½-pound) flounder fillet, cut into
   4 pieces

2 teaspoons extra-virgin olive oil

2 teaspoons kosher salt

1 lemon, thinly sliced

1 cup sugar snap peas

½ teaspoon freshly ground white pepper

Make the glaze: In a high-sided medium saucepan, combine the ham hock, ginger, cloves, white peppercorns, and garlic. Add enough water just to cover the ham hock. Bring to a boil over high heat, then reduce the heat to medium and partially cover the pot. Cook for 40 to 45 minutes, until the meat begins falling from the bone. Use tongs to remove the ham hock and set aside on a plate to cool.

Add the orange juice, brown sugar, sorghum, mustard, and lemon juice to the liquid in the pot. Bring the mixture to a boil over high heat. Boil for 20 seconds, then reduce the heat to medium and simmer for 20 to 25 minutes, until the glaze is thick enough to coat the back of a spoon. Remove the pot from the heat.

Make the fish: Preheat the oven to 425°F. Line a baking sheet with parchment paper.

Pat the flounder dry with paper towels. Drizzle with olive oil, then season on both sides with the salt. Arrange the fillets, lemon slices, and snap peas on the prepared baking sheet. Bake for 4 to 5 minutes, then remove from the oven and turn the temperature to broil. Brush the fillets generously with the ham hock glaze, then broil them until the fish is flaky and the edges are golden, 1 to 2 minutes, watching them carefully so they do not burn. Remove from the oven.

Brush the fillets with more glaze and season with the white pepper. Discard the lemon slices. Carefully transfer the fillets to individual plates.

Pick the meat from the ham hock, placing it in a small bowl. Transfer the snap peas to the bowl with the ham and stir to combine. Add a portion of the ham and snap peas to each plate and serve.

Muscadine grapes have a thick, tannic skin and plenty of seeds. The best way to remove the seeds is to use a pair of tweezers or a fork to pop them out after slicing the grapes in half. It's actually a fair amount of work to get to the goods of a muscadine, but the addictive, mouth-puckering juice is absolutely worthy of the labor. Paired with succulent, pan-seared duck breast, the acidity of the grapes and bitterness of the greens complement the fattiness of the bird. If you don't have the fortune of living in muscadine country, save this recipe for when you find yourself there. Regular grapes won't cut it—it's worth using the real thing here. **Feeds 4**

DUCK BREAST, MELTED MUSCADINE GRAPES, AND BITTER GREENS

4 duck breasts

3 teaspoons kosher salt

1 pound muscadine grapes, halved and seeded

2 teaspoons freshly ground black pepper

1 leek, white and light green parts only, well washed and minced

4 cups chopped turnip greens, mustard greens, or dandelion greens

1 tablespoon fresh lemon juice

Flaky salt, for serving

Using a paring knife, score the duck skin on an angle in a crosshatch pattern, spacing the cuts ⅛ inch apart and being careful not to pierce through to the flesh. Pat dry and season evenly on both sides with 2 teaspoons of the salt. Place the duck skin-side down in a medium skillet. Cook over low heat, pressing down on the duck to ensure the skin makes direct contact with the pan, until the fat is rendered, about 10 minutes.

Transfer the duck to a plate. Carefully pour the fat from the pan into a heatproof bowl and reserve, then return the duck to the pan, skin-side down. Increase the heat to medium and cook until the duck lifts easily from the pan and the skin is golden brown, 4 to 5 minutes. Flip and

cook on the flesh side for 30 seconds, then transfer to a cutting board to rest.

In the same pan, combine the grapes, the remaining 1 teaspoon salt, and the pepper. Cook over medium heat, stirring occasionally, until the grapes blister and wilt, about 7 minutes. Add the leek and 2 teaspoons of the reserved duck fat. Reduce the heat to low and cook until the leek is soft and translucent, 5 to 6 minutes more. Add the greens and lemon juice and cook, stirring, until the greens are wilted, about 3 minutes more.

Divide the grape mixture among four plates. Slice the duck breasts and place one on top of each serving. Finish with flaky salt.

When I think of summer, my mind is consumed with memories of aromatic juices running from fruit at the peak of their ripeness. Throughout my childhood, any family gathering was made complete by a bowl of freshly cut melon studded with berries at the end of the buffet table. In my rush to clean my plate so I could run off and play with my cousins, I'd carelessly swipe forkfuls of grilled seafood through streams of fruit juice on the way to my mouth. That counterintuitive pairing stuck with me, and I later saw similarities between other salt-and-sweet combinations: prosciutto and cantaloupe, Tajín and mango. This recipe is part of that long-standing tradition, pairing briny, gingery shrimp with the concentrated sweetness of grilled peaches and watermelon. **Feeds 4**

GINGERED SHRIMP, WATERMELON, AND PEACH SKEWERS

For the Shrimp

¼ cup grapeseed oil

1 tablespoon fish sauce

¼ cup packed dark brown sugar

1 (3-inch) knob fresh ginger, peeled and grated

3 garlic cloves

1 habanero chile, seeded

Juice of 3 limes

1 fresh lemongrass stalk, chopped

1 pound shrimp (preferably 21/25 red shrimp), peeled and deveined

For the Skewers

1 tablespoon olive oil

Zest and juice of 2 limes

1 teaspoon kosher salt

4 peaches, pitted and cut into 1-inch chunks

4 cups chopped watermelon (1-inch cubes)

Make the shrimp: In a small glass bowl, whisk together the grapeseed oil, fish sauce, brown sugar, ginger, garlic, chile, and lime juice. Bruise the lemongrass using the flat side of a butcher's knife to release its fragrance, then add it to the marinade. Add the shrimp and toss to coat. Allow the shrimp to marinate in the refrigerator for at least 1 hour or up to 2 hours.

Assemble the skewers: At least 30 minutes before you plan to grill, soak eight 10-inch wooden skewers in water to prevent them from burning; drain before using.

Heat a grill to medium-high (about 400°F) or heat a grill pan over medium-high heat.

In a large bowl, whisk together the olive oil, lime zest, lime juice, and salt. Add the peaches and watermelon and gently toss to coat.

Thread 4 shrimp on a skewer, piercing them through the tail and again through their thickest part; repeat with the remaining shrimp.

Thread the peach and watermelon cubes on skewers, alternating them as you go.

Grill the skewers over direct heat until the fruit is charred and the shrimp are no longer opaque, 2 to 3 minutes on each side. Remove from the grill. Remove and discard the skewers. Transfer the shrimp and fruit to a serving platter and enjoy.

I take research and development seriously. So while opening my first restaurant, Good Hot Fish, I also took a part-time job as a cook at a well-known fast-food franchise in Asheville—I wanted to learn the ins and outs of quick, consistent service to complement my fine-dining background. When I'm in, I'm all in, and another product of my research was these trout fingers. I set out to make a convenient, handheld version of one of my favorite childhood treats and landed on this very grown-up version of fish sticks. These fishy fingers hold their crunch well, turning fried fish into a handy grab-and-go snack. Try them (and any other fried thing, actually) slathered in creek sauce, which I created to be the mountain version of Alabama white sauce or Carolina Gold BBQ sauce. I wanted to make a version we could claim. Its tang meets the demand of an all-purpose sauce, and the sweetness is crowd-pleasing. Slather it on anything, not just fish. **Feeds 4 to 6**

CRISPY TROUT FINGERS
WITH CREEK SAUCE

For the Creek Sauce

1 cup Duke's mayonnaise

3 tablespoons buttermilk

¼ cup minced Foolproof Fridge Pickles (page 157)

4 parsley sprigs, minced

1 garlic clove, grated

1 teaspoon freshly ground black pepper

1 teaspoon paprika

½ teaspoon kosher salt

For the Trout

1 (1½-pound) steelhead trout fillet

2 teaspoons kosher salt

Neutral oil, such as canola or grapeseed, for frying

1 cup all-purpose flour

¼ cup rice flour

¼ cup fine yellow cornmeal

1 tablespoon Tajín seasoning

½ teaspoon dried sage

½ teaspoon dried parsley

½ teaspoon freshly ground black pepper

Lemon wedges, for serving

Make the creek sauce: In a small bowl, whisk together the mayonnaise, buttermilk, pickles, parsley, garlic, pepper, paprika, and salt. Cover and refrigerate until ready to serve.

Make the trout: Pat the trout fillet dry with a paper towel. Slice it with the grain into 1-inch-wide strips to make 12 "fingers." Season the trout fingers evenly with 1 teaspoon of the salt.

Fill a Dutch oven with 1 inch of oil and clip a deep-fry thermometer to the side. Heat the oil over medium heat to 375°F. Set a wire rack over a rimmed baking sheet.

Meanwhile, in a large bowl, combine the remaining 1 teaspoon salt, the all-purpose flour, rice flour, cornmeal, Tajín, sage, parsley, and pepper. Dredge each trout finger in the flour mixture, turning to coat and pressing to adhere, then shake off the excess. Working in batches, slowly add the breaded trout to the hot oil. Cook, flipping occasionally, until crispy and golden brown, 3 to 4 minutes. Transfer to the rack to drain. Repeat with the remaining trout, allowing the oil to return to 375°F between batches.

Serve the trout fingers with a side of creek sauce for dipping and lemon wedges for squeezing.

Watching the labor of love that is my wife preparing mole from scratch—that's what pretty much sealed the deal for me. I'm hundreds of moles in by now, and I'm never looking back. If you know anything about mole, you know making it is an undertaking that requires tending to each ingredient individually and with care. The process is long; if someone offers you this gift, I can assure you, they're in love. This dish is inspired by the peanut butter–based green mole that my wife's dad grew up eating in northwestern Mexico, which was often paired with small game. **Feeds 4 to 6**

RABBIT IN OKRA MOLE

2 poblano chiles

1 white onion, quartered

4 tomatillos, papery husks removed

1 cinnamon stick

2 whole cloves

6 rabbit legs

4 Mexican oregano sprigs

2 teaspoons kosher salt, plus more to taste

1 pound okra

1 teaspoon cumin seeds

1 teaspoon coriander seeds

1 teaspoon whole black peppercorns

¼ cup shelled raw peanuts

1 serrano chile, seeded and coarsely chopped

3 garlic cloves, peeled

¼ cup packed chopped fresh cilantro

1 tablespoon canola oil

Freshly cracked black pepper

For Serving

Charleston Ice Cream (page 45)

¼ cup thinly shaved white onion, soaked in cold water for 5 minutes, drained, and rinsed

Using tongs, char the poblanos, onion quarters, and tomatillos over an open flame or in an oven-safe pan under the broiler until blackened and charred all over, turning constantly, 2 to 3 minutes total. Set the onion quarters and tomatillos aside to cool. Transfer the poblanos to an airtight container or a paper bag, seal, and set aside to cool.

In a small pan, toast the cinnamon stick and cloves over medium-low heat, stirring continuously, until aromatic and fragrant, 2 to 3 minutes. Remove from the pan. Transfer the onion and tomatillos to a large stockpot. Add the rabbit legs, cinnamon, cloves, oregano, salt, and just enough

water to cover. When the poblanos are cool enough to handle, peel off their charred skins under running water, discarding the skins, then add the chiles to the pot. Bring to a boil over high heat, then reduce the heat to low, cover, and cook until the rabbit is tender and falling off the bone, about 2 hours.

Transfer the rabbit to a plate and let cool. Strain the cooking liquid through a colander set over a large bowl. Discard the cinnamon stick and cloves, then transfer the remaining solids to a blender along with 2 cups of the strained cooking liquid. Blend on medium speed until smooth, about 1 minute, then pour the pureed tomatillo

Recipe continues

mixture through a fine-mesh sieve set over a large bowl, using a ladle to gently push it through the sieve. Discard any lingering bits that are too big to pass through the sieve and stir in an additional 1 cup of the cooking liquid (reserve the remaining cooking liquid for the sauce). Set the strained tomatillo mixture aside and clean out the blender.

When the rabbit is cool enough to handle, shred the meat, discarding the bones.

Split the okra pods lengthwise and, using a small spoon or tweezer, free the okra seeds from the center membrane, reserving the okra scraps. Place the seeds in a small sauté pan and cook over medium heat, stirring continuously, until dried out, brown, and aromatic, about 5 minutes. Remove the okra seeds from the pan and let cool.

In the same pan, toast the cumin, coriander, and peppercorns over medium heat, stirring continuously, until aromatic and fragrant, 2 to 3 minutes. Remove from the pan. Repeat with the peanuts, toasting them for 4 to 5 minutes.

Set aside 2 tablespoons of the toasted okra seeds. Place the remainder in the blender along with the toasted spices, toasted peanuts, okra scraps, serrano, garlic, cilantro, and 1 cup of the reserved cooking liquid. Blend on high speed until smoothly pureed, adding more cooking liquid as needed, about 2 minutes.

Heat the canola oil in a large saucepan over medium-high heat. When it shimmers, carefully add the blended okra mixture. Cook, stirring often, until the sauce darkens and thickens, about 10 minutes. Stir in the strained tomatillo mixture, then reduce the heat to low. Simmer, uncovered, until the sauce thickens, 25 to 30 minutes. Stir in the rabbit meat and cook until the meat is heated through and incorporated into the sauce, about 15 minutes more. Taste and season with more salt and pepper.

Serve the mole over rice, garnishing each serving with some of the reserved toasted okra seeds and shaved white onion.

Soon after my short stint as a teenaged bartender began, I naturally gravitated toward the kitchen in search of more recklessness. By the time I turned seventeen, I had five months of kitchen experience and already felt like a real badass, a true back-of-house veteran. If things were slow, I'd happily and hungrily bop into the kitchen with as many cold Heinekens as I could fit between my fingers, trading beers for time on the hot line. My creation of this sandwich—featuring what I called fried chicken mayo—earned me the ridiculous nickname of FCM among my white coworkers. The "joke" was that I was fried chicken on the outside (Black) and mayo on the inside (white). To save face, I chuckled alongside them. But inside, I soaked up this reminder that culturally I was different—that because I defied their stereotypes, I was someone to ridicule. Since then, in my commitment to establish better workplaces for us all, I've worked hard to not just grow a thick skin but to call out these moments when they arise. That said, the frustrating thing was that this was a damn good sandwich! For me, that's what always mattered the most. **Feeds 4**

HOT CHICKEN BURGER
WITH FRIED CHICKEN MAYO

For the Marinated Chicken

2 boneless, skin-on chicken breasts

1 cup buttermilk

1 teaspoon kosher salt

½ teaspoon freshly cracked black pepper

For the Spice Mix

1 teaspoon cayenne pepper

½ teaspoon kosher salt

½ teaspoon paprika

¼ teaspoon chile powder

¼ teaspoon ground mustard

¼ teaspoon garlic powder

¼ teaspoon onion powder

For Breading and Frying

1 large egg

2 dashes of hot sauce

1 cup all-purpose flour

½ teaspoon kosher salt

1 teaspoon freshly cracked black pepper

Peanut oil or canola oil, for frying

For the Fried Chicken Mayo

1 large egg, at room temperature

2 teaspoons distilled white vinegar

¼ cup canola oil

Kosher salt

For the Cheese Spread

2 ounces cream cheese, at room temperature

2 ounces Gorgonzola cheese, at room temperature

¼ cup shredded cheddar cheese

1 tablespoon honey

¼ teaspoon red pepper flakes

For Serving

4 sesame seed buns

Finely shredded iceberg lettuce

½ cup Foolproof Fridge Pickles (page 157)

Recipe continues

Prepare the chicken: Preheat the oven to 450°F. Line a baking sheet with parchment paper.

Remove the chicken skins from the breasts and lay the skins flat in an even layer on the prepared baking sheet. Roast for 8 to 10 minutes, until the skins are crisp and golden brown. Pour off the chicken fat into a bowl and set the skins and fat aside to cool, then refrigerate them until needed.

Place the chicken breasts on a clean cutting board. Trim off and reserve any fat. Butterfly the chicken breasts, then slice them in half down the center, creating 4 very thin cutlets.

In a medium bowl, whisk together the buttermilk, salt, and pepper. Carefully add the chicken cutlets, then cover the bowl and marinate in the refrigerator for at least 3 hours or up to 8 hours.

Make the spice mix: In a small bowl, stir together the cayenne, salt, paprika, chile powder, ground mustard, garlic powder, and onion powder.

Set up your fry station: In a small bowl, whisk together the egg and hot sauce. In a large bowl, combine the flour, salt, and pepper.

Remove the chicken cutlets from the buttermilk, place them on a plate, and pat dry with paper towels.

Line up the chicken, egg mixture, and flour mixture in a row next to the stove. Set a clean wire rack over a baking sheet and set it nearby. Fill a Dutch oven or high-sided heavy-bottomed skillet with 1 inch of peanut oil and clip a deep-fry thermometer to the side. Heat the oil over medium-high heat to 350°F.

Working with one piece at a time, dip a chicken cutlet into the egg mixture and let any excess drip off, then press it into the flour mixture, turning to coat. Add the coated chicken to the hot oil and cook, flipping occasionally, until golden brown and crispy, 4 to 5 minutes. Transfer the chicken to the rack and immediately sprinkle generously with the spice mix. Repeat with the remaining chicken, allowing the oil to return to 350°F between batches.

Pull out your chicken skins and refresh them in the hot oil until crispy again, up to 2 minutes. Transfer the crispy chicken skins to the rack or to a plate lined with paper towels to drain.

Make the mayonnaise: In a blender, combine the egg, vinegar, and reserved rendered chicken fat. With the blender running on medium speed, very slowly pour in the canola oil in a thin, steady stream; the mixture will thicken. Transfer the mayo to a medium bowl.

Place the crispy chicken skins on a cutting board and crush them using the flat side of your knife. Fold the skin pieces into the mayonnaise, season with salt to taste, and set aside.

Make the cheese spread: In a small bowl, stir together the cream cheese, Gorgonzola, cheddar, honey, and red pepper flakes until well incorporated.

To assemble the burgers, slather the mayo on the bottom half of each bun. Top each with a chicken cutlet. Follow up with shredded lettuce, then pickles. Spread a generous amount of the cheese spread on the bun tops. Close up the burgers and enjoy.

I call spoonbread the unicorn of cornbread because of how special it is in an otherwise very casual genre of food. Its eggy, pudding-like texture distinguishes it, and traditional versions are baked in a soufflé, requiring extra care and a watchful eye. I finally nailed the plush, soufflé-like texture during my time as chef de cuisine at Benne on Eagle, after hotel pan after hotel pan of trial and error—Edna Lewis would have been proud. Once, for a restaurant special at a dinner service, I thought to create a dish that saw spoonbread baked inside of fish with a kind of complicated shiso-citrus butter. It was popular but time-consuming, which drove me to create this simpler but still stellar at-home version. The crab spoonbread provides a nice airy bite while maintaining its fluffiness, supplying a textural counterpoint to the well-seasoned roasted trout. I love a leafy green salad alongside this dish. **Feeds 4**

WHOLE TROUT STUFFED
WITH CRAB SPOONBREAD

For the Spoonbread

3 large eggs, separated, at room temperature

1 cup coarse yellow cornmeal

1 teaspoon baking powder

2 teaspoons kosher salt

4 tablespoons (½ stick) unsalted butter

½ cup boiling water

1 cup buttermilk, at room temperature

8 ounces jumbo lump crabmeat, picked over

½ cup sliced scallions (green parts only)

For the Trout

4 whole rainbow or golden trout, gutted, cleaned, and butterflied

1 tablespoon kosher salt

2 tablespoons extra-virgin olive oil

Make the spoonbread: Preheat the oven to 375°F.

In a medium bowl, beat the egg whites to soft peaks with a whisk. Place the egg yolks in a small bowl and lightly beat them with a fork. In a medium pot, whisk together the cornmeal, baking powder, salt, butter, and boiling water. Slowly whisk in the buttermilk. Cook over medium-low heat, stirring continuously to prevent the bottom of the pot from scorching and adding more water if the mixture becomes too thick to stir, until the cornmeal takes on the texture of mashed potatoes, about 30 minutes. Remove from the heat and let cool, then slowly drizzle in the beaten egg yolks and fold them into the mixture. Fold in the crabmeat and scallions, then gently fold in the egg whites.

Make the trout: Generously salt the trout inside and out. Stuff the cavity of each trout with the spoonbread mixture, dividing it evenly, and tie the fish closed with kitchen twine (or thread with skewers to hold closed). Drizzle the fish with the olive oil and bake until the fish is a bit browned and the flesh flakes easily, about 30 minutes. Remove from the oven and snip and discard the kitchen twine.

Transfer the stuffed fish to a serving platter and serve.

Potpie was always a welcome addition to our table. My mom often fitted flaky crusts onto skillets of chicken goulash, steak and cheese, and other variations that had likely come from the pages of an old issue of *Taste of Home*. While this was indeed a stealthy way to get me to eat vegetables, I simply saw these crispy shells as a catchall for the velvety sauces and gravies my taste buds had the pleasure of bearing witness to. My mom is the longest-reigning gravy queen of all time, and I assure you my research is up to date. While this recipe won't reveal her secret for whipping up a stunningly lump-free version in under ten minutes, it will lead you to a technique that yields something rich and soul-warming nonetheless. Next time you're in the mood, skip over the usual chicken potpie and give this hearty, earthy, decadent pie a go instead. **Feeds 6 to 8**

POTATO, LEEK, AND MUSHROOM PIE
WITH GIBLET GRAVY

4 red potatoes, diced

3 teaspoons kosher salt

1 cup chicken gizzards and livers, trimmed and diced

1½ teaspoons freshly cracked black pepper

3 tablespoons all-purpose flour

1 tablespoon canola oil

3 leeks, white and light green parts only, thinly sliced and washed well

2 medium carrots, diced

1 cup thinly sliced cremini mushrooms

2 celery stalks, diced

2 tablespoons minced fresh parsley

1 cup chicken stock, homemade (page 41) or store-bought

1 cup heavy cream

4 frozen puff pastry shells, defrosted

Preheat the oven to 400°F.

Place the potatoes in a medium pot and add enough water to cover by 1 inch and 1 teaspoon of the salt. Cover and bring to a boil over high heat, then reduce the heat to medium and cook until the potatoes are fork-tender, 6 to 7 minutes. Drain and set aside.

In a small bowl, season the chicken gizzards and livers with the remaining 2 teaspoons salt and the pepper. Add 1 tablespoon of the flour and toss to coat evenly.

Heat the oil in a large skillet over medium-high heat. When it shimmers, working in batches, add the chicken and cook, stirring occasionally, until the meat is browned on the outside, 3 to 4 minutes per side. Transfer to a plate.

In the same pan, combine the leeks, carrots, mushrooms, and celery. Cook over medium heat, stirring occasionally,

until the vegetables begin to soften, 4 to 5 minutes. Add the potatoes and browned chicken to the pan with the leek mixture. Stir in the parsley and the remaining 2 tablespoons flour. Stir in the stock and cream and scrape up any browned bits from the bottom of the pan. Reduce the heat to low and simmer until the cream thickens, about 15 minutes.

Lay 2 puff pastry shells over the bottom of a 9 × 13-inch casserole dish, overlapping them as needed to fit. Add the filling, then cover with the remaining 2 shells, crimping around the edges to seal and trimming any excess. Bake for 35 to 40 minutes, until the filling is bubbling and the crust is golden brown.

Allow the pie to rest for 15 to 20 minutes, then slice and serve family-style.

Fried pies, or hand pies, depending from where you hail, are one of the many delicious roadside snacks of the South. Right alongside steaming vats of boiled peanuts, you'll likely find these precious, flaky delights bursting at the seams with gooey, delicious stewed fruit. Magically preserved in time due to ungodly amounts of sugar, these shelf-stable snacks are the grab-and-go the South welcomes you with all along Route 17 or any country road you find yourself on. Like all my Homeland recipes, this fried apple pie scoffs at the idea of tradition. Schmaltz lends flakiness to the crust and makes the glaze the fatty, guilty pleasure it's supposed to be. I have never really been one for desserts, but the savory elements here suit my salty-sweet tooth. **Makes 12 pies**

FRIED APPLE PIE
WITH SCHMALTZ ICING

For the Filling

4 large Granny Smith apples, peeled, cored, and diced

1 cup packed dark brown sugar

1 cinnamon stick

For the Dough

4 cups self-rising flour, sifted, plus more for dusting

1 tablespoon cornstarch

¼ cup chicken schmaltz (see Note, page 41)

3 large egg yolks, lightly beaten

½ teaspoon kosher salt

⅔ cup whole milk, warmed

For the Icing

1 cup confectioners' sugar

¾ cup whole milk

¼ cup chicken schmaltz (see Note, page 41)

1 large egg, lightly beaten

Neutral oil, such as canola or grapeseed, for frying

Make the filling: In a small saucepan, combine the apples, brown sugar, and cinnamon stick. Cook over medium heat until the apples begin to soften, 5 to 6 minutes. Remove from the heat.

Meanwhile, make the dough: In a large bowl, mix together the flour and cornstarch. Use your fingertips to work the schmaltz into the mixture until small pea-size pieces form.

In a separate large bowl, whisk together the egg yolks and salt. Slowly pour the milk into the eggs, whisking vigorously. One cup at a time, add the flour mixture to the egg mixture,

stirring frequently to form a dough. Turn out the dough on a floured surface and knead until soft, 5 to 6 minutes.

Divide the dough into 12 equal-size pieces and roll each piece into a ball. Using a bowl or a ring mold, punch each dough ball out into a roughly 6-inch circle.

Spoon 3 tablespoons of the filling onto one side of each circle, then fold the dough over itself to create a half-moon. Pinch the edges together, then seal with the beaten egg. Crimp the edges with a fork. (At this point, you can place the pies on a baking sheet and freeze until solid, then wrap them tightly in plastic wrap and store in the freezer for up to 3 months. Thaw completely before frying.

Fill a Dutch oven with 2 inches of oil and clip a deep-fry thermometer to the side. Heat over medium heat to 350°F. Set a wire rack over a baking sheet. Working in batches, carefully drop the pies into the hot oil and fry for 2 to 3 minutes on the first side, then flip and cook for 2 to 3 minutes more, until they're flaky and golden brown on the outside. Transfer to the rack to cool. Repeat with the remaining pies, allowing the oil to return to 350°F between batches.

Meanwhile, make the icing: In a small bowl, whisk together the confectioners' sugar, milk, and schmaltz until smooth.

Pour the icing over the pies while they're still hot. Let the icing set for a few minutes, then serve warm. Any leftover pies can be stored in an airtight container in the fridge for up to 4 days.

BLACK GIRL, CHEF WHITES

Digging into my culinary roots to write this book finally gave my work, at least in my view, the authenticity I'd been missing while hiding under a weighted chef coat of imposter syndrome. After crass kitchens, culinary school, Michelin stars, and stages around the world, I've finally reached a point at which I proudly subject myself to this culinary pilgrimage—an alternative learning style in which resourcefulness, tradition, and homage are the curriculum.

Writing this book sent me on seemingly endless searches for the histories and provenance of the food I grew up eating. In the end, I realized that, more than learning the actual recipes for anything, it was the not-knowing that kept me continually intrigued. I found myself quite literally going back home, both where I spent the most time and where I wished I could've spent more, eating at the spots I knew and loved. Instead of using yet another work excuse, I found the time to attend hot, sticky family reunions, lending an ear to generations-old family stories and peeking over shoulders into simmering pots. I sailed my coastal waters and visited the fisherfolks who witnessed my first catch and taught me to shuck oysters for silver dollars. I already knew you could learn by doing, but I found out sometimes you can only *really* learn by going.

For too long, I had unwittingly and unintentionally eschewed anything these special places had to offer, thinking my tiny worldview was far higher than that of my past. Then, in my worldly estimation, nothing good could be scooped and served from a steam table or slung at you in a grease-soaked brown paper bag. But through a renewed and now far more mature lens, I discovered years of recipe development and technique formed by need and a flavor-driven palate shaped by place. It is easy to approach my own food from a creative and honest lens because these are my people. I speak the language, if you will. Somehow, the places I'd so quickly and desperately traded in for what I thought would be more fertile soil ultimately served as the driving force in creating my own style of food. I aim to create food worthy of a platform, with rich history and vivid storytelling steering the way. I'll tell stories of all these places, letting them collide beautifully on one plate.

And most important, I'll share my own story: that of a chef who is no longer pretending to be anyone but herself.

ACKNOWLEDGMENTS

Any level of success I've achieved or could ever humbly claim, I owe to an entire village.

To my sweet wife, Meaghan, whose encouragement, patience, and thoughtfulness are unmatched. I look at you and feel instant gratitude.

Thank you to my incredible family for their constant support, and to my loving parents for the safe space of my childhood home in which to write this book. I wouldn't be here if not for your belief in and support of my vision and for you instilling within me perseverance, integrity, and courage. You are all the world to me.

My fearless photography team and dynamic duo, Johnny and Charlotte Autry—you helped making this book a visual representation of who I am. Special thanks to my phenomally talented and bold food stylist, Micah Morton. And to Nick Iway, Bri Blythe, and Sydney Taylor for the many assists and "save the day" moments.

To my frequent advocate, sometimes therapist, and actual literary agent, Rica Allannic of David Black Agency. Thank you for pushing me with a touch of gentleness and seeing in me the writer that I hadn't.

Thank you to my editor, Amanda Englander, who believed in this project from the very beginning, pulling every lever in the publication of this book just like she said she would. And to Ivy McFadden, for precisely and carefully sifting through these pages with a fine-tooth comb.

To Lisa Forde, Renée Bollier, and Kevin Iwano of Union Square & Co., for helping to bring my very first cookbook to life.

To Soleil Ho, for patiently helping me take this book to this finish line in the nick of time, all the way from the other side of the country.

To my dear loved ones and friends, who helped make all these moving parts work together: Tina Teasley, Jeanie and Tyrone Thorne, Janiece Benjamin, Sarah Point, Sandra and Dennis Harris, Tia Clark, Connie Matisse, Captain John Fuss, Captain Chris Ludford, Tamarya Sims, and Anne and Aaron Grier.

To my stellar Good Hot Fish team, who held down the shop during the initial months of our opening and ran with the vision, helping to bring life to these recipes in the restaurant space.

To my faithful Asheville community. Thank you for rooting for me and entrusting me to carry the torch of our region's foodways. Here on this transformative land, doors have been opened that I could have never imagined, and everlasting connections have been made that I will continue to value, deeply, for eternity. This liberal Southern community is a thriving one that consists of farmers, makers, writers, and artists, some of the most prolific people I've ever come across and who inspire me daily, and I'm thankful to be welcomed into it with open arms.

INDEX

Note: Page references in *italic* indicate photographs.

UNION
SQUARE
& CO.

NEW YORK

Text © 2024 Ashleigh Shanti
Photographs © 2024 Johnny Autry

ISBN 978-1-4549-4912-1
ISBN 978-1-4549-4913-8 (e-book)

Library of Congress Control Number: 2024936675

For information about custom editions, special sales, and premium purchases,
please contact specialsales@unionsquareandco.com.

Printed in China

2 4 6 8 10 9 7 5 3 1

unionsquareandco.com

Editor: Amanda Englander
Designer: David Brown
Photographer: Johnny Autry
Prop Stylist: Charlotte Autry
Food Stylist: Micah Morton, with exception of the following recipes, which were styled by
Charlotte Autry: *Kilt Lettuce; Vinegar Bars; Oyster Dressing Cakes with Red Onion Soubise; Smoky Ham BBQ Oysters
on the Half Shell; Blueberry Ricesicles; Red Rum Punch; Foolproof Fridge Pickles; Carrot Salad with Honeyed Peanuts;
Melon Salad with Pistachio–Melon Seed Granola; Herby Peach and Tomato Salad with Pickled Shallots; Collard and
Sweet Potato Chowder; Sweet Potato Bargain; Winter White Salad; Gingered Shrimp, Watermelon, and Peach Skewers*
Food Styling Assistant: Sydney Taylor
PA: Bri Blythe
Photo Assistant: Nick Iway
Art Director: Renée Bollier
Project Editor: Ivy McFadden
Production Manager: Kevin Iwano
Copy Editor: Mark McCauslin